# Sustainable Renovation

## STRATEGIES FOR COMMERCIAL BUILDING SYSTEMS AND ENVELOPE

**Lisa Gelfand** and **Chris Duncan**

**WILEY**

John Wiley & Sons, Inc.

100%
TOTAL RECYCLED PAPER
100% POSTCONSUMER PAPER

This book is printed on acid-free paper. ∞

Copyright © 2012 by John Wiley & Sons, Inc. All rights reserved.

Published by John Wiley & Sons, Inc., Hoboken, New Jersey.

Published simultaneously in Canada.

For general information on our other products and services, or technical support, please contact our Customer Care Department within the United States at 800-762-2974, outside the United States at 317-572-3993 or fax 317-572-4002.

Wiley publishes in a variety of print and electronic formats and by print-on-demand. Some material included with standard print versions of this book may not be included in e-books or in print-on-demand. If this book refers to media such as a CD or DVD that is not included in the version you purchased, you may download this material at http://booksupport.wiley.com. For more information about Wiley products, visit www.wiley.com.

*Library of Congress Cataloging-in-Publication Data:*

Gelfand, Lisa.
  Sustainable renovation : strategies for commercial building systems and envelope / Lisa Gelfand and Chris Duncan.
     p. cm. —(Wiley series in sustainable design)
  Includes index.
  ISBN 978-0-470-87261-1 (cloth : alk. paper); 978-1-118-10011-0 (ebk); 978-1-118-10013-4 (ebk); 978-1-118-10217-6 (ebk); 978-1-118-10218-3 (ebk); 978-1-118-10219-0 (ebk)
  1. Buildings—Repair and reconstruction. 2. Commercial buildings—Remodeling. 3. Sustainable buildings—Design and construction. I. Duncan, Chris, 1962- II. Title. III. Title: Strategies for commercial building systems and envelope.
  TH3401.G45 2012
  690'.24—dc22

                                                                                        2011010962

Printed in the United States of America

10 9 8 7 6 5 4 3 2 1

# CONTENTS

ACKNOWLEDGMENTS   ix

PREFACE   xi

CHAPTER **1**

**INTRODUCTION** ——————— 1

**Sustainability Defined   1**

**The Urgency of Sustainability in Buildings   4**

**The Importance of Existing Buildings   6**

Renovation Contrasted with Replacement   8

Facility Management and Incremental
Renovation   9

**The Benefits of Sustainable Renovation   10**

Health and Comfort   10

Economic Returns   12

Reduction of Climate Change Impact   14

CHAPTER **2**

**WHOLE BUILDING DESIGN** —————— 17

**Introduction   17**

**Existing Building Context   19**

Climate and Function   19

Building Energy Simulation Models   22

Testing and Benchmarking Performance   22

**Understanding Existing Building Strategies   29**

Daylight   32

Ventilation   35

Permanent Materials   36

Building Envelope   38

Building Systems   39

**Modern Building Code Implications   40**

CHAPTER **3**

**FACILITY MANAGEMENT UPGRADES** —— 49

**Introduction   49**

**Immediate Improvement   51**

Behaviors   51

Testing and Analyzing Performance   52

Retrocommissioning   55

Lighting   56

Plug Loads   59

Heating, Ventilating, and Air-Conditioning   60

Water Use   62

**Beyond Energy—Green Operations and
Maintenance   62**

Indoor Environmental Quality   63

Regional Issues   65

Putting Your Program Together   65

CHAPTER **4**

**BUILDING ENVELOPE REDESIGN** ———— 77

**Introduction   77**

**Air Infiltration Losses   78**

**Insulation Strategies   78**

Cold Climate   79

Humid Middle Latitude Climate   81

Hot Humid Climate   82

Hot Dry Climate   83

Continental Climate   83

**Pre-War Buildings   84**

Thermal Mass and Climate Zones   84

Masonry Wall Design   85

Window Replacement and Shading   86
Roof Structure and Insulation   88
Roofing   89

## Mid-Century Modern Buildings   92
Curtain Wall Replacement, Modification, and Shading   92
Insulation Options   93
Window Replacement   95
Roofing   95

## Late Modern Buildings   96
Introducing Daylight   96
Correcting Roof Structures and Slope   98
Insulation Options   99
Window Replacement   100
Roofing   101

CHAPTER **5**
## BUILDING SYSTEMS REPLACEMENT ____109
### Building System Needs   109
Thermal Comfort   110
Water Use   112
Light   112
Building Controls and Environmental Responsiveness   114

### Pre-War Buildings   114
Renovation or Replacement of Steam and Hydronic Systems   115
Improving Ventilation and Fire Safety   117
Restoring or Improving Daylighting   118
Water Saving Strategies   118
Electric Power and Controls Replacement   120

### Mid-Century Modern Buildings   120
Renovation or Replacement of Hydronic Systems   120
Creating New Passive Ventilation Options   122
Improving or Replacing Forced Air Heating, Ventilation, and Air-Conditioning   122
Restoring or Improving Daylighting   124

Water-Saving Strategies   124
Electric Power and Controls Replacement   126

### Late Modern Buildings   127
Strategies for Deep Floor Plates   127
Creating New Passive Ventilation Options   128
Improving or Replacing Forced Air Heating, Ventilation, and Air-Conditioning   130
Restoring or Improving Daylighting   130
Water-Saving Strategies   132
Electric Power and Controls Replacement   133

### Systems Replacement Summary   133

CHAPTER **6**
## BUILDING MATERIALS _____141
### Environmentally Beneficial Products   141
Rating Systems and Lifecycle Assessment   142
LCA Tools   145
Recycling, Salvage, and Reuse   146
Resource Efficiency   149
Reduction in Operational Energy and Waste   150

### Low-Emitting Materials   151
"Natural" Materials   152
Concrete and Stone   152
Metals   152
Wood   153
Carpet   155
Resilient Flooring   155
Wall Finishes   156

### Pre-War Buildings   157
Salvage of Masonry and Finishes   157
Strategies for Obsolete Plaster and Partition Systems   159

### Mid-Century Modern Buildings   162
Disassembly Options   162

### Late Modern Buildings   163
Hazardous Material Issues163
Disposal Reduction   164

CHAPTER **7**

## CONSTRUCTION OPERATIONS ———173

**Introduction 173**

**Initial Construction Activities 174**

Assembling the Team 174

Exploratory Demolition and Investigations 176

Demolition Documents versus Site Discussions 177

Hazardous Materials Abatement 178

**Construction Debris 185**

**Occupied Rehabs 186**

Relocation 186

Phasing 187

Separation and Noise 189

Notification 189

Elevators 189

**Commissioning 191**


CHAPTER **8**

## HIGH PERFORMANCE RENOVATION ———201

**Transformation 201**

Renovation versus Transformation 201

Change of Use 202

Additions and Deletions 205

Preservation of Significant Historic Characteristics 207

**Retrofitting Active Energy Systems 208**

Combined Heat and Power 209

Solar Heating and Power 211

Wind Power 216

Geothermal Heat Exchange 218

**Waste Water Strategies 219**

Graywater Recirculation 220

Reuse of Building System Wate 221r

Living Machine Waste Water Treatment 221

**Passive House (Passivhaus) Design and Existing Buildings 222**

Passive Solar Design 223

Superinsulation 224

Sealing the Envelope 226

Introducing Fresh Air—Heat and Energy Exchange 227


CHAPTER **9**

## THE FUTURE OF RENOVATION ———239

**Introduction 239**

**Energy Conservation and Building Lifecycle Strategy 241**

Low and No Cost Strategies 241

2025 Improvements 243

2040 Improvements 245

Building Integrated Power Generation 246

**Deconstruction 248**

**Conclusion 250**


**INDEX** ———265

# PREFACE

THE GREEN BUILDING COMMUNITY has generated excitement through the promotion of highly sustainable new buildings, but the truth is that for industrialized nations the vast majority of the buildings of the future already exist. Furthermore, existing buildings are a large contributor to the disproportionate use of energy by the developed world. If we are to mitigate the effects of buildings on the environment, we must improve the performance of existing buildings.

About half of the U.S. energy demand in the building sector comes from single-family homes. Other resources such as water, the materials that go into construction, and products and services used by residents also have significant impact on the environment. Since energy use translates directly into family utility bills, and indoor air quality, waste, and water use have direct effects on family finances and well-being, the benefits of green renovation are equally direct. As a result, a great deal of information is available to homeowners who wish to improve the energy performance, the health, and the comfort of their homes. In this book we will study the other half of the market, the commercial sector, where we work, learn, shop, and recreate.

But these buildings come in many shapes and sizes. Sometimes they are built of materials that no one uses anymore, or there may be no record of how they were built. They occur in all geographies and climate zones. They serve many different purposes. Contractors, architects, and engineers may have lost the skills and knowledge needed to work with their materials and components. Their financial value may be associated with their location and cash flow more than with their design or performance for their users.

These obstacles are all surmountable. In this book we provide a tool case:

- An analysis of the environmental impact of existing buildings
- Illustrations of the benefits of sustainable renovation
- Methods for measuring, modeling, and monitoring building performance
- Descriptions of low and no cost measures that gain rapid results
- Common systems and materials found in prewar, postwar, and more recent buildings
- Strategies and examples achieving high performance in various buildings
- A road map for reducing the impact of the building sector by 80 percent in the next thirty years

While every existing building is a little different from the one next door, we wish to demystify some of the uncertainty that surrounds renovation. Just like new construction, there are a finite number of ways to make buildings functional, light, thermally comfortable, safe, and sanitary. Understanding what exists in any given building, owners and designers can plan for low cost and high yield immediate improvements, major renovations, transformative change, or a phased approach that creates incremental improvements as critical elements of the building systems age and fail.

The first three chapters in the book introduce the concept of sustainability, provide an understanding of whole buildings, and illustrate potential immediate upgrades. Chapters four through six examine strategies for upgrading building envelopes, systems, and materials relative to different climates and different eras of original construction. This is the *how to* heart of the book. We hope the reader will synthesize this specific information on building technics as related to individual buildings to better understand how to implement a sustainable renovation for the reader's own combination of climate, building type, and use.

Our emphasis is on improvements in building energy performance, indoor environmental quality, and impacts on the outside environment. These are the areas where the biggest changes are needed. Promising new building integrated power generation options exist. We include such options. However, at the highest rate of production currently forecast for our electrical system, they provide only 10 percent of the improvement needed to reach our target for building sector energy reduction. It is hoped that new breakthroughs will improve power generation efficiency, storage of energy, and links with the grid, but in the mean time, energy conservation delivers a much bigger bang.

Lastly, we look at construction operations, examples of exemplary performance, and how the numbers add up in the aggregate for all existing buildings in the United States. Sustainable renovation can be done; we show in the case studies how it has been done, and we argue that it must be done more widely in the future. The goal of 80 percent reduction in building energy use may sound audacious, but it is nothing more than the sum of all the things we already know how to do, implemented over the next generation.

# ACKNOWLEDGMENTS

I WOULD LIKE TO THANK my coauthor, Chris Duncan, for his research, expertise, humor, and hard work on this book. It would also never have come about had Chris not known from the beginning of our practice that what is now known as sustainable renovation was the most effective thing we could do.

My thanks to all our clients, contractors, and fellow professionals who have envisioned what could be done with existing buildings, crawled through their interstices, and worked with us to transform them. We bring the experience of architectural practice to this book, but very little of what we've learned here was learned in the office. I want to thank all the dedicated nonprofit developers who have made sustainability a priority among all their competing needs, and the project teams who have made it happen.

My particular thanks to Ken Rackow and Sandy Kovtun, for roping in the pictures and the paperwork; Rosanna Lerma for her invaluable insights, and for years of fruitful collaboration; and Deven Diliberto for a summer of productive research. I also want to thank the rest of our partners for their patience in putting up with another research project as we busily try to keep our practice rolling.

Thanks to the team at Wiley for their support. And finally, I would like to thank Andrew and Zach, my sons, for giving me an urgent stake in the future.

LISA GELFAND

I thank my wife Donna Graves for wrangling a fellowship that allowed me the time to investigate the broad spectrum of sustainable strategies that can be applied to existing buildings. The Loeb Fellowship at the Harvard Graduate School of Design provided me "affiliate" status—giving me free reign to attend classes and access to the libraries of Harvard University—making invaluable resources available while providing an energizing break from a hectic work life. In particular I appreciate the inspiration of Kenneth Kao and Bill Dunster, whose ZED class set the bar high, and Christoph Reinhart who provided a refresher course in building physics and led me to a number of valuable insights.

Of course my time in Cambridge could not have occurred without the extra efforts put in by the principals and staff at Gelfand Partners Architects who allowed me to mostly disappear for ten months while supporting all my ongoing projects. Thank you. I thank as well the architecture and engineering firms around the world who are developing and applying the sustainable renovation techniques we illustrate in this book. While they continue to provide inspiration to the communities in which they work, they provided us with practical advice and useful examples included in our book. On a more local level, I am grateful to live in the Bay Area where so many architects and engineers are working to make our buildings more sustainable.

I especially thank Russell Bayba, who let me babble on about the book and helped steer me back on course.

I thank Doug Montalbano for careful reading and advice on a late draft of this work. Lastly, my children Alice and Malcolm put up with a distracted father through many days of writing, perhaps hearing a bit more about buildings and energy than they would prefer. I hope that this book can help transform our relationship with existing buildings and allow my children to grow up in a world where environmental degradation becomes a distant memory.

CHRIS DUNCAN

# chapter 1

# INTRODUCTION

We shape our buildings, and afterwards our buildings shape us.

—*Winston Churchill*[1]

Mt. Jhomolhari in the Himalayas in 2009. During the last five years retreating glaciers and melting snow have exposed cliffs on this recently white peak. *Gelfand Partners Architects.*

## SUSTAINABILITY DEFINED

In 2010, a chunk of ice three times the size of Manhattan broke off the Greenland ice cap and floated out to sea. Scientists were excited—the event occurred as predicted, and would soon be followed by another Manhattan-sized ice floe. Every three hours updates appeared on the Internet. Reporters asked anxiously if the ice would crash into some unlucky coastline. They seemed relieved to hear that nine-tenths of the iceberg was underwater, and that it would melt or drift aground far away from any coast. Asked if the event was an indication of global warming, the

1

scientist paused for a moment and answered, "Yes, obviously," but the significance was really the accelerated ice melt caused by the warming of the ocean, that great heat sink, which, though itself more gradual, was a far more rapid agent of change than the atmosphere.[2]

While it is exciting to see a theory validated, the implications for rising waters, changing climates, and disruption of habitat are frightening indeed. In the years since the world population began meeting to define *sustainability*, environmental change has accelerated, as has the need to limit human impacts. In 1987, the United Nation's Brundtland commission defined sustainability as: "meeting the needs of the present without compromising the ability of future generations to meet their own needs."[3] This careful humanist definition encompassed the needs of people in developing countries to continue to improve their welfare and happiness and for people in wealthy and industrialized nations to maintain their comfort and well-being. However, overwhelming scientific evidence shows that our influence on the future extends beyond our ability to make ourselves more or less comfortable. Today we influence the ability of the biosphere of which we are a part to continue to flourish or even perhaps to survive.

Science depends upon the cautious accretion of observations and knowledge and cannot answer the question of whether or which species can adapt fast enough to thrive in a drastically altered environment. Gambling on the acceleration of 50,000 years of evolution into 100 years seems risky. We are in this together with the plankton and the polar bears. It seems only prudent to maintain or restore atmospheric and oceanic dynamics close to those to which we are all adapted. The Hippocratic oath to do no harm was first sworn in an era when physicians could do very little good. Our new environmental compact, consistent with our new powers, must go beyond the ancient Hippocratic standard, and find ways to heal.

Climate change appears to be tracking along the predictions of the worst-case scenarios. And so sustainability discussions today focus more sharply on carbon and energy than the resource depletion or air and water quality issues of earlier environmentalists. Deforestation, over-hunting and over-fishing, contamination of air and water with waste, and introduction of toxins arouse sorrow, outrage, and no small amount of action. But despite lack of progress in some areas, we can in fact substantiate considerable progress in slowing the destruction of the Amazon, cleaning up toxic emissions, and restraining chemical pesticide and fertilizer pollution.

Progress in these areas should encourage us to see that some damage that seemed catastrophic was at least partially reversible. We can still slow or halt climate change, although studies have shown that even a successful leveling of carbon emissions (such that increased emissions in the developing world would be fully offset by reduced emissions in the United States and Europe) would not change significantly the effect of already present greenhouse gases on climate change.

An 80 percent reduction of greenhouse gas emission by 2100 is required to turn around the engine of climate change and produce a stable concentration of greenhouse gases.

Recognizing the strains we have already imposed on the future, we suggest it is time to reverse the Brundtland definition and say:

---

**Sustainability is the restoration of the ability of future generations to meet their needs without compromising our ability to meet our own.**

---

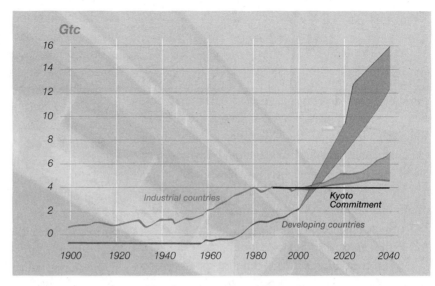

Developing countries' emissions are projected to greatly exceed industrial countries' emissions by 2040.[4] *Energy Visions 2030, VTT Technical Research Centre of Finland, 2003.*

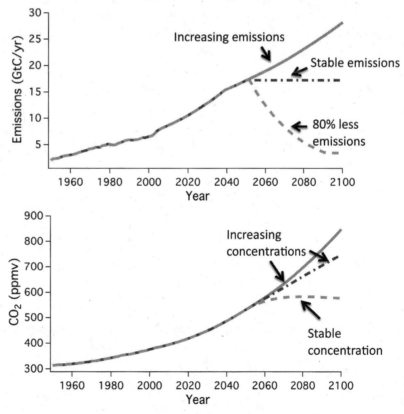

Eighty percent less emissions produces a stable concentration of $CO_2$. *National Academy of Sciences.*

# THE URGENCY OF SUSTAINABILITY IN BUILDINGS

Reducing air and water pollution in the industrialized world began by targeting the largest single polluters—factories, automobiles, untreated sewage from cities. Today, smaller or distributed polluters—runoff from road salt, pollution from tractors and lawnmowers, diesel boat engines, and the like—have become significant, even as developing nations wrestle with more traditional pollution occurring in the midst of rapid and unregulated economic growth. Greenhouse gas emission is another multifaceted problem.

Major contributors to greenhouse gas emission are tied to the building sector, including producers of electricity and heat, land use change, and industry (production such as iron, steel, and cement). Reducing these contributions requires reducing building energy use during operation (electricity, heat, cooling), reducing use of high energy construction materials (reusing existing buildings, using low-impact materials), and reducing sprawl that paves over productive land.

Buildings in the United States used 39.4 percent of total energy consumption and 67.9 percent[6] of generated electric power in 2002, directly consumed fossil fuels for heating and cooling, and are composed of materials that consumed large amounts of energy during their extraction, refinement, manufacture, transportation, and erection. Buildings consume considerably more than the 30 percent[7] of energy used by the entire transportation sector in 2008. Buildings are also major users of potable water. In addition to concerns about the sustainability of the supply of potable water due to the effects of climate change, the greenhouse gas contributions of our current system of water treatment and delivery are significant. Reducing water use in buildings is a priority for both reasons.

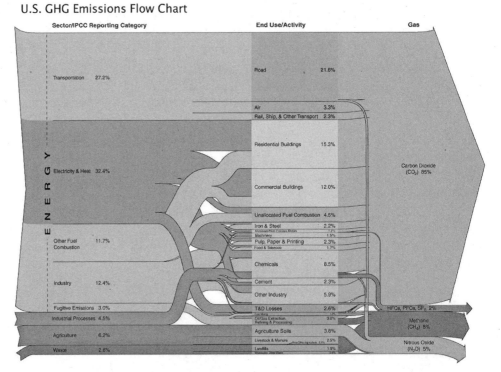

U.S. GHG Emissions Flow Chart

Building sector carbon emission occurs in electricity and heat, other fuel combustion, industry (iron, steel, aluminum/nonferrous metals, cement), and land use change.[5] *World Resources Institute.*

This office renovation is light, airy, and quiet while preserving the qualities of the historic building. *Gelfand Partners Architects.*

The size of the $CO_2$ reduction needed means that to effect meaningful change we need to do everything now, but we will concentrate in this book on reducing greenhouse gas emissions directly due to the construction, reconstruction, and operation of buildings, strategies for reducing the use of externally generated power in buildings, and strategies for reducing the use of resources with high embodied energy. If an 80 percent reduction in emissions is required overall, we suggest that buildings must do no less. We will show how this can be done in a three-phase process encompassing low and no cost improvements, limited replacement of systems and building components, and finally, major renovations affecting building physics through their systems and envelopes.

The first round of attention to energy conservation design following the oil crisis of the 1970s focused on tight building envelopes and recycled air in heating and cooling systems. This exacerbated a trend of increasingly unhealthy indoor air, leading to "sick buildings" that made their occupants unproductive, uncomfortable, and unhealthy. Because of inattention to off-gassing by building components and to moisture issues, indoor air may often have pollutant concentrations two to four times worse, and occasionally up to 100 times worse, than outdoor air.[8] Current building technologies have developed to enhance energy efficiency without sacrificing indoor air quality or occupant comfort. Such technologies can be adopted in buildings at every price point, making it reasonable to set building code targets at much higher levels than they are today.

Beyond energy efficiency sustainable design sets a standard of health and well-being for building environments that includes high quality indoor air, and comfortable and productive places to live, work, learn, and enjoy oneself.

## THE IMPORTANCE OF EXISTING BUILDINGS

Consistent with the practice of looking at the big sources first, within the building sector the existing building stock is where the opportunity for improvement is largest. Because the vast majority of the buildings to be occupied during the next thirty years are already constructed, existing buildings are the most important places to realize big changes now and in the near future. Great new buildings are the equivalent of doing no harm. Great renovations begin to heal the planet.

Renovation has never had the same high profile as new construction. With the exception of preservation of culturally significant structures the particular skills and related knowledge needed for renovation are learned more in the field than taught in schools of architecture or engineering. Usually the building techniques employed in previous periods are not studied. But existing buildings have useful commonalities that can help suggest both what is likely to be found within

Small infill projects are the only new construction this mature San Francisco cityscape is likely to see for another generation. *Gelfand Partners Architects.*

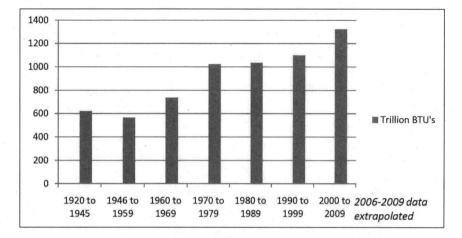

This graph shows energy use by buildings constructed in different periods. The U.S. DOE Commercial Buildings Energy Consumption Survey (CBECS) demonstrates the postwar leap in building energy consumption.[9] *U.S. Department of Energy.*

their basements, walls, and attics, and the potential choices of renovation strategies.

It is our intention to help define and apply sustainable renovation strategies for buildings of various periods. We will describe the building assemblies likely to be found in pre-World War II buildings, the immediate postwar period, and in late-century modern buildings. As can be seen in the chart, buildings of these periods created an escalating need for energy. A similarly escalating need for energy improvement applies to each period. A prewar building designed for daylight, natural ventilation, and characterized by high thermal mass, often has more need for its old logic to be restored in a renovation than to be completely rethought. Later buildings became more and more dependent on oversized mechanical systems and cheap electric lighting and their shapes and envelopes changed as well. These produce different challenges for a sustainable renovation.

It should also be clear that percentage improvement targets are more useful when looking at buildings in the aggregate than when looking at an individual building. A building that started off working pretty well needs less improvement than a building that is extremely inefficient. What is needed is a target energy use for the building that represents its fair share of energy demand

in an energy-thrifty world. The Architecture 2030 Challenge sets targets by occupancy. The combination of use (occupancy), climate and local geography, and building type and condition will be different in each individual building. Each building needs to be studied, measured, and modeled to optimize its energy use. But benchmarks do exist and can be very useful in focusing the sustainable design effort for each building. We advocate setting goals beyond the 2030 Challenge, which targets improvement for modernization at only 50 percent of that for new construction.[10] We then apply the individual analysis of the building to the higher goals of 80 percent reduction.

Equivalent performance to new construction is technically achievable in many, if not most, cases. The barriers are often more financial than design based. It is difficult to see why financial barriers should be addressed by lowering design standards rather than reforming financial strategies. Direct attention to financial barriers has yielded interesting new approaches. Where structures of loans, leases, and building valuation have more to do with setting rates of investment than the actual cost of building improvements or the lifecycle benefits they will bring, changing financing may be feasible. Creative financing and leasing solutions are being developed to share both the costs and the benefits of sustainable improvements. Part of changing the way renovation is done is changing the way the economics are analyzed and realized.

Phasing in sustainability improvements with reference to the preexisting service life of building systems and components is another approach to financial feasibility. Building systems wear out. They also represent considerable embodied energy. Looking at medium-term replacement (fifteen years from now) can be part of a strategy that is both financially sensible and sustainable. Taking a staged approach does not require vastly different investment strategies from what is conventional today. The first stage is low or no cost change and probably provides net savings to the owner. The second stage is replacement of systems and components that are reaching the ends of their service lives and need to be replaced in any case. The third stage is major renovation encompassing changes to all building systems, physics, and patterns of use.

## Renovation Contrasted with Replacement

At the level of improvement we are suggesting for major renovation, the replacement cost of a building may be close to or even exceeded by the cost of the renovation. A cultural bias for something exciting and new may kick in at this point. Why pay almost as much for an old building as for a new one? In some cases replacement will be a more obvious financial option, although many older buildings have cultural associations that give them unrecognized value in the com-

Even with a renovation that removed all finishes and replaced all systems, the structure of the building was there to be reused. *Gelfand Partners Architects.*

munity. On the other hand, many existing buildings were not designed for longevity. Their envelopes or even structural systems may have shorter projected service lives than the proposed improvements. Further, many were designed without optimal orientation or building configurations.

Where settlement patterns, transportation infrastructure, or zoning rules have changed, the existing building stock may have lost value completely independent of the quality of the structure itself. Suburban development poses significant challenges in this connection. Increasing density to improve pedestrian experience and increase transit efficiency is a sustainable strategy that may call for the replacement of existing buildings. Ironically, the replacement of prewar Main Street development with suburban shopping malls was an example of a new land use that abandoned an intrinsically more sustainable pattern, and leaves us with two problems—what to do with the big box retail development and its acres of parking lots and highways, and what to do with originally sound buildings that are now deteriorated and more challenging to renovate.

Change happens, and it is no use refusing to acknowledge it. While successful adaptive reuse has transformed warehouses into live work developments, shopping centers into schools, factories into art studios, or office buildings into apartment buildings, some buildings may be the wrong thing in the wrong place and it might be the right thing to demolish them.

Yet inherent sustainability benefits do derive from renovation rather than replacement. Construction debris accounted for nearly 60 percent of total non-industrial waste generation in the United States in 1996.[11] The embodied energy of a building created during its construction accounts for 10 to 20 percent of the energy consumed by the building over its entire existence.[12]

The decision to replace a building should meet the following criteria:

- The total energy used in demolition and waste disposal of the existing building plus construction and operation of the new building will save more energy than the energy used in renovating and operating the existing building.
- It will have additional benefits in increasing the sustainability of the site and local community.
- The components of the existing building can be productively reused.

## Facility Management and Incremental Renovation

The need to make big changes in the performance of the building sector can be met on many schedules. Major modernizations replacing entire building systems and/or envelopes are almost as rare as new construction. However, the first phase of small changes can be implemented without major modernization. Widespread adoption of sustainable operation practices and the steady improvement of building performance through incremental renovation will make larger changes than a few exemplary projects.

Many of these improvements yield rapid payback in reduced costs and tangible benefits. There are many resources that can help building managers improve their practices and cut energy use. As in looking at energy use as a whole, it is useful to look for the biggest benefits that can be gained through incremental improvement.

Lighting upgrades, heating improvements, occupancy controls, and basic envelope improvements are all strategies that can yield almost immediate benefits in energy consumption and energy costs. In addition to organized campaigns for energy conservation, a masterplan for sustainability and energy improvement can map conservation into the future. A new central heating and cooling plant in a commercial office building will not yield its full benefits until all the terminal units are modified. They may be dependent on tenant improvements. But providing the infrastructure for sustainable tenant systems is an important first step in increasing sustainability in the future. When a masterplan exists, each small renovation can provide an increment toward the overall sustainability goals without the need to rethink each component of each project.

## THE BENEFITS OF SUSTAINABLE RENOVATION

### Health and Comfort

The health and comfort benefits of sustainable renovation are shared with sustainable design in general. Studies have shown that the benefits of green buildings are direct:

- The Heschong-Mahone study showed that daylighting in classrooms in three cities improved student performance up to 20 percent.

- Herman Miller found that worker productivity improved 7 percent after a move to a green, daylit facility.

- A Lawrence Berkeley National Laboratory study found that U.S. businesses could save as much as $58 billion in lost sick time and an additional $200 billion in worker performance if improvements were made to indoor air quality.[13]

Americans spend an average of 87 percent of their time indoors.[14] The health risks of exposure to high chemical concentrations, biological contaminants, and carbon monoxide and other gases, include short-term illness such as sick building syndrome, asthma, and infectious disease, as well as development of long-term illness such as cancer from exposure to radon, asbestos, and chemicals such as formaldehyde. During the same period that outdoor air quality has improved substantially, indoor air quality has declined. The truly sustainable building achieves energy conservation improvements while reducing exposure to toxic chemicals, biological agents, and unhealthy concentrations of gases. Building occupants experience better health and well-being.

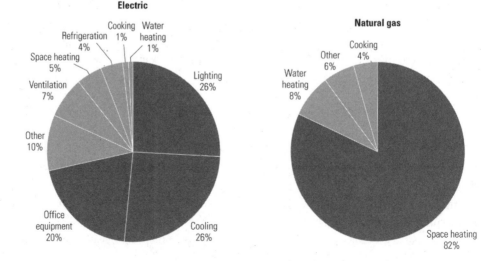

The lion's share of direct use of fossil fuels in buildings is in space heating while electricity demand (often generated from coal or natural gas) is focused on lighting, cooling (and fans), and plug loads. *Used with permission, ©2010 eSource Companies LLC.*

Daylit workspaces are associated with higher worker productivity. *Gelfand Partners Architects.*

Comfort is a different measure than exposure to unhealthy air. Buildings exist to give us a comfortable environment when the outdoor environment is uncomfortable. Keeping out the rain is a basic function of building envelopes. Keeping temperatures and humidity within a zone that allows us to do what we'd like to do while dressed the way we'd like to be dressed is the goal of heating, ventilating, and air conditioning. In a sense the building maintains internal homeostasis similar to the actions and structures of our skins and internal organs. And just as our bodies maintain temperature and gases internally within the band that allows us to survive and thrive, so buildings shelter us from the surrounding environment. Automated systems have been developed that add heat when it is cold, remove heat when it is hot, and regulate humidity. Building envelopes can now respond automatically to the need to shade or admit sunlight, adjust windows and ventilation openings, and maintain comfort without the need for inhabitants to monitor the building conditions.

However, comfort is subjective, and a degree of control on the part of building occupants helps them feel more comfortable even when the measurements are very close to what a building automation system might provide. Each of the major sustainable design

In a very basic example of envelope automation, the campus energy management system opens the clerestory windows when classroom temperatures rise. *Gelfand Partners Architects.*

scorecard systems recognize both the need to maintain comfort and the desire for control on the part of the occupants. The first green buildings of the 1970s included a strategy of designing for a broader range of comfort (assuming sweaters and shorts as acceptable adaptations, for example), as well as an expectation that occupants would pay attention to their building environment with actions such as drawing shades when the sun came onto that side of the building or turning on and off fans when air should or shouldn't stratify. The current green building provides or exceeds the comfort to which we are accustomed and includes more or less automation in adjusting to changes in external weather, climate, and time of day. Discomfort is not a sustainable state.

## Economic Returns

The economic benefits of green building are substantial. For renovation, the picture is more complicated than a straight cost benefit analysis. Commercial real estate is an investment. It is undertaken for economic benefit, and must show a return on investment that makes it worth the investor's risk and capital. The current structure of the business is also deeply intertwined with taxation. Buildings are assets that are treated as having declining value as their systems and materials age and require replacement or repair. These paper losses offset the income the building generates and are so basic to building economics that the expiration of building depreciation is often an event that triggers a sale or major renovation.

For an owner/occupier it is easy to show that the premium for green building (averaging less than 2 percent of construction cost in new buildings[15]) is easily outweighed by economic benefits. Greg Kats developed the accompanying chart as part of a report to the California Sustainable Building Task Force. In the report the most substantial benefits clearly can be seen to derive from the health and productivity benefits of green buildings. These benefits in employment terms include fewer sick days and reduced turnover, as well as measured productivity increases in tasks. Entities that benefit from these improvements include major building owners such as governments, educational institutions, and hospitals. They have been early enthusiasts of green design as a requirement for their building programs. Individual homeowners have also shown considerable interest in the energy savings and health benefits they can obtain through weatherization and other modest measures as well as campaigns for radical improvement such as net zero energy buildings.

Rents and occupancy rates can be shown to be higher in green buildings than in their conventional counterparts. For real estate developer Hines, sustainable design has contributed to an 8 percent higher occupancy rate than nongreen competitors.[16] Building green is also correlated with rents up to 10 percent higher than comparable nongreen buildings.[17] Neither of these has the overwhelming present value of the improved work environment. Yet including the energy savings that are realized by the owner of the building, reduction in risk of healthier environments, the savings in maintenance of durable construction, and the increase in equity value, a strong case can still be made for the business benefits to the investor of green building.

Commercial real estate developers and investors have not been as quick as owner/occupiers in adopting green building practices. Green financiers have been working on the development of interesting new tax incentives, bond financing, and green leases to try to create a more direct path for the financial rewards of sustainability to track with the financial costs. Making sure that conserving energy benefits the party that makes the investment and changes their behavior is one of the challenges in commercial real estate.

In the big picture, saving energy and achieving greater health and productivity benefit the whole economy. In order to encourage deeper market penetration and more rapid adoption of these practices it is important to structure deals so that profit is part of the persuasion.

| Financial Benefits of Green Buildings<br>Summary of Findings (per sf) | |
| --- | --- |
| **Category** | **20-year NPV** |
| Energy Value | $5.79 |
| Emissions Value | $1.18 |
| Water Value | $0.51 |
| Waste Value (construction only)  1 year | $0.03 |
| Commissioning O+M Value | $8.47 |
| Productivity and Health Value (Certified and Silver) | $36.89 |
| Productivity and Health Value (Gold and Platinum) | $55.33 |
| Less Green Cost Premium | -$4.00 |
| **Total 20-year NPV (Certified and Silver)** | **$48.87** |
| **Total 20-year NPV (Gold and Platinum)** | **$67.31** |

*Gregory Kats, Capital-E.*

## Reduction of Climate Change Impact

What does climate change mean to us? It is frankly unknown. The ice caps are melting. Tropical glaciers are disappearing. If precipitation came as rain the snow packs in the Himalayas would no longer be available as melt water during dry seasons in rivers like the Yangtze and Brahmaputra. The snows in the Sierra and Rocky Mountains do the same for California and other parts of the arid West of the United States. Rising ocean temperatures are freeing fast ice from polar seas. In purely human terms many billions of dollars of investment would be required by 2100 in coastal areas such as Bangladesh, Cairo, Shanghai, Florida, and the Netherlands to cope with a modest rise of 2 feet in sea level (as predicted in Intergovernmental Panel on Climate Change (IPCC) models that entirely neglect the polar or Greenland ice caps).

In the case of a rise in sea level of seven feet, as predicted by Rob Young and Orrin Pilkey in *The Rising Sea*,[19] cultural and ecological impacts are vast. Dense populations in all of the great river deltas from the Mississippi to the Mekong will be displaced. Coastal cities such as Miami will face the choice of relocation or trying to hold back the ocean. In the case of a three-foot rise in sea level, downtown Miami would be an island, and Miami Beach a sandbar.

Hurricanes draw their energy from the warm waters of the Gulf of Mexico. What happens when the hundred-year storm is an annual occurrence?

Nations of the world came together in Copenhagen in 2009 to discuss agreements to limit emission of greenhouse gases. No treaty was made. Perhaps that is because the reality of the extent of change required finally has begun to sink in. In the short term, no one nation wants to limit their own economic system while others continue to profit. While the rapid industrialization of China and India and Brazil are certainly adding tinder to the fire, it is important to remember that the per capita consumption of energy by individuals in the world's wealthy nations exceeded that of individuals in developing nations by five times in 2005.[20]

The Sierra snowpack forms a natural reservoir for dry season water users. "Currently, state operators maintain ≈ 12km³ of total vacant space in the major reservoirs to provide winter and early spring flood protection, a volume approximately equal to that stored in the natural snowpack reservoir by April 1st. Capturing earlier runoff to compensate for future reductions in the snowpack would take up most of the flood protection space, forcing a choice between winter flood prevention and maintaining water storage for the summer and fall dry period use."[18] *Gelfand Partners Architects.*

This Bangkok water market occurs at the border between the river and the land. *Gelfand Partners Architects.*

The diverse geographies of the world provide homes to many billions of creatures in addition to ourselves. We have not begun to describe all the ways that they interact with each other now, much less the consequences that attend the disappearances of species in the future. We still cannot understand the workings of the isolated ecology of the islands of New Zealand well enough to manage the problems caused by introducing rabbits.

What we are doing to the climate is much worse than introducing rabbits. In the hope that we can bet-ter learn how to live on the planet without destroying it, we need time. Changing light bulbs buys a little time. But changing the way we build, get around, produce things, and generate energy, if it can be done now, gives our children's children a chance to experience health and prosperity in a world with wild fish, tropical rain forests, coral reefs, and tigers.

This world that was the birthright of the generation now in power around the globe is within our capability to hand down to our children. We must start with the buildings that are all around us.

## ENDNOTES

1. Winston Churchill, Speech to the House of Commons, October 28, 1943.

2. NPR story, August 12, 2010.

3. Commission reference.

4. UNEP Buildings and Climate Change.

5. "Navigating the Numbers: Greenhouse Gas Data and International Climate Policy," 2005, Washington, DC: World Resources Institute, © 2005 World Resources Institute.

6. EPA Building Statistics Compiled by U.S. Environmental Protection Agency Green Building Workgroup, December 20, 2004.

7. New York State Energy Research and Development Authority, Patterns and Trends, New York State Energy Profiles: 1994–2008, January 2010.

8. EPA Building Statistics Compiled by U.S. Environmental Protection Agency Green Building Workgroup, December 20, 2004.

9. www.eia.doe.gov/emeu/cbecs/cbecs2003/detailed_tables_2003/2003set19/2003pdf/e1-e11.pdf .

10. *Architecture 2030 Implementation Guidelines*, p. 1.

11. EPA Building Statistics Compiled by U.S. Environmental Protection Agency Green Building Workgroup, December 20, 2004.

12. Buildings and Climate Change—Status, Challenges and Opportunities, United Nations Environment Programme (UNEP).2007, p. 7.

13. Kats, Greg, Capital E, A Report to California's Sustainable Building Task Force, October 2003, p. viii.

14. Klepeis, N.E., W.C. Nelson, W.R. Ott, J.P. Robinson, A.M. Tsang, P. Switzer, J.V. Behar, S.C. Hern, and W.H. Engelmann. 2001. "The National Human Activity Pattern Survey (NHAPS): a resource for assessing exposure to environmental pollutants." *Journal of Exposure Analysis and Environmental Epidemiology*, 11: 231–252. [LBNL-47713]

15. Kats, op cit, p. viii.

16. www.nrdc.org/buildinggreen/bizcase/com_occupancy.asp, accessed August 21, 2010.

17. www.nrdc.org/buildinggreen/bizcase/com_rent.asp, accessed August 21, 2010.

18. www.ncbi.nlm.nih.gov/pmc/articles/PMC514653/, accessed January 23, 2011.

19. http://e360.yale.edu/content/feature.msp?id=2230, accessed August 21, 2010.

20. EarthTrends, http://earthtrends.wri.org.

# chapter 2

# WHOLE BUILDING DESIGN

"The greatest challenge to any thinker is stating the problem in a way that will allow a solution."

—*Bertrand Russell*

## INTRODUCTION

For most engineers the best way to define a design problem is to narrow the definition of both the problem and the solution to measurable quantities. For example, a problem such as the design of a heating, ventilating, and air conditioning (HVAC) system can be framed as finding the least expensive way to condition space so that 80 percent of the occupants of the building feel comfortable in 95 percent of the weather conditions the building is likely to encounter. Similarly, a building envelope can be required to be waterproof for fifteen years, allow views of the nearby mountains from 75 percent of occupied spaces, and be secure against car bombs set off within fifty feet.

While a final building design must solve each one of such narrowly defined problems, in almost every case the solution will be found through a process of compromise and prioritization that may cause some of the original problems to be restated or adjusted.

The goal of integrated design is a solution that transcends quantitative descriptors and is the best balance of all the sometimes competing requirements. In an ideal solution, not only are all individual requirements met, but the total result is coherent, and each individual requirement is enhanced by the rest of the design.

In the context of renovation, many general parameters of the building exist. Some logic informed the design of the building when it was originally constructed and has probably survived further remodels. The building owner may have replaced a boiler or a roof. But even when focusing on such limited problems it is worth thinking about the way each system contributes to the whole, and the effect that any new element will have on the performance of parts of the building that appear to be untouched.

While it is not practical or necessary to calculate a whole energy model of a building every time someone needs a new roof, it is important to put such improvements in context. A rough order of magnitude estimation of the local climate and the loads and costs of an existing HVAC system will be enough to test whether a cool roof or added insulation will be worth considering, and whether potential advantages support an additional cost benefit analysis.

Renovations to this building include rebuilding a stair that a previous renovation removed. This restores the connection from the street to the central daylit atrium and helps the building circulation make sense again. *Gelfand Partners Architects.*

As the scope of remodeling grows, the benefits of a holistic understanding of the building also grow. When a new building is designed, the design team models it in a variety of ways—for energy perfor-

mance, structural performance, appearance, function, smoke control, fire exiting, and so on. Since it doesn't yet exist, it is obvious that investigation of a model is more cost effective than trial and error on an actual building scale. But renovation is often conducted without such whole building models. Available energy and structural modeling tools are often very weak when confronted with historic or obsolete construction types.

One advantage that existing buildings have is that they do exist, with the potential to observe and measure actual performance. Such performance includes actual energy and water use as well as the subjective experience of people using the building. Utility bills are an obvious first source of energy use data, but must be analyzed carefully so that utility rate structures that vary by season and time of day do not mislead the designer. In addition, the rate of energy use could be very good for a building of its type, or very bad. Such comparisons with similar model buildings help the designer target the potential performance, and how much improvement is needed. Benchmarking the building, or a comparison of actual performance indicators with expected values, is the process that can help identify the most important improvements to make.

The steps that the design team takes in renovation include:

- Analyze the site, climate, and building user needs.
- Analyze modern building regulations and their implications for the existing building.
- Model the actual and designed building performance.
- Integrate the building design strategies.

## EXISTING BUILDING CONTEXT

### Climate and Function

The first step in understanding an existing building is the same as the first step in designing a new one. What outside conditions and internal program needs affect the building? The climate zone and the cultural mores of the area interact to produce parameters for building comfort and function.

Clothing, fire, and shelter have enabled human beings to inhabit every climate zone on earth. Over

---

### Koeppen Climate Classifications

**A–Moist** Tropical Climates are known for their high temperatures year-round and for their large amount of year-round rain.

**B–Dry** Climates are characterized by little rain and a huge daily temperature range. Two subgroups, S–semiarid or steppe, and W–arid or desert, are used with the B climates (designated in lowercase).

**C–Humid** Middle Latitude Climates in which land/water differences play a large part. These climates have warm, dry summers and cool, wet winters.

**D–Continental** Climates that can be found in the interior regions of large land masses. Total precipitation is not very high and seasonal temperatures vary widely.

**E–Cold** These climates are part of areas where permanent ice and tundra are always present. Only about four months of the year have above-freezing temperatures.[1]

Mesa Verde cliff dwellings, built around 900 AD at approximately 8,000 feet elevation in a Bw climate, take advantage of orientation, overhangs, and thermal mass to moderate winter cold and avoid summer sun. *Kotaro Nakamura.*

most of our history we have done this by adopting strategies specific to each geography. Geographies vary in cultural history, geological and topographical configuration, and climate. Climates vary in average temperature, swings of temperature, amount and timing of precipitation, hours of daylight, and seasonal change. These factors interact with topography to form local microclimates. Plants and animals must adapt to meet these conditions, creating ecosystems and habitats; our buildings should be designed to react similarly.

One commonly used system for climatic context is the Koeppen Climate Classification. It identifies five major climate types, along with a number of subgroups. These classifications occur both within and across national boundaries, allowing us to see a variety of solutions to similar climate problems around the world. Continental climates tend to have greater swings of temperature both across day and night and from season to season. Humid Middle Latitude climates often include the marine or coastal climates that are moderated by the adjacent ocean and its com-

▲ Vernacular buildings in cold Oppland County, Norway (Dfc), hunker down into the ground where temperatures are more stable. They use sod roofs to increase insulation. *Kotaro Nakamura.*

◀ The Sochinkyo teahouse in Kyoto, Japan, built around 1600, catches cooling breezes through sliding shoji doors and large overhangs to provide comfort in a humid subtropical (Cfa) climate. *Kotaro Nakamura.*

parative coolness in the summer and warmth in the winter. In humid climates the moist air retains heat during the night, whereas desert nights can be very much colder than the day. During some parts of our history populations exploited this variability by moving between climates seasonally or by conducting their greatest activity during the coolest or warmest times of the day.

Once settled in a particular climate though, people want comfort through all the variations. Inside the building we want to have an environment that is light (or dark) on demand, varies in temperature by only a few degrees during occupied hours, and varies by only a little more between day and night. In addition, we want a relative humidity that is finely tuned to our bodies' systems for staying comfortably moist but not overly sweaty.

The climatic classification helps the designer relate a given building to other examples. A sustainable building in Northern Europe, like many of the best examples in this book, looks very different from the Japanese teahouse. Examples of existing buildings will be found where designers were probably motivated more by a formal or historicist reference to a building precedent than by a more appropriate inspiration from a similar climatic zone. Such buildings require a different kind of renovation from buildings that originally were designed for their own climate.

## Building Energy Simulation Models

Building energy models require the input of a location for the building. Most energy software choices have a good deal of built-in information about climates or can accept standardized statistical tables. Such models are detailed enough to account for seasonal precipitation or diurnal/nocturnal variations in temperature rather than averages. For example,

EnergyPlus includes 2,100 discrete locations for weather data. Half of those locations are in the United States. The building model allows the designers to test various scenarios. What will be the energy use with a particular HVAC system? How will it change with new windows, a cool roof, or additional insulation in the attic? Will such improvements allow the HVAC system to be downsized?

The software then requires entry of building function to provide additional information such as hours of operation, functional needs of activities within the building, potential seasonal differences in use, and habits or requirements of building users. These vary greatly depending on building occupancy. Energy demands in residential buildings may be exactly complementary to office buildings, at least in terms of hours of use. On the other hand, senior housing may have few working individuals and much more daytime energy use by residents than other types of housing.

Culturally based expectations shape perceptions of comfort. Americans are thought by many Europeans to overheat and overcool their buildings. Within the United States, cooling of residential units, not even available before World War II, is now considered a basic necessity in many climates, and a requirement of subsidized housing. In San Francisco, with a July average maximum temperature of 63 degrees and only 160 cooling degree days annually (compared to New York City, with 335 in August alone),[4] developers generally provide cooling in luxury apartments.

## Testing and Benchmarking Performance

Benchmarking databases allow a building owner or design team to look at building performance relative to similar occupancies across the country. Test-

## Thermal Behavior of Buildings—Whole Building Modeling Software

U.S. DOE, Energy Efficiency and Renewable Energy

*Building Energy Software Tools Directory[2]:*

**Energy Plus:** A new-generation building energy simulation program from the creators of BLAST and DOE-2.

**DOE-2:** An hourly, whole-building energy analysis program which calculates energy performance and lifecycle cost of operation. The current version is DOE-2.1E.

**Building Design Advisor:** Provides building decision-makers with the energy-related information they need beginning in the initial, schematic phases of building design through the detailed specification of building components and systems.

**Energy-10:** A program for small commercial and residential buildings that integrates daylighting, passive solar heating, and low-energy cooling strategies with energy-efficient envelope design, and mechanical equipment. This allows for detailed simulation and performance analysis.

**SPARK:** Models complex building envelopes and mechanical systems that are beyond the scope of EnergyPlus and DOE-2. Good for modeling short time-step dynamics. Runs 10–20 times faster than similar programs.

*Model Validation and Testing:*

**BESTEST (Building Energy Simulation TEST)[3]:** Software for comparison of various modeling programs. Compares simulations to measurements in test rooms.

ing performance in the real building also allows the team to see how users actually operate the systems. On-site measurements are highly significant numbers—we note that BESTEST relies on actual measurements in test buildings to validate energy simulation software.

Several tools are available for understanding and ranking building performance. One of the most popular is ENERGY STAR's Portfolio Manager, a program that uses basic building information and utility bills to create a score from 1 to 100. This number indicates the building's performance relative to a theoretical group of comparable buildings [based on the Department of Energy's Commercial Buildings Energy Consumption Survey (CBECS) Database]. The Information Exchange from the Building Owners and Managers As-

sociation (BOMA) International is another database of commercial building performance.[5]

Architecture 2030, an organization founded in 2002 by architect Edward Mazria, seeks to change the way the building sector performs in the United States and internationally. Performance goals set by Architecture 2030 have been adopted by industry groups, state and local governments, and form part of the American Clean Energy and Security Act of 2009. These goals escalate as the years go by, aiming for new buildings to be carbon neutral by 2030. Providing an aggressive set of targets, the 2030 Challenge has promoted progress toward common goals in reduction of energy consumption, clarifying energy use for many building types not included in Portfolio Manager.

# 2030 Challenge Targets: U.S. National Averages

The 2030 Challenge aims to reduce the effects of building energy use and fossil fuel consumption for construction of new buildings and renovations to zero by 2030. This chart shows reductions from current average building energy consumption figures for various types of buildings.[6]

| Primary Space / Building Type[2] | Available in Target Finder[3] | Average Source EUI[4] (kBtu/Sq.Ft./Yr) | Average Percent Electric | Average Site EUI[4] (kBtu/Sq.Ft./Yr) | 2030 Challenge Site EUI Targets (kBtu/Sq.Ft./Yr) | | | | |
|---|---|---|---|---|---|---|---|---|---|
| | | | | | 50% Target | 60% Target | 70% Target | 80% Target | 90% Target |
| **U.S. Averages for Site Energy Use and 2030 Challenge Energy Reduction Targets by Space/Building Type[1]** From the Environmental Protection Agency (EPA): Use this chart to find the site fossil-fuel energy targets | | | | | | | | | |
| Administrative / Professional & Government Office | ✓ | | | | | | | | |
| Education | | 170 | 63% | 76 | **38.0** | 30.4 | 22.8 | 15.2 | 7.6 |
| College / University (campus-level) | | 280 | 63% | 120 | **60.0** | 48.0 | 36.0 | 24.0 | 12.0 |
| K-12 School | ✓ | | | | | | | | |
| Food Sales | | 681 | 86% | 225 | **112.5** | 90.0 | 67.5 | 45.0 | 22.5 |
| Convenience Store (with or without gas station) | | 753 | 90% | 241 | **120.5** | 96.4 | 72.3 | 48.2 | 24.1 |
| Grocery Store / Food Market | ✓ | | | | | | | | |
| Food Service | | 786 | 59% | 351 | **175.5** | 140.4 | 105.3 | 70.2 | 35.1 |
| Fast Food | | 1306 | 64% | 534 | **267.0** | 213.6 | 160.2 | 106.8 | 53.4 |
| Restaurant / Cafeteria | | 612 | 53% | 302 | **151.0** | 120.8 | 90.6 | 60.4 | 30.2 |
| Health Care: Inpatient (Specialty Hospitals, Excluding Children's) | | 468 | 47% | 227 | **113.5** | 90.8 | 68.1 | 45.4 | 22.7 |
| Hospital (Acute Care, Children's) | ✓ | | | | | | | | |
| Health Care: Long Term Care (Nursing Home / Assisted Living) | | 225 | 54% | 124 | **62.0** | 49.6 | 37.2 | 24.8 | 12.4 |
| Health Care: Outpatient | | 183 | 72% | 73 | **36.5** | 29.2 | 21.9 | 14.6 | 7.3 |
| Clinic / Other Outpatient Health | | 219 | 76% | 84 | **42.0** | 33.6 | 25.2 | 16.8 | 8.4 |
| Medical Office | ✓ | | | | | | | | |
| Lodging | | 194 | 61% | 87 | **43.5** | 34.8 | 26.1 | 17.4 | 8.7 |
| Dormitory / Fraternity / Sorority | ✓ | | | | | | | | |
| Hotel, Motel or Inn | ✓ | | | | | | | | |
| Mall (Strip Mall and Enclosed) | | 271 | 71% | 107 | **53.5** | 42.8 | 32.1 | 21.4 | 10.7 |
| Office | ✓ | | | | | | | | |
| Bank / Financial Institution | ✓ | | | | | | | | |
| Public Assembly | | 143 | 57% | 66 | **33.0** | 26.4 | 19.8 | 13.2 | 6.6 |
| Entertainment / Culture | | 265 | 63% | 95 | **47.5** | 38.0 | 28.5 | 19.0 | 9.5 |
| Library | | 246 | 59% | 104 | **52.0** | 41.6 | 31.2 | 20.8 | 10.4 |
| Recreation | | 136 | 55% | 65 | **32.5** | 26.0 | 19.5 | 13.0 | 6.5 |
| Social / Meeting | | 102 | 57% | 52 | **26.0** | 20.8 | 15.6 | 10.4 | 5.2 |

| | | | | | | | | | |
|---|---|---|---|---|---|---|---|---|---|
| **Public Order and Safety** | | 189 | 57% | 90 | **45.0** | 36.0 | 27.0 | 18.0 | 9.0 |
| **Fire Station / Police Station** | | 157 | 56% | 78 | **39.0** | 31.2 | 23.4 | 15.6 | 7.8 |
| **Courthouse** | ✓ | | | | | | | | |
| **Service** (Vehicle Repair / Service, Postal service) | | 150 | 63% | 77 | **38.5** | 30.8 | 23.1 | 15.4 | 7.7 |
| **Storage / Shipping /** **Nonrefrigerated Warehouse** | | 56 | 56% | 25 | **12.5** | 10.0 | 7.5 | 5.0 | 2.5 |
| **Self-storage** | | 12 | 44% | 4 | **2.0** | 1.6 | 1.2 | 0.8 | 0.4 |
| **Non-refrigerated Warehouse** | ✓ | | | 1 | **0.5** | 0.4 | 0.3 | 0.2 | 0.1 |
| **Distribution / Shipping Center** | | 90 | 61% | 44 | **22.0** | 17.6 | 13.2 | 8.8 | 4.4 |
| **Refrigerated Warehouse** | ✓ | | | | | | | | |
| **Religious Worship** | | 83 | 52% | 46 | **23.0** | 18.4 | 13.8 | 9.2 | 4.6 |
| **Retail Store** (Non-mall Stores, Vehicle Dealerships) | | 191 | 67% | 82 | **41.0** | 32.8 | 24.6 | 16.4 | 8.2 |
| **Retail Stores** | ✓ | | | | | | | | |
| **Other**[5] | | 213 | 56% | 104 | **52.0** | 41.6 | 31.2 | 20.8 | 10.4 |
| **Secondary Space / Building Type**[2] | | | | | | | | | |
| **Ambulatory Surgical Center** | ✓ | | | | | | | | |
| **Computer Data Center** | ✓ | | | | | | | | |
| **Garage** | ✓ | | | | | | | | |
| **Open Parking Lot** | ✓ | | | | | | | | |
| **Swimming Pool** | ✓ | | | | | | | | |
| **Residential Space / Building Type**[6, 7] | | | | | | | | | |
| **Single-Family Detached** | | 76.6 | - | 43.8 | **21.9** | 17.5 | 13.1 | 8.8 | 4.4 |
| **Single-Family Attached** | | 70.7 | - | 43.7 | **21.9** | 17.5 | 13.1 | 8.7 | 4.4 |
| **Multi-Family, 2 to 4 units** | | 93.2 | - | 58.2 | **29.1** | 23.3 | 17.5 | 11.6 | 5.8 |
| **Multi-Family, 5 or more units** | | 99.4 | - | 49.5 | **24.8** | 19.8 | 14.9 | 9.9 | 5.0 |
| **Mobile Homes** | | 153.2 | - | 73.4 | **36.7** | 29.4 | 22.0 | 14.7 | 7.3 |

*Notes*

1. This table presents values calculated from the Energy Information Administration in the Commercial Building Energy Use Survey (CBECS), conducted in 2003; using the Environmental Protection Agency's Table 1: 2003 CBECS National Average Source Energy Use and Performance Comparisons by Building Type.

2. Space/Building Type use descriptions are taken from valid building activities as defined by the Energy Information Administration in the Commercial Building Energy Use Survey (CBECS), conducted in 2003.

3. A "✓" indicates that this Space/Building Type is included in Target Finder. On the input page, use the 2030 Challenge EnergyReduction Target option and select 50%.

4. The average Source EUI and Site EUI are calculated in kBtu/Sq.Ft./Yr as weighted averages across all buildings of a given space type in the CBECS 2003 data set.
Source Energy is a measure that accounts for the energy consumed on site and the energy consumed during generation and transmission in supplying energy to the site.
Converting Site to Source Energy:
Source Energy values are calculated using a conversion for electricity of 1 kBtu Site Energy = 3.34 kBtu Source Energy; a conversion for natural gas of 1 kBtu Site Energy = 1.047 kBtu Source Energy; a conversion factor for district heat of 1 kBtu site energy = 1.40 source energy and a conversion factor for fuel oil of 1 kBtu site energy = 1.01.

5. Other: For all building types not defined by the list above, these buildings may choose to use the performance benchmark categorized by "other". Note that this category is not well defined therefore source energy use varies greatly with source EUI ranging over 1500 kBtu/Sq.Ft. As categorized by EIA, "other" may include airplane hangers, laboratory, crematorium, data center, etc.

6. Energy Information Administration (EIA), U.S. Residential Energy Intensity Using Weather-Adjusted Primary Energy by Census Region and Type of Housing Unit, 1980-2001, Table 8c.

7. Energy Information Administration (EIA), U.S. Residential Energy Intensity Using Weather-Adjusted Site Energy by Census Region and Type of Housing Unit, 1980-2001, Table 6c.

EUI: Energy Use Intensity

When working with similar buildings in the same region, study of utility bills across a portfolio of buildings yields interesting results. After modernizations to their nine similar schools, Los Altos School District compared the utility bills for schools modernized to meet the Collaborative for High Performance Schools (CHPS) criteria and schools modernized to meet the normal building code. As illustrated in the accompanying chart, the middle school saves $23,000 per year and the elementary schools save an average of $50,000 per year (Bullis Elementary School is much smaller than the others) in energy costs when compared to the typical schools. Performing an analysis and comparison such as this *before* modernization can pinpoint existing facilities that have the most room for improvement.

The Collaborative for High Performance Schools, consistent with their mission to make schools a better place to learn and provide school districts with the information and tools necessary to build and renovate schools in a sustainable way, has put together a Web-based benchmarking and continual improvement tool for all existing schools known as the Operations Report Card. It is a kit of measuring instruments, directions, survey questions, and score sheets to enable school staff to make their own analyses of building performance.

"Since the ORC is designed specifically for schools, it allows administrators to assess their schools with both an occupant survey and technical classroom audits. Teachers and staff respond with

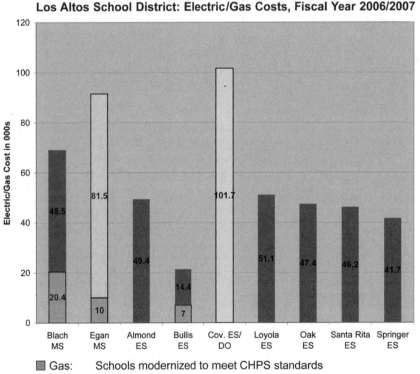

**Los Altos School District: Electric/Gas Costs, Fiscal Year 2006/2007**

Construction budgets for the CHPS schools were the same as budgets for the Title 24 schools. Schools modernized to meet CHPS criteria saved thousands of dollars a year in energy costs compared to schools modernized to meet the basic building code. *Los Altos School District.*

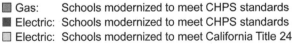

■ Gas: Schools modernized to meet CHPS standards
■ Electric: Schools modernized to meet CHPS standards
▫ Electric: Schools modernized to meet California Title 24

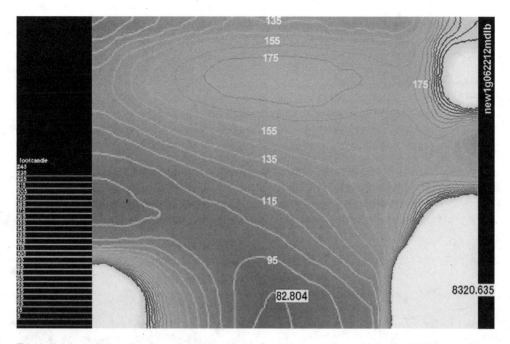

This daylighting software plot of an existing classroom indicated hotspots that needed to be shielded to avoid glare. Modeling software can analyze natural light as well as artificial light to provide key information necessary for successful modernization. *Gelfand Partners Architects.*

their opinions of the school, and the maintenance staff receives training on how to operate common tools like light meters or infrared thermometers. The ORC also suggests improvements that the school might undertake to improve its performance. By viewing those improvements through the lens of the occupant survey, schools can identify which options fit both their budget and the needs of those who use the building."[7]

The Operations Report Card goes beyond energy use to measure acoustic and lighting/daylight performance, thermal comfort, and indoor air quality as well as to gather subjective responses from building users. CHPS puts measuring tools in the hands of building operators and users and also provides a database for comparison of individual building performance. A growing number of individuals and companies also offer this kind of service, although usually focused strictly on energy and often known as an energy audit, and can help building owners see where their building performance stands.

Daylighting has its own suite of specialized computer modeling programs that can be incorporated in a building analysis before modernization. These programs produce plots that map the light levels at various locations within a room.

Many of these programs require considerable time and effort to develop good information. One way designers can shortcut the analysis time is to build a physical model and place sensors inside. The model can be put onto an accurate mount to set angles for sunlight to visualize changes of sun angle due to

## DAYLIGHTING Modeling Software ©2010 Austin Energy Green Building™

### ADELINE

Lawrence Berkeley National Laboratory
Building Technologies Program
Mail Stop 90-3111
1 Cyclotron Rd.
Berkeley, CA 94720
(510) 486-7916

Daylighting, electric lighting, and whole building analysis, provides 3-D CAD modeling of a space, automatically generates SuperLite and Radiance input files, calculates interior luminance levels.

### Lightscape

1054 South DeAnza Blvd.
San Jose, CA 95129
(800) 859-9643

Lighting design tool with high-quality visual simulation.

### Lumen Micro

Lighting Technologies
David DiLaura
2540 Frontier St., Ste. 107
Boulder, CO 80301
(303) 449-5791

Graphics-oriented indoor lighting design that analyzes complex interior lighting systems, including sidelighting, direct/indirect lighting mixed, and even-aimed luminaires. User-friendly input.

### Radiance

Building Technologies Program
www.radsite.lbl.gov/radiance

A suite of programs designed at Lawrence Berkeley National Labs for the analysis and visualization of lighting in design. Input files specify the scene geometry, materials, luminaires, time, date, and sky conditions (for daylight calculations). Calculated values include spectral radiance (i.e., luminance + color), irradiance (illuminance + color), and glare indices. Simulation results may be displayed as color images, numerical values, and contour plots. Radiance has no limitations on the geometry or the materials that may be simulated. Radiance predicts illumination, visual quality, and appearance of innovative design spaces, and can evaluate new lighting and daylighting technologies. Radiance is UNIX software; for PC software, use ADELINE.

This apparatus allows the building model to be tilted to the correct angle for various times of day and seasons so that daylighting inside the model can be measured. *Gelfand Partners Architects.*

season and time of day. Tiny fiber-optic cameras can record time lapse movies showing the changing daylighting conditions within a model, providing a visual record further verified by the quantitative sensors.

However the targets are set and performance calculated or verified, it is important to consider all the major contributors to building sustainability when developing a sustainable renovation masterplan. Using the right tools provides the information needed to assess building strengths and weaknesses. But making the renovation plan requires prioritizing, compromising, and integrating HVAC, lighting/daylighting, envelope upgrades, and interior finishes into a single coherent strategy.

# UNDERSTANDING EXISTING BUILDING STRATEGIES

Analysis and benchmarking of building performance indicates how a given building compares to other similar buildings. The objective is to focus on areas where the building may be weak (i.e., high cooling demand, or excessive electricity use). But the next step is to analyze how the whole building produces those results. An element of forensic or diagnostic thinking goes into this. Often it starts with figuring out how the building was meant to work when it was built.

Different priorities have driven building design, leaving a legacy of buildings that solve problems that we may have forgotten, or ignore issues we deem important today. For example, one of the problems for postwar builders in Europe and North America was to overcome shortages caused either by the war itself or the postwar expansion as soldiers returned home, formed families, and economies began to grow again.

Suburban development in the United States was fueled by government-aided home-buying and highway construction, making up for years of stagnant growth. This produced not only homes and roads but an urgent need for schools and businesses. Loyola Elementary School, in Los Altos, California, was constructed in 1948 as part of this building boom. The school was built using repetitive mass-production techniques and a highly rational layout of daylit, naturally ventilated classrooms. It met the needs of its community at that time. But by 2002 it was showing significant wear. Educational ideas embraced diversity instead of repetition. The building was analyzed and found likely to perform poorly in the event of a moderate earthquake.

In renovating Loyola we took advantage of the sustainable daylighting and ventilation that were intrinsic to its original design. We also wanted to stay comfortably within the expressive language of the building and its straightforward functionality, while improving its scale and introducing a rhythm that would create a more engaging campus. Once we knew that the building needed a structural improvement, it was clear that renovation work would include changes to the building envelope, including new sheathing on the roof and new shear panels in the walls. The new shear panels would unbalance the even daylight distribution so we decided to include new monitors in the roof, rebalancing the classroom daylighting scheme. We coordinated the monitor location with existing roof framing.

Within the classrooms the changes resulted in great daylighting, natural ventilation, and better acoustics. Another choice the team made was to leave the old window system in place even though it had single-pane glazing with nothing high-performance about it. This was an economic choice, and also recognized the frequency with which glazing gets replaced on school sites. In this mild California climate not a great deal of additional heat is needed once lights, children, and computers heat up the classroom. Since the roof was replaced, we did upgrade to R-30 insulation. The project is modeled at over 30 percent better than the California energy code in place at the time (Title 24-accepted along with ASHRAE 90.1 as a LEED prerequisite). Its actual utility bills are closer to 50 percent below the code-complying elementary school across town, modernized at the same time. The building energy performance is based chiefly on the greatly reduced lighting requirements. Electric lighting, with daylight compensation and occupancy sensors, rarely runs at greater than 10 percent capacity in this day-

Loyola Elementary School, 1948 (before modernization). Existing north-facing classroom walls were glazed for daylighting but lacked an adequate seismic bracing system. *Gelfand Partners Architects*.

Loyola Elementary School, 2006 (after modernization). New shear walls provide structural improvement, while new roof monitors replace lost daylight and provide new passive ventilation opportunities. *Photo Mark Luthringer*.

This classroom demonstrates an integrated design solution to needs for structural improvements, daylighting, and natural ventilation. *Gelfand Partners Architects.*

time use. Additionally, natural ventilation is created when the energy management system opens a clerestory window instead of running a fan.

Loyola Elementary was designed using two-dimensional drafting software, cardboard models, a three-dimensional computational structural model, and an energy model. These models allowed exploration of modifications that affect such disparate elements as structure and daylighting, ventilation, and energy. By understanding the goals and limitations of the original design, the various models were able to capture beneficial aspects of the existing building within the context of the current program, prioritizing needs and maximizing results.

Computer software today is converging toward a point where a Building Information Model (BIM) will be a computer simulation that can be shared by the various disciplines that are involved in design. A single computational representation of a building will be used to explore the interrelationships between energy, structure, daylight, and materials. At the end of construction the model will also be usable by a facility manager to find out what is in the walls, what kind of equipment was installed, what warranties exist, and what maintenance is required. Such a model will be a big asset in developing energy conservation strategies that are implemented over time, or in buildings where tenants change, or modifications are required for other reasons.

## Daylight

Daylight was clearly a defining problem in the original design of Loyola. But that was not unusual. Until efficient fluorescent lighting became widely available, most buildings depended on daylighting for a great deal of their daytime illumination. For smaller buildings the distance from a window was never far. But for larger buildings, configuring the envelope so that light could be brought into the deepest part of the building was a major design task.

Larger prewar buildings were generally built in the relatively dense centers of towns and cities. Built close together, or with multiple stories, fire was a major concern. Exterior walls were usually masonry, and might be either load bearing (as in supporting the floors and roof), or at least carrying their own substantial weight. Windows were only as large as steel lintels or masonry arches could span carrying heavy bricks or stone above. With limited ability to ventilate or light areas far from windows, buildings were folded and hollowed out to create more exterior walls. They end up resembling letters such as "E" or "H" with many interior lightwells and courts. Floor and roof assemblies varied from wood to brick vaults to concrete.

The higher the daylight source in the wall, the deeper the light can penetrate into the room. High ceiling heights were part of the system. In working with buildings from this era it is effective to extend their strategies. In the Marlton Manor senior housing renovation in San Francisco, the program called for increased resident social space. Residents did not want to use the full-height basement because it was dark and felt unsafe. Our solution included dropping the lightwell roof and skylight one floor to bring daylight to the basement, along with allowing oversight of the space by windows in the ground floor offices. One physical change can solve many needs, illustrating the power of integrated design.

▲▶ Prewar civic and institutional buildings were often constructed of brick no matter their climate zone. This 1908 building made use of maximum window size, light courts, setbacks, and skylights to introduce daylighting to all spaces. *Gelfand Partners Architects.*

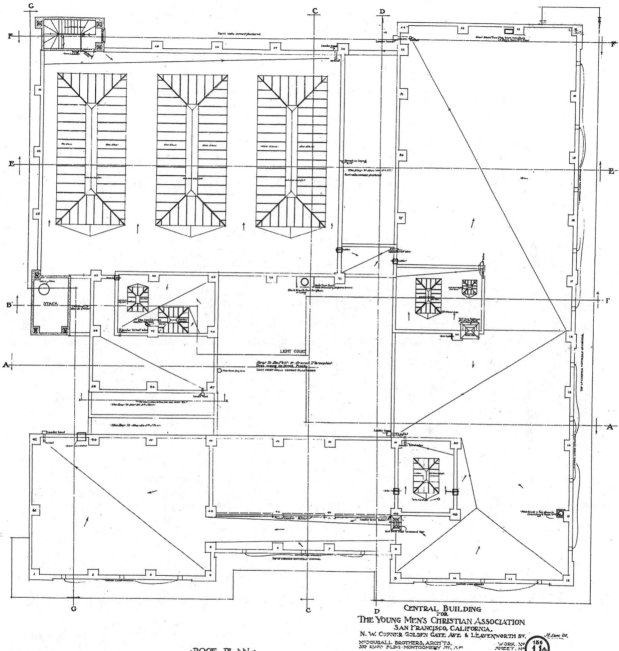

· ROOF PLAN ·
· SCALE ⅛ IN = 1 FOOT ·

CENTRAL BUILDING
FOR
THE YOUNG MEN'S CHRISTIAN ASSOCIATION
SAN FRANCISCO, CALIFORNIA.
N. W. CORNER GOLDEN GATE AVE & LEAVENWORTH ST.

McDOUGALL BROTHERS, ARCH'TS.

WORK. N°  156
SHEET. N°  11A

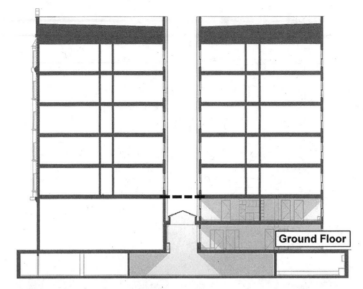

Marlton Manor, renovated 2002. The original lightwell extended down to the dashed line. By dropping the roof and adding a skylight we added a dwelling unit with code-required light and air, and connected the basement and first floor spaces with daylight and without a fire separation. *Gelfand Partners Architects.*

**Ground Floor**

▲ The basement of the Marlton was frightening and unused. *Gelfand Partners Architects.*

▶ Opening the basement to the skylight and to observation from the first-floor offices made the space feel safe and bright. *Gelfand Partners Architects.*

## Ventilation

In addition to daylight, another driver of older buildings was ventilation. Like daylighting, ventilation systems were designed with narrow floor plates to allow cross ventilation. Passive or natural ventilation that is not assisted by fans requires a pressure difference. In cross ventilation there are windows on two sides of a space. Chances are that one side is the windward side and the other the leeward side and that air will naturally flow from high to low pressure.

In *stack ventilation* the pressure difference is created by convection. Hot air rises. When it rises it creates low pressure; air from higher pressure areas flows toward the low pressure. This can occur in one-story rooms with high ceilings, or in connected stacks within multistory buildings. It is also at work in fireplaces and combustion appliances. Air is needed for combustion and is usually sucked into a space and sent up the chimney by the stack pressure difference. This is why combustion air for furnaces, hot water heaters, and fireplaces should come from outside the conditioned space. Otherwise we are just sending conditioned air (and the energy used to condition it) up the chimney and out of the building.

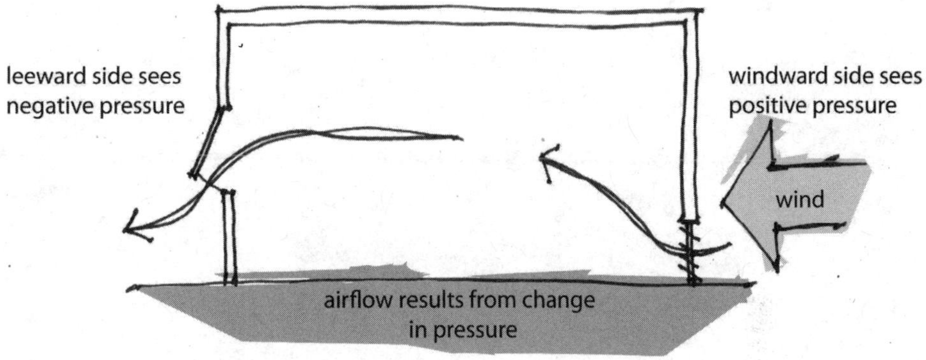

Cross ventilation is seen in vernacular buildings in most warm climates. In the Japanese teahouse sliding panels could be opened and closed to adapt to changing wind patterns. *Gelfand Partners Architects.*

leeward side sees negative pressure

windward side sees positive pressure

wind

airflow results from change in pressure

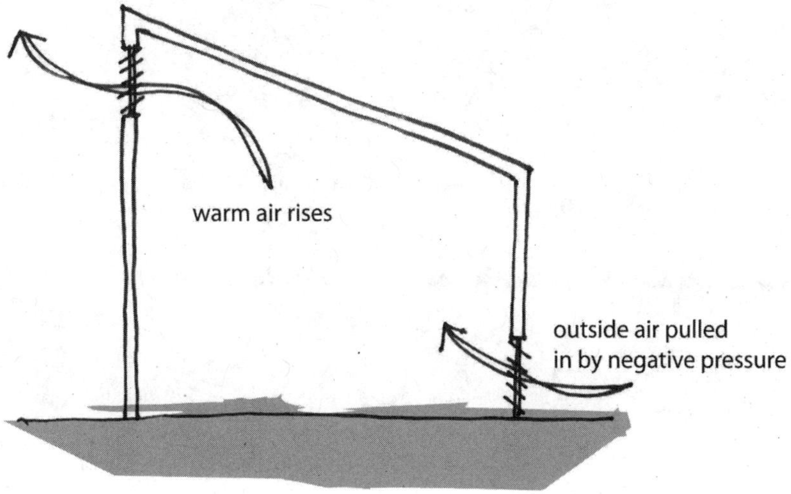

With an adequate ceiling height, hot air in a room rises. If there is a high opening and a low opening, air flow will be created without the need for fans. *Gelfand Partners Architects.*

warm air rises

outside air pulled in by negative pressure

Before forced air heating systems, ventilation and the natural physics of air movement provided fresh air throughout buildings. Solutions included wind scoops in desert areas, and the use of shafts and towers to promote stack ventilation. Building codes have evolved since the early part of the twentieth century, often requiring separation of floors and of disparate occupancies to prevent spread of smoke and fire. This results in buildings that are more difficult to ventilate naturally. Modernized buildings often will require fire or smoke dampers between spaces or magnetic hold-opens on doors separating corridors from stairs to achieve the required fire separations while enabling passive ventilation strategies.

## Permanent Materials

Building components vary in their expected service life. The structure of a steel or concrete building might be expected to last indefinitely if protected from water and properly designed for extreme events such as earthquakes and hurricanes. The exterior walls of a masonry building have a similar longevity. Even a wood building can last for centuries if properly maintained. But finishes, systems, equipment, roofing, windows and doors, and furniture are all building components that need to be maintained, repaired, or replaced on a regular basis.

In addition to wear and tear, buildings also become stylistically and functionally obsolete. Retail and hospi-

Windscoops in Hyderabad, Pakistan, have been channeling prevailing winds for at least 500 years. *Fred Bremuer, 1880s, © harappa.com.*

The steel frame and wooden floors of this former department store remain to be repurposed into an office building with new central daylit atrium. *Gelfand Partners Architects.*

tality buildings are rebranded frequently. The longevity of their materials may have little to do with their condition and everything to do with the desired image. A substantial amount of renovation activity is caused by the desire to refresh the look of a building, accommodate changes in the function of the building, and allow upgrades in rapidly developing data and other infrastructure. While considering otherwise permanent materials as disposable is on the face of it unsustainable, the competitive nature of some businesses means that such pressures should be considered by the designers.

Permanent materials have sustainability advantages that include their lack of need for ongoing investment of energy and resources in maintenance, the fact that they won't be transported anywhere else for disposal, and the fact that they won't become landfill. However, it is the lifecycle assessment that truly measures sustainability over time.

Over the life of a material, another way of looking at permanence embraces flexibility. The Cradle to Cradle (C2C) approach articulated by McDonough and Braungart carries materials through their reconstitution into

something else, prioritizing disassembly and reuse. As in an ecosystem, the waste of one creature is the food of another. Nothing is truly wasted. This approach is realized in such materials as office workstations that must be truly reconfigurable—at least three times—and carpet tiles that can be both repurposed in the building and ultimately returned to the factory to be remade into new carpet tiles.

One way of combining the two approaches is to think of the most permanent parts of a building as providing the skeleton for uses that change more often. Office buildings with their regular grids of columns and systems risers provide such a skeleton for many different kinds of tenants. The original tall buildings of the 1920s are now too narrow for large floor plate office users. But they often work for housing. Their high ceilings, deep daylight, and systematic design can be readily adapted to a residential use. The opposite situation is found in a sloped floor concrete parking garage that is virtually permanent in terms of its materials, but cannot be repurposed as transportation needs change. Permanence lasts only as long as the building can serve a purpose.

## Building Envelope

The light and energy that pass (or do not pass) through the building envelope create the need for artificial lighting or mechanical systems. Changing the performance of the building envelope influences the design of building systems, or may even make it unnecessary to upgrade them. If the envelope is part of the scope of work of a renovation, it can create a major opportunity.

Renovation of building envelopes ranges from repair to replacement. Where a masonry building may need cleaning and repointing, leaving the major materials intact, a curtain wall building may require complete replacement of the wall system. Many interesting approaches involve transformation of the envelope. Adding insulation to the outside of a masonry wall optimizes its potential as thermal mass. Rather than reradiating its heat to the exterior, heat stays in the building. While desirable in cold climates, especially in

Busby and Associates added an outer skin to the Telus building starting in 1998 as a pioneer in this method of reusing buildings while significantly improving their performance. *Courtesy Busby Perkins+Will Architects Co.*

winter, heat retention could be disastrous in a warm, humid climate. Some renovations have layered glass on the outside of concrete or masonry, increasing heat gain in some seasons and exhausting it in others.

Changing the building envelope in isolation can create major problems. Understanding and designing the envelope to manage water vapor is a key task. Moisture condensing out of warm moist air onto cold surfaces is the cause of much water damage wrongly diagnosed as leaking. Older buildings were not hermetically sealed. When sealing up buildings to prevent infiltration of outside air or leaking of inside air, the walls or roof must be double checked to be sure they will still manage moisture properly.

As in all other design problems, the envelope performance must be considered in context. Users, systems, and appearance all impose requirements on the building envelope. The sustainable envelope manages thermal separation, visual transparency, vapor transport, and design appearance while requiring limited user attention and very low energy use.

## Building Systems

No part of building technology has changed as much as the systems that provide indoor climate control. As machines increased our ability to heat and cool and light, wholly enclosed space became more common. In an era when energy seemed cheap, little thought went into this transition away from natural ventilation and daylighting. But now there is pressure to rethink building systems so that they are more energy efficient while maintaining a healthier indoor environment. Heating systems at first were simple heated surfaces, followed by forced air that could rapidly change the temperature in a space. These systems worked by replacing cold air with warmed air, often exhausting (throwing away) great quantities of heat and energy. The first wave of energy consciousness modified heat-

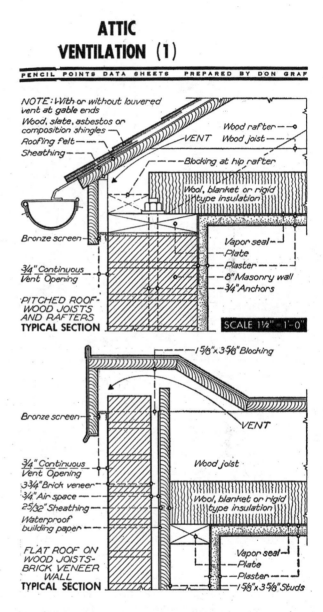

This 1947 detail illustrates the correct venting of attic or crawl spaces with a vapor seal on the warm side of the ceiling insulation in a cold climate. While adding insulation inside the masonry wall, it would be important to avoid creating a vapor seal on the cold side of the existing masonry or sheathing, trapping condensation within the cavity. *Dan Graf's Data Sheets, 1944, Reinholt Publishing Corporation.*

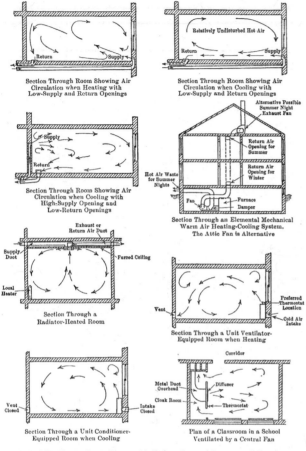

Typical Air Distribution in Rooms with Various Types of Systems. (Taken from "American Society of Heating and Ventilating Engineers' Guide.")

These 1944 diagrams illustrate the systems likely to be found in buildings of that era. *Kidder-Parker Architects' and Builders' Handbook, 1947, John Wiley & Sons, Inc.*

ing systems to recycle heated building air. But now systems can be designed that bring in entirely fresh air, passing it through heat or energy recovery systems that transfer the heat but not the gases or particles from the "used" room air.

Lights have progressed from being controlled by simple on or off switches to computerized systems that sense daylight and occupancy. HVAC systems have similarly added functions that respond not only to a switch but to sensors for temperature, occupancy, and even carbon dioxide concentration. While these system controls are generally separate now, the trend is toward greater convergence. Power, data, telephone, fire alarm, building automation, public address, security, and cable television may all have separate cable infrastructures now, but in the future, it is likely that they will be consolidated and building managers may be able to control them all on a single computer dashboard. These systems will also respond to the environment around buildings, taking into account daylight and exterior temperature and wind while assessing previous use to estimate upcoming needs. Planning for such changes by providing empty pathways (conduits) is a prudent way to future-proof a building.

## MODERN BUILDING CODE IMPLICATIONS

When changing the occupancy of a building (from office to residential, for example), a full upgrade to current building codes may be required. Other code upgrade triggers include renovations that affect a certain percentage of existing walls or finishes or an addition of a certain size. Certain other requirements, typically safety- or accessibility-related, have been imposed on buildings whether or not they are being renovated. In some states, multifamily housing owners were required to add smoke detectors and/or fire sprinklers to existing buildings. Jurisdictions with earthquake danger identified particularly vulnerable buildings and gave time limits for structural upgrades before they would be denied continued occupancy. And successful lawsuits by disability advocates have forced the accelerated renovation of entrances, restrooms, and other accommodations within public buildings.

A historic building code exists in most jurisdictions to give flexibility to owners of culturally significant buildings over fifty years old so that character-defining elements can be maintained despite their incompatibility with modern codes. Safety is still the top priority but the historic building code allows alternate methods to be used to achieve performance goals.

Many of the results of building code–enforced renovations can be seen in the exposed sprinkler pipes, boarded up transoms, and awkwardly enclosed stairwells of some older buildings. As systems were added over time, often in the convenient space of corridor ceilings, and fire hazards were remedied, original ventilation schemes were abandoned. Where transoms once opened to corridors that connected to fire stairs that went the height of the building, there is now no cross ventilation for apartments. Although these units still have operable windows, it is the pressure difference caused by the stack of air rising up through the stair shafts that moved the air. In the building shown here, the new renovation will add exhaust fans to toilet rooms in each room and use fire-safe shafts to reach the roof. This will restore pressure differences and allow stack ventilation to work once again.

Building code changes have come about in response to problems. After every catastrophe—fire, earthquake, hurricane, or terrorist attack—the building codes evolve to address causes of building failure. It might be argued that the profligate use of energy by the building sector is another building failure. This is not a reason to discard the older building stock, nor is it a reason to ignore the ideas that organized these buildings. A strategic and integrated approach to building function, systems, and envelopes can make sense of these buildings and make continued use of the great amount of energy embodied in their fabric.

This residential hotel corridor carries nonoriginal power, phones, cable TV, and hot and cold water for fan coil units. Sprinkler piping is hung beneath and crossing the rest of the piping. Transoms over the doors have been boarded up and provide the pathway for the piping. *Gelfand Partners Architects.*

CASE STUDY

# Gårdsten Apartments

**Owner**  Gårdstensbostäder, Kastanjgården 3, 424 39 Angered, Sweden gbg@gardstensbostader.goteborg.se

**Renovation Architect**  CNA – Christer Nordström Arkitektkontor AB; Gårdstenbostäder

**Original Building Type**  Multifamily Housing

**Renovation Building Type**  Multifamily Housing

**Original Construction Date**  1970s

**Renovation Date**  2006

**Location**  Göteborg, Sweden

**Climate**  Oceanic (Köppen Cfb)

**Area**  205,000 square feet

**Achievement**  none

**Key Indicators**  Solar Air–Heated Double Envelope

    Solar Heating Intake Air

    Solar Hot Water

    Heat Recovery Ventilation

    Efficient Insulation

    Low-e Windows

**Energy Achievement**  44 percent less than comparable building

**Total Energy Use**  15.33 kWh/sf/year  (165 kWh/m²/year)

**Total Energy Use Before**  25.55 kWh/sf /year   (275 kWh/m²/year)

**Renewables**  Solar Hot Water

The transformation of the ten buildings and 255 apartments in the Gårdsten public housing project in Göteborg, Sweden, was performed in careful coordination with the residents. Focused on energy efficiency, renewable energy systems, and improvements to indoor environmental quality, the project achieved impressive results. Energy efficiency was advanced through installation of a conventional exterior insulation system with insulated low-emissivity glazing. Walls facing the prevailing winds were provided with additional insulation. At the south façade of a three-story building, an innovative solar air–heated double envelope protects the building. The solar panels heat air that is circulated between the new insulation and the existing exterior walls. The thermal mass of the original building retains and spreads the heat while triple-insulated windows complete the enclosure.

New south-facing skin includes insulation and a double-walled panel that preheats incoming air, which is circulated between the existing building wall and the new insulation, reducing heating loads. © *CNA Christer Nordstrom Architects, www.cna.se.*

New panelized pitched roof elements include solar hot water panels. © *CNA Christer Nordstrom Architects, www.cna.se.*

Three seven-story buildings received a new modular pitched roof system with integrated solar panels on their south sides. The solar panels preheat domestic hot water stored in a basement tank, then distributed throughout the complex during colder periods of the day. The panel system provides additional attic insulation. Balconies added to south façades provide solar preheating of fresh air. A heat recovery ventilation system rounds out the ventilation scheme.

The complex instituted provisions for composting and recycling by residents, and provides a community greenhouse. Finally, space heating and domestic hot water are now monitored for each apartment, further encouraging energy conservation. Overall, energy consumption was reduced from 275 to 165 kWh/m², a reduction of 44 percent.

▲ Glazed balconies combine with ground-floor greenhouse and added insulation to passively heat south-facing apartments. Rooftop solar collectors preheat domestic hot water that is stored in a basement tank for distribution during colder periods of the day. © CNA Christer Nordstrom Architects, www.cna.se.

▶ Ground-floor greenhouse provides a winter garden for residents while preheating air that travels up the apartment faces, reducing heating needs. © CNA Christer Nordstrom Architects, www.cna.se.

CASE STUDY

# Trees Atlanta Kendeda Center

**Owner**  Trees Atlanta Kendeda Center

**Renovation Architect**  Smith Dalia Architects

**Original Building Type**  Warehouse

**Renovation Building Type**  Office, Multiuse

**Original Construction Date**  1950s

**Renovation Date**  2008

**Location**  Atlanta, GA

**Climate**  Humid Subtropical (Köppen Cfa)

**Area**  12,000 square feet

**Achievement**  LEED NC 2.2 – Platinum (54 points)

**Key Indicators**  Daylighting

Geothermal Heat Exchange, Solar Thermal Hot Water

Green Roof

IAQ

Local Materials

Rainwater Collection—Toilet Flushing

**Energy After**  25 to 35 percent savings

**Renewables**  none

An organization dedicated to the promotion and preservation of urban forestry, Trees Atlanta brought their ecological focus to the development of their Kendeda Center outside Atlanta, Georgia. Beginning with a 1950s warehouse in an industrial neighborhood, Smith Dalia Architects saw the opportunity for transformation, demolishing about one-third of the building while sustainably renovating the remainder. Situated in a humid subtropical climate, the designers prioritized energy savings through minimization of heat gain and conservation of water.

Sun shades and "light boxes" were installed around windows to reflect sunlight away from the building and to reduce the urban heat island effect. Greater than normal insulation protects roofs and walls. Large windows and sun tubes in restrooms, hallways,

Trees Atlanta Kendeda Center grew within a 1950s warehouse building. New insulation, sunshades, and a vegetated roof limit heat gains in the humid subtropical climate. A shallow pipe geothermal heat exchange system heats and cools the complex while using 25 to 35 percent less energy than a comparable building. © 2010 John Clemmer / www.johnclemmer.net.

and the boardroom emphasize natural light throughout. A sheltered interior courtyard provides additional daylight while presenting sample tree varieties. Demonstration installations of three kinds of green roofing with differing planting methods and plant types augments reflective cool roofing. An on-site rainwater collection system stores 7,500 gallons of water from the rooftop for flushing toilets and for irrigation. Bioswales, porous hardscape, and native trees planted around the site further manage stormwater.

Finally, a geothermal heating and cooling system harnesses the near-constant temperature of the earth through shallow piping loops installed under the parking area. Making site disturbance do double duty, the system results in 25 to 35 percent energy savings. Interior air quality is protected through installation of low-emitting materials and a ventilation system that exhausts through the copy room to limit spread of particulates.

Low-emitting finishes combine with natural ventilation and mechanical exhaust through the copier room to preserve indoor air quality. Every room has high-quality access to natural light. © 2010 John Clemmer / www.johnclemmer.net.

One-third of the existing structure was carved away, a central courtyard grounds the plan, drawing daylighting into every room. Collected rainwater irrigates a site that focuses on native trees that illustrate the organization's mission. Bioswales and porous landscaping limit stormwater runoff. © 2010 John Clemmer / www.johnclemmer.net.

## ENDNOTES

1. www.blueplanetbiomes.org/climate.htm (3 of 12) [7/5/2010 2:54:23 PM].

2. http://apps1.eere.energy.gov/buildings/tools_directory/doe_sponsored.cfm.

3. Testing and Validation of a New Building Energy Simulation Program, http://gundog.lbl.gov/dirpubs/rio4.pdf.

4. www.ncdc.noaa.gov/oa/climate/online/ccd/nrmcdd.html, accessed January 10, 2011. Cooling Degree Days (CDD) are used to measure the energy likely needed for cooling. CDD measure the difference between the average daily temperature and 65 degrees each day. If a day's average temperature is 78 degrees, that day would have 13 CDD. Totaling each day for a year gives the total CDD for a location.

5. www.facilitiesnet.com/energyefficiency/article/Benchmark-Energy-Data—10270.

6. Architecture 2030, www.architecture2030.org/.

7. Notes, Nick Semon, phone interview August 29, 2010.

chapter **3**

# FACILITY MANAGEMENT UPGRADES

## INTRODUCTION

The objective of green design and construction is a building that can be maintained in a healthy and efficient manner. Without a green approach to management and maintenance, even the greenest design will fail to achieve its potential. To a large extent the reverse is also true—with green management even an inefficient building can be improved. We advocate raising the sustainability targets for renovation to match new construction, and we advocate a similar level of ambition for management and maintenance. The truth is that wise management of energy, resources, and waste can produce savings equal to many of the new building components with minimal capital investment.

Leaks consume eight times as much indoor water as baths in the United States. *Gelfand Partners Architects.*

For example, potable water is not only an increasingly scarce resource in many regions, but a substantial energy user. And yet leaks constitute 13.7 percent of U.S. daily indoor water use.[2] Similarly, "energy vam-

49

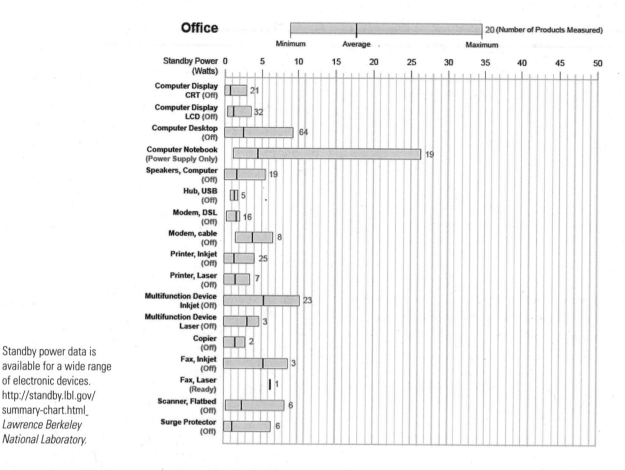

Standby power data is available for a wide range of electronic devices. http://standby.lbl.gov/summary-chart.html_ *Lawrence Berkeley National Laboratory.*

pires," electronic devices [with power supplies, light emitting diodes (LEDs), etc.] that draw power whenever they are plugged in account for between 5 and 10 percent of U.S. residential electricity use. It is a smaller fraction in the commercial sector as a whole, but particularly significant in common office devices such as printers, copiers, and computers.

In addition to fixing the electricity and water "leaks," similar attention to air leaks both in the building envelope (weatherization) and within heating, ventilating, and air-conditioning (HVAC) systems (retrocommissioning) can contribute to substantial savings.

The United States Green Building Council (USGBC) Leadership in Energy and Environmental Design (LEED) for Existing Buildings: Operation and Maintenance (LEED-EBOM) rating system helps facility managers map comprehensive environmental improvement across their facility. Unlike the other LEED checklists, it is possible to earn up to LEED Silver recognition with almost no capital investment. USGBC describes the scope of the rating system: "Specifically, the rating system addresses exterior building site maintenance programs, water and energy use, environmentally preferred products and practices for cleaning and alterations, sustainable purchasing policies, waste stream management, and ongoing indoor environmental quality."[3]

Should a building get coveted LEED Silver recognition just by fixing what's broken and changing existing operations and management practices? The rating system is set up to enable this achievement. There is an important point here: While green design is an important tool in reducing the energy and resource demands of the building sector, green operations and management (O&M) can lead to substantial improvements long before a building owner or manager considers it economically feasible to renovate a building thoroughly. Green O&M will also be needed to maintain a renovated building at its heightened level of performance. There is no reason to wait.

Behavior changes, immediate lighting and HVAC control improvements, and repair or one-for-one replacement of existing equipment and fixtures, can repay owners and tenants very quickly. Saving resources through better management of trash and recycling, and water conservation can also produce immediate environmental benefits. A step-by-step facility improvement program can fill in the gaps before major building systems such as HVAC reach the end of their service life and are replaced.

# IMMEDIATE IMPROVEMENT

## Behaviors

Daylight savings time is an example of an attempt to change energy use through changing behavior. In 1784 Benjamin Franklin first noted in a letter to the *Journal of Paris* the "immense sum that the city of Paris might save by the economy of using sunshine instead of candles."[4] People simply needed to wake earlier, substituting hours of daylight activity for hours of darkness. Other examples of immediate ways to change energy consumption through behavioral changes include the low speed limits and right-turn-on-red laws that followed the oil embargo of the 1970s.

Conscious changes of habits also occur. Submetering individual housing units within previously master-metered apartment buildings results in energy and utility bill savings. The New York State Energy Research and Development Authority (NYSERDA) found that 73 percent of the residents of a newly submetered apartment building used less than the average amount of energy per unit than when utilities were master-metered.[5] Extending such submetering to commercial tenants or divisions within large institutions could achieve the same improvements.

Spurred on by submetering, people do the following to save energy:

- Turn off lights, computers, appliances, and HVAC units when not in use
- Open blinds and turn off lights
- Close blinds and turn down air-conditioning
- Reduce thermostat settings in winter
- Increase thermostat settings in summer
- Change thermostat settings at night

Submetering provides a financial incentive for people to change their habits. But consciousness without financial benefit can also change habits. As part of university-wide energy conservation, the *NORESCO Energy Conservation through Behavior Change* team worked with students at Kutztown University in Pennsylvania to achieve improvements of more than 12 percent. The biggest improvements were gained through turning off fans, air-conditioners, printers, and audio speakers when not in use.[6]

In commercial settings, changing workplace schedules can also cut down on energy use during peak hours (i.e., by starting earlier in the morning and cutting down on cooling hours). Exterior doors should be kept closed when air-conditioning is on. Computers should be turned off completely at night (this can be done by switching off the power strip after shutting down the

computer). People can use stairs instead of elevators. In hotels guests can be given the choice of reusing towels and linen rather than having them laundered daily.

In addition to energy use, behavior influences water use, and waste and pest management. The same habits that are advocated in the home work in commercial and institutional facilities—turn off the faucet while brushing teeth or scrubbing pots, water plants with cold water otherwise wasted waiting for hot water, avoid bottled water, separate trash into recycling and compost, print double-sided copies and documents, clean up food waste and standing water to limit attraction to pests.

Behavior change does something else. The limited improvements possible through these conscious efforts help raise expectations for the improvements possible in the systems themselves. Commitment to change needs to come from both the users and the managers. Investments in conservation that are repaid by employee satisfaction and pride have benefits beyond the immediate balance sheet. Students who see their own efforts matched by university staff are rein-

forced in the authenticity of university commitments. Residents, tenants, and employees of sustainable organizations bring that knowledge and commitment to their other enterprises.

## Testing and Analyzing Performance

The same benchmarking analysis that is an important first step in creating an integrated design for a major renovation helps in planning the low cost changes that can be made right away. The EPA Energy Star benchmarking tool Portfolio Manager helps building operators and managers make a quick start in comparing performance against a national average for buildings of the same type. During the process of benchmarking, building managers examine their utility bills and identify the different rates that apply. This may yield important cost information: for instance, usage reduction levels that eliminate peak or premium pricing and can help target the highest return for improvements.

The person within an organization who is responsible for tracking and monitoring performance plays a vital role. Measurement of the outcome of energy

**PALO ALTO UNIFIED SCHOOL DISTRICT
FACILITIES MASTER PLAN**

Addison Elementary School    *enrollment 426*

**Utilties Data Sheet**

**Utilites Use and Cost**

*summaries and trends*

**Utilites Use/Cost Totals (FY 06, 7/05 thru 6/06)**

| | use units | cost |
|---|---|---|
| Electric | 212,516 kWh | $21,366 |
| Gas | 9,737 therms | $11,362 |
| Water | 1,013 ccf | $4,077 |
| Garbage | N.F.S. bins | $9,534 |
| Storm | | $0 |
| Sewer | | $2,712 |
| *per student $115* | **TOTAL** | **$49,051** |

Pie chart: Storm 0%, Sewer 6%, Garbage 19%, Water 8%, Gas 23%, Electric 44%

**Electric**

| | |
|---|---|
| Peak Demand (KW) | 70 |
| Annual kWh | 212,516 |
| Annual Electric Cost | $21,366 |
| Main Service Size (AMPS) | - |
| Service Voltage | - |
| Meter # 1 | 02131 |
| Meter # 2 | N/A |

**Gas**

| | |
|---|---|
| Annual therms | 9,737 |
| Annual Gas Cost | $11,362 |
| Meter # 1 | 36558 |
| Meter # 2 | N/A |

**Water**

| | |
|---|---|
| Irrigation Water Meter # | 31778 |
| Potable Water Meter # | 27234 |
| Annual CCF (irrigation) | 328 |
| Annual CCF (potable) | 685 |
| Annual CCF (total) | **1,013** |
| Annual Cost of Irrigation | $1,320 |
| Annual Cost of potable | $2,757 |
| Annual Cost (total) | **$4,077** |
| Service Pipe Size (irrigation) | - |
| Service Pipe Size (potable) | - |

**Sewer**

| | |
|---|---|
| Annual cost | $2,712 |
| Service Pipe Size | - |

**Storm**

| | |
|---|---|
| Annual cost | $0 * |
| Service Pipe Size | - |

*Storm Drain Costs calculated from Hardscape S.F.

**Garbage**

| | |
|---|---|
| Annual cost | $9,534 |
| Number of Bins | N.F.S. |

**4 Year Electric Use Trend**

**4 Year Gas Use Trend**

**4 Year Water Use Trend**

**Weekly Utility Use Profile**

Reference Documents
CPAU CARE Audit: *Energy Efficiency Report, Addison Elementary, Salas O'Brien Engineers, Inc.*

The City of Palo Alto financed utility audits for all of the Palo Alto public schools as part of the public school facility masterplan. *Palo Alto Unified School District.*

conservation strategies identifies which ones should be continued or extended, and where improvement is needed. Motivation for staff and users can include financial benefit that is passed along, or the sense that their workplace or school or apartment complex is doing better than others at solving environmental problems. It is important to have the data to communicate where the facility started and what has been achieved.

## U.S. EPA Five-Step Building Upgrade Program

■ Retrocommissioning

Retrocommissioning is the first stage because it provides an understanding of how a facility is operating and how closely it comes to operating as intended. Specifically, it helps to identify improper equipment performance, equipment or systems that need replacing, and operational strategies for improving the performance of the various building systems.

■ Lighting

Lighting upgrades, which may include new light sources, fixtures, and controls, come early in the process because the lighting system has a significant impact on other building systems. Lighting affects heating and cooling loads and power quality.

■ Supplemental Load Reductions

Supplemental load sources, such as building occupants and electronic equipment, are secondary contributors to energy consumption in buildings. They can affect heating, cooling, and electric loads. With careful analysis of these sources and their interactions with HVAC systems, equipment size and upgrade costs can be reduced.

■ Air Distribution Systems

Air distribution systems bring conditioned air for heating or cooling to building occupants, and therefore directly affect both energy consumption and occupant comfort. Fan systems can be upgraded and adjusted to optimize the delivery of air in the most energy-efficient way.

■ Heating and Cooling Systems

If the steps outlined in the first four stages have been followed, cooling and heating loads are likely to have been reduced. That reduction, coupled with the fact that many existing HVAC systems are oversized to begin with, means that it may be possible to justify replacing an existing system with one that is properly sized or retrofitting a system so that it operates more efficiently. In addition to saving energy, proper sizing will likely reduce noise, lower the first costs for equipment, and optimize equipment operation, often leading to less required maintenance and longer equipment lifetimes.[7]

Energy audits performed by utility companies or private contractors can also be a helpful resource. Such audits identify the major offenders in energy use in a facility, such as lighting, inferior windows, energy wasting practices in commercial kitchens such as continuously running ovens and hoods, or missing pool covers. Managers should look for auditors with qualifications such as Certified Energy Manager (CEM), and Certified Measurement and Verification Professional (CMVP), or various engineering licenses such as Professional Engineer, Electrical Engineer, Mechanical Engineer (PE, EE, ME, respectively).

The first step in the LEED-EBOM system is also benchmarking building performance. Unlike new construction or major renovation, a major part of the data is recorded performance of the building rather than energy models or calculations. Twelve months of utility bills show how and when the building uses energy and water. LEED-EBOM may not be the best product to use if an owner is taking over a building that has been vacant or has been used by a very different enterprise (for example, a developer planning to convert an office building into an apartment building). LEED-NC (New Construction) may be the better choice.

Looking at the building performance and its relationship to other buildings of its class helps focus attention when examining the systems themselves. If a building is using a large amount of water with no apparent cause, building managers and occupants can be more alert for leaks, faulty valves, or poor management practices. The building upgrade program can focus on the areas that compare the worst to other facilities. This may be an indicator of where the biggest returns can be found.

## Retrocommissioning

Checking utility bills allows a rough tabulation of how much energy building systems draw. It is important to read bills carefully because rate structures differenti-

ate between times of day and seasons while the actual machinery may not. But the next stop is looking at and testing the systems themselves. Commissioning new buildings or systems is the process that tests the performance of systems against their targets, identifies problems, and assists in clearing them. Existing building systems should be retrocommissioned on a regular basis. Although some problems are immediately obvious, some can lurk within systems, reducing efficiency or equipment life by many years.

In the renovation of our office in San Francisco we consolidated spaces that formerly served different programs. In an area that had been office space we elected to reuse and retrocommission an existing functioning HVAC system. The tests on the units

Building energy system deficiencies: A recent study of retrocommissioning revealed a wide variety of problems—those related to the overall HVAC system were the most common type (A). Energy and non-energy benefits: Retrocommissioning provided both energy and non-energy benefits—the most common of these, noted in one-third of the buildings surveyed, was the extension of equipment life (B).

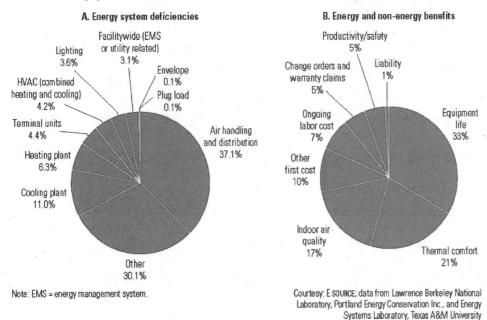

**A. Energy system deficiencies**

Facilitywide (EMS or utility related) 3.1%
Lighting 3.6%
HVAC (combined heating and cooling) 4.2%
Terminal units 4.4%
Heating plant 6.3%
Cooling plant 11.0%
Envelope 0.1%
Plug load 0.1%
Air handling and distribution 37.1%
Other 30.1%

Note: EMS = energy management system.

**B. Energy and non-energy benefits**

Productivity/safety 5%
Change orders and warranty claims 5%
Liability 1%
Ongoing labor cost 7%
Other first cost 10%
Equipment life 33%
Indoor air quality 17%
Thermal comfort 21%

Courtesy: E SOURCE; data from Lawrence Berkeley National Laboratory, Portland Energy Conservation Inc., and Energy Systems Laboratory, Texas A&M University

Retrocommissioning delivers immediate economic benefits to building owners and operators. *Used with permission, ©2010 eSource Companies LLC.*

Curtains can be opened when stack ventilation is desired, or closed to conserve heat. *Gelfand Partners Architects.*

themselves showed that they were working fine—the right volumes, velocities, and temperatures were being achieved. However, workers in the room were still cold. Commissioning agents distributed data loggers throughout the space and identified the problem. Our renovation combined an adjacent space with the office. Through the open passage the air had found a way to escape up a forty-foot-tall tower. Heated air was rushing up the stack and sucking more cold air into the space. We hung a curtain over the opening to reduce the loss of heated air and adjusted the performance of the HVAC system to remedy the performance prob-

lem. This illustrates an important difference between *testing and balancing equipment* and *commissioning*. Commissioning focuses on performance of the system compared with its goals. It was too cold for users. The HVAC contractor was right—his equipment was fine, but the system was not meeting its goal for thermal comfort.

Other important tasks in retrocommissioning include training and documentation. Many buildings have a shelf full of equipment manuals that describe how each piece of equipment should work. Building management staff need a building systems manual that describes how all the equipment works together. This can be created by the retrocommissioning agent. It can also detail the scheduled maintenance procedures such as cleaning of filters and chiller coils that are necessary to keep systems running efficiently. These tasks may require some initial investment, however, they have been shown to have some of the fastest paybacks of any measures building owners can take.

## Lighting

Electric lighting draws between 20 and 30 percent of the energy in most commercial buildings in the United States. It is a vital element in most built environments. It makes it possible for us to do tasks at any time of day or night. It helps make outdoor spaces safer and more accessible. It affects the way we perceive space and the attention that we pay to various elements in the space. Lighting upgrades in the sustainable sense accomplish the same goals that all lighting does, but accomplish them using less energy. Merely reducing expectations (and light levels) is not the sustainable strategy.

Energy codes and industry standards have set increasingly stringent standards for power demands by lighting. With new light sources, controls, and design approaches these standards can be met by lighting designs that are more comfortable, functional, and easy on the eyes than former high-energy approaches.

Lighting retrofits discussed here do not require changing ceilings, fixtures, and circuits. These actions may be part of a more comprehensive modernization, or even a focused lighting replacement, but there are immediate steps that can be taken without going that far. The familiar advice to replace incandescent light bulbs with compact fluorescent bulbs recognizes the wide disparity among the sources themselves.

Upgrades of existing fluorescent light fixtures are a mainstay of commercial lighting upgrades. In many cases this also requires the replacement of the ballast in the lighting fixture. The original magnetic ballasts reg-

ulated the current in fluorescent lamps but were also the source of the annoying flicker and hum that light fixtures sometimes produced. The modern electronic ballasts have much higher cycle rates and generally do not flicker or hum. Different ballasts are required with different lamps. Replacing both together produces the best result.

In addition to changing the sources, changing the environment and the way lighting is delivered are both potentially powerful strategies. In a space with a suspended ceiling with a grid of direct lighting four lamp fixtures, one approach is to reduce the ambient light-

| Lamp type | Lamp property | | | | | |
|---|---|---|---|---|---|---|
| | Mean efficacy, including ballast (mean lm/W) | Lumen maintenance (%) | Rated life (hours) | Color rendering index | Correlated color temperature (K) | Typical applications |
| Full-size fluorescent (T5, high-performance T8) | 80 to 97 | 92 to 93 | 20,000 to 30,000 | 80 to 85 | 2,700 to 6,500 | General area lighting of all kinds, including open and closed offices, classrooms, and high-bay areas |
| Compact fluorescent | 43 to 71[a] | 86 | 6,000 to 12,000 | 80 to 85 | 2,700 to 6,500 | Incandescent replacements in table and floor lamps, cans, wall washers, and sconces |
| Quartz pulse-start metal halide | 60 to 80[a] | 65 to 75 | 20,000 | 65 to 70 | 2,900 to 4,200 | Outdoor lighting, high-bay lighting, and remote-source lighting |
| Ceramic pulse-start metal halide | 60 to 80[a] | 80 | 20,000 | 85 to 94 | 2,900 to 4,200 | Where color is critical, including high-bay and retail applications |
| High-pressure sodium | 60 to 110[a] | 85 to 90 | 24,000 | 22 | 1,900 to 2,200 | Outdoor lighting and in high-bay applications where color is not critical |
| Induction | 50 to 60[a] | 70 at 60,000 hours; 55 at 100,000 hours | 100,000 | 80 | 2,700 to 4,100 | Where maintenance costs are high, including roadways and tunnels, parking garages, escalator wells, warehouses, and malls |
| LED | 15 to 30 | 70 | 50,000[b] | 80 to 90 | 2,700 to 10,000 | In color-based applications such as exit signs, niche applications such as outdoor signage, task lamps, and accent lighting |

Notes: K = kelvin; LED = light-emitting diode; lm/W = lumen per watt.
a. Higher efficacies for higher-wattage lamps.
b. Time at which output has degraded to 70 percent of initial output.

Courtesy: E SOURCE

In addition to selecting lamps that will save energy, compatibility with existing fixtures and color rendition will inform choices. *Used with permission, ©2010 eSource Companies LLC.*

Fewer tubes in existing fixtures could improve lighting in this community college classroom. Lighting at the counter could substitute one tube for the existing eight in fixtures at that end of the room. *Gelfand Partners Architects.*

ing produced in the ceiling and add task lighting at work areas. This can be accomplished by using fewer tubes in the existing fixtures. At the same time the efficiency of the remaining tubes can be increased if they are replaced by better lamps and ballasts.

The amount of electric light needed in a space also depends on daylight entering the space or on the color of the walls and ceiling. High contrast in a room is both uncomfortable and inefficient (when not intended as in retail or theater spaces). When occupants' eyes are adjusted to the brightest area in the scene the dimmer areas look dark even if they would be quite comfortable without the contrast. Lighting walls and ceilings rather than work surfaces alone reduces the level of ambient light needed for comfort. When walls and ceilings are light colors this strategy works better. Changing the paint from dark to light in an existing room can have a major influence.

Of course the biggest difference in energy use is between on and off. As noted above, users can turn off lights when they leave the room. Occupancy sensors accomplish this automatically. Occupancy sensors can now detect motion and/or infrared radiation. Installing adequate numbers of dual technology sensors that detect both can help reduce annoyance caused by switching off lights in occupied rooms. For years European buildings have run corridor and exit lighting on motion sensors. U.S. building occupants may find it disturbing to enter a dark hallway and then have the lights turn on, but perhaps the base state for these spaces should be the emergency light levels and lighting should increase from there as occupants enter the area.

LED technology is rapidly improving. It is already a proven source for exit lighting. The challenge for lamp designers has been to develop a truly white LED light. "White" LEDs are available, as well as clusters of red/green/blue LEDs. Many of these products are subjectively well-received while achieving low scores for the standard colors used to quantify the Color Reflectance Index (CRI), where more established light sources now score high. For colored lighting such as exit lighting, LEDs are perfect with their long service lives and high efficiency.

Retrofits for lighting include:

- Change or reduce the number of lamps (remove lamps in multi-lamp fixtures and add fluorescent task lighting for up to 50 percent energy improvements)
- Replace lamps and ballasts in standard fluorescent fixtures with new high-efficiency lamps and electronic ballasts
- Install dimmers and dimmer compatible bulbs (incandescent and screw-in fluorescent)
- Install dimmers and dimming ballasts for fluorescent fixtures
- Replace exit signs with LED exit signs
- Retrofit hallway and security lighting (reduce to emergency levels and use an occupancy sensor to increase light level when occupied)
- Install occupancy sensors in break rooms, restrooms, and conference rooms

## Plug Loads

In addition to the energy savings that users can achieve by truly turning off their gadgets when not in use, selecting Energy Star appliances and equipment reduces power demands. Such devices typically have power saving "sleep" modes, and/or greater intrinsic efficiency. For example, flat-screen computer monitors use one-third the energy of a cathode ray tube (CRT) monitor. Care should be taken to compare actual listed energy use among products since Energy Star criteria span a wide range.

High-efficiency T-5 and T-8 fluorescent lamps fit in older light fixtures but require replacement of the original ballasts with electronic ballasts *Gelfand Partners Architects.*

Even sleep modes use energy. Vampires are devices that remain connected to the electric power lines while not doing any useful work. The EPA estimates that up to 11 percent of U.S. electricity use goes to powering these vampires. While purchase of Energy Star devices can reduce these loads tremendously, plug load control systems can be built into the electrical system or be provided as occupancy sensor power strips that turn off all power when no one is using a location.

Offices, restaurants, retail, warehouses, and shops all have different individual quirks. Energy Star data show that restaurants typically use 2.5 times more en-

A manual power strip (easily switched off) can be used to reduce consumption from vampires (transformers that continuously suck small amounts of power). Better still are occupancy sensor power strips that turn off power if no one is present. *Gelfand Partners Architects.*

ergy per square foot than other commercial buildings.[8] Commercial kitchens have a range of easily adopted changes that can greatly reduce the energy needed for their operation. Energy Star's top five strategies are:

1. Install compact fluorescent lamps.
2. Install a high efficiency pre-rinse spray valve.
3. Fix water leaks immediately, especially hot water.
4. Perform walk-in refrigerator maintenance.
5. Replace worn-out cooking and refrigeration equipment.[9]

Like building operations in general, the main strategies are to maintain equipment so that it operates as intended, fix leaks, replace obsolete equipment with Energy Star equipment, and adopt specific, targeted improvements. Tips such as making ice at night in bulk help distribute energy demand out of peak hours and rates, lowering bills and improving efficiency of electric distribution.

As in many other areas of renovation, reducing plug loads starts with studying your own business or facility and finding the biggest energy draws.

## Heating, Ventilating, and Air-Conditioning

Fans and chillers are major users of electricity. Heating is a major direct user of natural gas and other fossil fuels. While major envelope improvements are beyond the scope of maintenance or operations change, the reduction in demand caused by lighting improvements is readily achievable and can be significant. Between retrocommissioning systems to ensure that they are working as well as they can, and reducing heat gain from lights and office equipment, HVAC equipment may be relieved of some of its load. This may mean that it is unnecessary to upgrade.

Depending on the equipment that is installed, different levels of benefit will be attainable. As an example, PG+E, the utility serving Northern California, published a guide to energy savings in packaged HVAC units. These ubiquitous rooftop equipment installations serve many office, retail, and institutional facilities (see sidebar).

Projects that tackled maintenance of 25 rooftop units each in heating-dominated New England and cooling-dominated Louisiana brought substantial savings: an average of 11 percent in New England, and between 22 and 42 percent in Louisiana.[12] These studies used qualified trade workers to perform the checks and adjustments but paid back their owners in lower utility bills within six months or less. While these studies were done on package rooftop units, the idea that major building systems should be regularly maintained is applicable to boilers, chillers, exhaust fans, and all the other machinery that maintains comfort and safety in buildings.

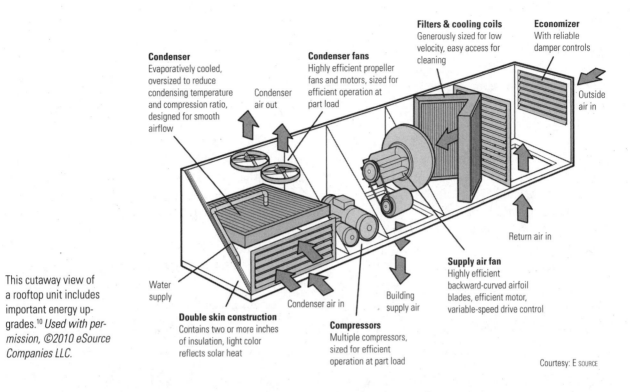

**Condenser**
Evaporatively cooled, oversized to reduce condensing temperature and compression ratio, designed for smooth airflow

Condenser air out

**Condenser fans**
Highly efficient propeller fans and motors, sized for efficient operation at part load

**Filters & cooling coils**
Generously sized for low velocity, easy access for cleaning

**Economizer**
With reliable damper controls

Outside air in

Return air in

**Supply air fan**
Highly efficient backward-curved airfoil blades, efficient motor, variable-speed drive control

Water supply

**Double skin construction**
Contains two or more inches of insulation, light color reflects solar heat

Condenser air in

Building supply air

**Compressors**
Multiple compressors, sized for efficient operation at part load

This cutaway view of a rooftop unit includes important energy upgrades.[10] *Used with permission, ©2010 eSource Companies LLC.*

Courtesy: E SOURCE

## Operations and Maintenance Steps

1.  Air side
    a.  Clean/replace filters regularly.
    b.  Inspect/clean evaporator coils annually to maintain cooling capacity.
    c.  Clean condenser coils. (Dirty coils can reduce compressor efficiency 15 percent.)
    d.  Fix leaks in cabinet and supply duct. (Losing 200 cfm from a 10-ton unit cuts capacity about 5 percent.)
    e.  Clean and adjust dampers.
    f.  Fans, bearings, and belts
        i.  Make sure fans are running in the correct direction (power leads are often switched, leading to a 50 percent reduction in efficiency).
        ii.  Replace bearings when causing excessive noise, vibration, or heat.
        iii.  Properly adjust belts, or replace with notched V-belts that increase drive efficiency by 2 to 10 percent.
    g.  Check airflow (should be within the expected range).

2.  Check compressor
    a.  Check refrigerant levels.
    b.  Check electrical system and analyze oil.
    c.  Check case temperature (common sign of impending compressor failure).

3.  Heat pumps
    a.  Check defrost function of outdoor coil.[11]

## Water Use

Low- and no-cost improvements in water use center on the same three approaches as other systems: behavior, retrocommissioning, and one-for-one fixture replacement with water-saving fixtures and fittings. Major users of water include not only use inside buildings but outdoor uses such as irrigation of ornamental plantings such as lawns. Changing whole landscapes is a major undertaking, but modifying controllers to avoid irrigation while it is raining, is not.

Within buildings, leak control can make big improvements. Commercial buildings vary more than houses, but much water use overlaps and can be cut in much the same way.

## BEYOND ENERGY—GREEN OPERATIONS AND MAINTENANCE

LEED-EBOM looks at user or owner behavior: buying or moving into a LEED building, reducing conventional commuting, sustainable purchasing and waste management, no smoking, and consulting a LEED accredited professional. Without changing the building these measures could add up to 36 points (40 are required for certification).

Building managers typically have control over the next level of improved practices. They can adopt integrated pest management, commissioning, measuring and monitoring of building systems, various manage-

### Daily Indoor per Capita Water Use in the Typical Single-family Home[13]

| Use | Typical Use | | Typical Conservation Measures | | | |
| --- | --- | --- | --- | --- | --- | --- |
| | Gallons per Capita | Percentage of Total Daily Use | Gallons per Capita | Percentage of Total Daily Use | Reduced Use (g/cap) | % Reduction |
| Toilets | 18.5 | 26.7% | 8.2 | 18.0% | 10.3 | 55.7% |
| Clothes Washers | 15.0 | 21.7% | 10.0 | 22.1% | 5.0 | 33.3% |
| Showers | 11.6 | 16.8% | 8.8 | 19.5% | 2.8 | 24.1% |
| Faucets | 10.9 | 15.7% | 10.8 | 23.9% | 0.1 | 0.9% |
| Leaks | 9.5 | 13.7% | 4.0 | 8.8% | 5.5 | 57.9% |
| Other Domestic Uses | 1.6 | 2.2% | 1.6 | 3.4% | — | 0.0% |
| Baths | 1.2 | 1.7% | 1.2 | 2.7% | — | 0.0% |
| Dishwashers | 1.0 | 1.4% | 0.7 | 1.5% | 0.3 | 30.0% |
| TOTAL | 69.3 | 99.9% | 45.3 | 99.9% | 24.0 | 34.6% |

*American Water Works Association*

Replacement of plumbing fixtures and fittings make 30 to 40 percent water savings readily achievable. Leak repair alone can result in significant water savings.

**Figure XI-1. Summary of Findings (per ft²)**

| Category | 20-year NPV |
|---|---|
| Energy Value | $5.79 |
| Emissions Value | $1.18 |
| Water Value | $0.51 |
| Waste Value (construction only) - 1 year | $0.03 |
| Commissioning O&M Value | $8.47 |
| Productivity and Health Value (Certified and Silver) | $36.89 |
| Productivity and Health Value (Gold and Platinum) | $55.33 |
| Less Green Cost Premium | ($4.00) |
| **Total 20-year NPV (Certified and Silver)** | **$48.87** |
| **Total 20-year NPV (Gold and Platinum)** | **$67.31** |

Greg Kats' detailed report to the California Sustainable Building Task Force quantified the costs of energy, water, waste diversion or disposal, and productivity and health value for state buildings and substantiated the benefit to the state of adopting green building standards.[14] *Gregory Kats, Capital-E.*

ment upgrades to specific systems, and best practices in maintenance and operations protocols. Potential points for these changes could add up to 20 more points, or a cumulative total of 56 points (LEED Silver).

LEED-EBOM thus reinforces the value of the choices that users, owners, and managers make in the operation of their facilities. Most of these choices require very little capital investment. Although they do assume time and attention spent in different ways than may be common practice in the industry, results such as the retrocommissioning studies substantiate the potential to recover these investments in time in the lowered costs of operating the facility. That is even before factoring in the gains in employee health and productivity.

Architects focus on the fabric of the building. But the research that Greg Kats (see table) did in quantifying the costs and benefits of green building emphasizes that the first costs of building are minute compared to the costs of operating and maintaining a building. Even *those* costs are minute compared to the expenditure that will be made on personnel in the building over its life. Thus the changes that can be made to improve productivity (healthy indoor environmental quality, comfort,

lighting, and so forth) are the ones with the biggest real payback for owner/occupiers of green buildings.

## Indoor Environmental Quality

Indoor air quality is a problem in many buildings. Building-related diseases include specific illnesses such as Legionnaire's Disease, but also include exposures to toxins such as formaldehyde, asbestos, radon, lead, cleaning products, mold and mildew, and unhealthy mixtures of normal atmospheric gases (i.e., higher concentrations of carbon dioxide). Some of these problems are exacerbated by inappropriate energy-saving techniques that reduce infiltration of fresh air without offsetting reductions with increased controlled ventilation. But building housekeeping is also a strong influence on indoor air and, like many of the immediate improvements that can be made in energy use, it can be modified very quickly.

Source control is the first step in limiting pollutants in the indoor environment. Areas near building entrances should be kept clean and swept outside, and walk-off mats should be used inside to reduce the amount of dirt tracked into buildings. Carpets and

---

A housekeeping program is more than just a cleaning program. It involves:

- Actions to prevent dirt from entering the environment as well as its removal once it is there

- Choices of products and methods that minimize the introduction of pollutants into the environments that the housekeeping program is designed to clean

- Tasks designed for health and safety as well as tasks designed for appearance

- Training, negotiating, and monitoring performance.[15]

This Energy Star printer powers down when not in use. *Gelfand Partners Architects.*

walk-off mats near entrances should be deep cleaned daily. Smoking should not be allowed in the building or near building entrances, windows, or air intakes. Indoor pollutant sources such as high-volume copiers should be isolated, exhausted, and negatively pressured with respect to the rest of the building. Sources of biological contamination such as kitchens and bathrooms need their own protocol.

The housekeeping program should not introduce its own pollutants via unhealthy products or methods that spread dirt rather than removing it. Carpets require particular attention. Vacuum cleaners should meet the requirements of the Carpet and Rug Institute "Green Label" Testing Program. Such vacuum cleaners are capable of capturing 96 percent of particulates 0.3 microns in size. The vacuum must not release more than 100 micrograms of dust particles per cubic meter of air.[16] Moisture on carpets should be removed with water extraction vacuum cleaners within forty-eight hours to avoid mold growth. Use dusters that capture dust (e.g., not feather dusters) and use mops with dust covers.

According to the Janitorial Products Pollution Prevention Project, each year in the United States, 6 out of every 100 professional janitors are injured by the chemicals they use.[17] Use environmentally preferable cleaning products such as those tested by Green Seal. Use products with a moderate pH and minimize products such as ammonia, chlorine, and volatile acids. Minimize aerosols and particles that become airborne.

Regularly clean areas that are not visible, such as spaces behind and under furniture. Blinds, shelves, and furniture itself can accumulate dirt. Dust and contamination in these areas can become part of the indoor atmosphere just like the dust in areas that are visible.

It is critical to train cleaning staff in the appropriate use of cleaning products and equipment. Outside contractors should be able to detail their training methods and the products they use. Even users should be involved in training so that they do not introduce some of the dangerous and unhealthy products that are readily available on the home market.

Mold and microbes require special consideration. Mold and microbes are alive. Mold spores are present in the environment all around us. The best approach to mold growth is prevention. Disinfecting with nonpolluting cleaning and antimicrobial agents can provide some protection against mold growth. But controlling moisture indoors is the key strategy. Condensation from water vapor inside rooms or wall or ceiling cavities is one source of moisture in a building that is not leaking. Particularly if setting back the thermostat at night is part of the energy strategy, careful design of ventilation and humidity control systems is needed to keep air flowing and prevent condensation. U.S. EPA recommends replacement of both ceiling tiles and insulation if they get wet, because they cannot be cleaned and dried effectively. This means a maintenance department needs a stock of tiles to be used for replacement or they will not match. And they need to be stored someplace dry.

Like molds, the first strategy against pests is prevention. Pests should not find hospitable habitats, and they should be blocked from access to buildings. Where pests are present, an integrated pest management (IPM) program is the way to deal with them. IPM depends on knowledge about the pests and their biology. The recommended EPA IPM program includes:

- Eliminate leakage
- Fix moisture problems
- Install barriers to pest entry and movement
- Monitor for pests and report problems[18]

A potential attraction for pests is food garbage. A hose bib and area drain helps maintenance keep the trash collection area clean. But some water districts protect water quality by requiring a roof over dumpster enclosures so that stormwater does not wash contaminants from the garbage down the drain. Design of the enclosure must be coordinated with the local scavenger service so that the equipment it uses to empty dumpsters will not conflict.

Once pests have arrived, best practices in pest eradication should be followed. The U.S. EPA has developed Worker Protection Standards that must be followed. These standards include training and protection of the workers as well as the environment. Even products that are relatively benign if used occasionally can be dangerous at occupational frequency or at concentrations that workers may encounter before they dilute the products for application.

## Regional Issues

LEED-EBOM awards credit for innovations including educational efforts and documentation. New in the latest version are four possible points automatically awarded by USGBC for projects earning credits that are identified as priorities for their region. This recognizes that some regions are more sensitive to issues such as energy sources or water or transit, and provides an additional point for projects that achieve strategies important to their region.

## Putting Your Program Together

Using LEED-EBOM as a framework, sustainable building operations and maintenance consists of:

### Sustainable Sites

- Choose a building that is already sustainably designed (i.e., has access to daylighting)
- Choose a building close to public transportation and create policies that support carpools, car share, pedestrians, and bicyclists
- Reduce stormwater, heat island, and light pollution impacts

### Water Efficiency

- Upgrade plumbing fixtures and fittings
- Monitor water use
- Reduce irrigation through plant selection and high efficiency irrigation
- Improve cooling tower operation

### Energy and Atmosphere

- Measure, retrocommission, and monitor system performance
- Manage refrigerants
- Report results

### Materials and Resources

- Adopt a sustainable purchasing policy including health impacts, regional impacts, and end-of-use disposal
- Adopt a sustainable waste management policy including consumables, durable goods, and alteration or construction waste

### Indoor Environmental Quality

- No smoking
- Adopt a green housekeeping policy
- Adopt integrated pest management

### Innovation in Operations Regional Priority

- Respond to the needs of your region

## LEED 2009 for Existing Buildings: Operations & Maintenance

Project Checklist

Project Name

Date

| 0 | 0 | 0 | | Sustainable Sites | Possible Points: | 26 |
|---|---|---|---|---|---|---|
| Y | N | ? | | | | |
| | | | Credit 1 | LEED Certified Design and Construction | | 4 |
| | | | Credit 2 | Building Exterior and Hardscape Management Plan | | 1 |
| | | | Credit 3 | Integrated Pest Management, Erosion Control, and Landscape Management Plan | | 1 |
| | | | Credit 4 | Alternative Commuting Transportation | | 3 to 15 |
| | | | | Reduce by 10% | | 3 |
| | | | | Reduce by 13.75% | | 4 |
| | | | | Reduce by 17.5% | | 5 |
| | | | | Reduce by 21.25% | | 6 |
| | | | | Reduce by 25% | | 7 |
| | | | | Reduce by 31.25% | | 8 |
| | | | | Reduce by 37.5% | | 9 |
| | | | | Reduce by 43.75% | | 10 |
| | | | | Reduce by 50% | | 11 |
| | | | | Reduce by 56.25% | | 12 |
| | | | | Reduce by 62.5% | | 13 |
| | | | | Reduce by 68.75% | | 14 |
| | | | | Reduce by 75% | | 15 |
| | | | Credit 5 | Site Development—Protect or Restore Open Habitat | | 1 |
| | | | Credit 6 | Stormwater Quantity Control | | 1 |
| | | | Credit 7.1 | Heat Island Reduction—Non-Roof | | 1 |
| | | | Credit 7.2 | Heat Island Reduction—Roof | | 1 |
| | | | Credit 8 | Light Pollution Reduction | | 1 |

| 0 | 0 | 0 | | Water Efficiency | Possible Points: | 14 |
|---|---|---|---|---|---|---|
| Y | N | ? | | | | |
| Y | | | Prereq 1 | Minimum Indoor Plumbing Fixture and Fitting Efficiency | | |
| | | | Credit 1 | Water Performance Measurement | | 1 to 2 |
| | | | | Whole building metering | | 1 |
| | | | | Submetering | | 2 |
| | | | Credit 2 | Additional Indoor Plumbing Fixture and Fitting Efficiency | | 1 to 5 |
| | | | | Reduce by 10% | | 1 |
| | | | | Reduce by 15% | | 2 |
| | | | | Reduce by 20% | | 3 |
| | | | | Reduce by 25% | | 4 |
| | | | | Reduce by 30% | | 5 |
| | | | Credit 3 | Water Efficient Landscaping | | 1 to 5 |
| | | | | Reduce by 50% | | 1 |
| | | | | Reduce by 62.5% | | 2 |
| | | | | Reduce by 75% | | 3 |
| | | | | Reduce by 87.5% | | 4 |
| | | | | Reduce by 100% | | 5 |
| | | | Credit 4 | Cooling Tower Water Management | | 1 to 2 |
| | | | | Chemical Management | | 1 |
| | | | | Non-Potable Water Source Use | | 2 |

LEED Scorecard[19] *U.S. Green Building Council (USGBC).*

| 0 | 0 | 0 | **Energy and Atmosphere** | Possible Points: | **35** |
|---|---|---|---|---|---|

| Y | N | ? | | | |
|---|---|---|---|---|---|
| Y | | | Prereq 1 | Energy Efficiency Best Management Practices | |
| Y | | | Prereq 2 | Minimum Energy Efficiency Performance | |
| Y | | | Prereq 3 | Fundamental Refrigerant Management | |
| | | | Credit 1 | Optimize Energy Efficiency Performance | 1 to 18 |
| | | | | ENERGY STAR Rating of 71 or 21st Percentile Above National Median | 1 |
| | | | | ENERGY STAR Rating of 73 or 23rd Percentile Above National Median | 2 |
| | | | | ENERGY STAR Rating of 74 or 24th Percentile Above National Median | 3 |
| | | | | ENERGY STAR Rating of 75 or 25th Percentile Above National Median | 4 |
| | | | | ENERGY STAR Rating of 76 or 26th Percentile Above National Median | 5 |
| | | | | ENERGY STAR Rating of 77 or 27th Percentile Above National Median | 6 |
| | | | | ENERGY STAR Rating of 78 or 28th Percentile Above National Median | 7 |
| | | | | ENERGY STAR Rating of 79 or 29th Percentile Above National Median | 8 |
| | | | | ENERGY STAR Rating of 80 or 30th Percentile Above National Median | 9 |
| | | | | ENERGY STAR Rating of 81 or 31st Percentile Above National Median | 10 |
| | | | | ENERGY STAR Rating of 82 or 32nd Percentile Above National Median | 11 |
| | | | | ENERGY STAR Rating of 83 or 33rd Percentile Above National Median | 12 |
| | | | | ENERGY STAR Rating of 85 or 35th Percentile Above National Median | 13 |
| | | | | ENERGY STAR Rating of 87 or 37th Percentile Above National Median | 14 |
| | | | | ENERGY STAR Rating of 89 or 39th Percentile Above National Median | 15 |
| | | | | ENERGY STAR Rating of 91 or 41st Percentile Above National Median | 16 |
| | | | | ENERGY STAR Rating of 93 or 43rd Percentile Above National Median | 17 |
| | | | | ENERGY STAR Rating of 95+ or 45th+ Percentile Above National Median | 18 |
| | | | Credit 2.1 | Existing Building Commissioning—Investigation and Analysis | 2 |
| | | | Credit 2.2 | Existing Building Commissioning—Implementation | 2 |
| | | | Credit 2.3 | Existing Building Commissioning—Ongoing Commissioning | 2 |
| | | | Credit 3.1 | Performance Measurement—Building Automation System | 1 |
| | | | Credit 3.2 | Performance Measurement—System-Level Metering | 1 to 2 |
| | | | | 40% Metered | 1 |
| | | | | 80% Metered | 2 |
| | | | Credit 4 | On-site and Off-site Renewable Energy | 1 to 6 |
| | | | | 3% On-site or 25% Off-site Renewable Energy | 1 |
| | | | | 4.5% On-site or 37.5% Off-site Renewable Energy | 2 |
| | | | | 6% On-site or 50% Off-site Renewable Energy | 3 |
| | | | | 7.5% On-site or 62.5% Off-site Renewable Energy | 4 |
| | | | | 9% On-site or 75% Off-site Renewable Energy | 5 |
| | | | | 12% On-site or 100% Off-site Renewable Energy | 6 |
| | | | Credit 5 | Enhanced Refrigerant Management | 1 |
| | | | Credit 6 | Emissions Reduction Reporting | 1 |

| Y | N | ? | | | Possible Points: | 10 |
|---|---|---|---|---|---|---|
| **0** | **0** | **0** | **Materials and Resources** | | | |
| Y | | | Prereq 1 | Sustainable Purchasing Policy | | |
| Y | | | Prereq 2 | Solid Waste Management Policy | | |
| | | | Credit 1 | Sustainable Purchasing—Ongoing Consumables | | 1 |
| | | | Credit 2.1 | Sustainable Purchasing—Durable Goods | | 1 to 2 |
| | | | | 40% of Electric | | 1 |
| | | | | 40% of Furniture | | 1 |
| | | | Credit 3 | Sustainable Purchasing—Facility Alterations and Additions | | 1 |
| | | | Credit 4 | Sustainable Purchasing—Reduced Mercury in Lamps | | 1 |
| | | | Credit 5 | Sustainable Purchasing—Food | | 1 |
| | | | Credit 6 | Solid Waste Management—Waste Stream Audit | | 1 |
| | | | Credit 7 | Solid Waste Management—Ongoing Consumables | | 1 |
| | | | Credit 8 | Solid Waste Management—Durable Goods | | 1 |
| | | | Credit 9 | Solid Waste Management—Facility Alterations and Additions | | 1 |

| Y | N | ? | | | Possible Points: | 15 |
|---|---|---|---|---|---|---|
| **0** | **0** | **0** | **Indoor Environmental Quality** | | | |
| Y | | | Prereq 1 | Minimum IAQ Performance | | |
| Y | | | Prereq 2 | Environmental Tobacco Smoke (ETS) Control | | |
| Y | | | Prereq 3 | Green Cleaning Policy | | |
| | | | Credit 1.1 | Indoor Air Quality Best Management Practices—Indoor Air Quality Management Program | | 1 |

| Y | N | ? | | | Possible Points: | 4 |
|---|---|---|---|---|---|---|
| **0** | **0** | **0** | **Regional Priority Credits** | | | |
| | | | Credit 1.1 | Regional Priority: Specific Credit | | 1 |
| | | | Credit 1.2 | Regional Priority: Specific Credit | | 1 |
| | | | Credit 1.3 | Regional Priority: Specific Credit | | 1 |
| | | | Credit 1.4 | Regional Priority: Specific Credit | | 1 |

| | | | | | Possible Points: | 110 |
|---|---|---|---|---|---|---|
| **0** | **0** | **0** | **Total** | | | |
| | | | Certified 40 to 49 points | Silver 50 to 59 points | Gold 60 to 79 points | Platinum 80 to 110 |
| | | | Credit 3.2 | Green Cleaning—Custodial Effectiveness Assessment | | 1 |
| | | | Credit 3.3 | Green Cleaning—Purchase of Sustainable Cleaning Products and Materials | | 1 |
| | | | Credit 3.4 | Green Cleaning—Sustainable Cleaning Equipment | | 1 |
| | | | Credit 3.5 | Green Cleaning—Indoor Chemical and Pollutant Source Control | | 1 |
| | | | Credit 3.6 | Green Cleaning—Indoor Integrated Pest Management | | 1 |

| 0 | 0 | 0 | **Innovation in Operations** | Possible Points: | **6** |
|---|---|---|---|---|---|
| Y | N | ? | | | |

| | | | Credit 1.1 | Innovation in Operations: Specific Title | 1 |
|---|---|---|---|---|---|
| | | | Credit 1.2 | Innovation in Operations: Specific Title | 1 |
| | | | Credit 1.3 | Innovation in Operations: Specific Title | 1 |
| | | | Credit 1.4 | Innovation in Operations: Specific Title | 1 |
| | | | Credit 2 | LEED Accredited Professional | 1 |
| | | | Credit 3 | Documenting Sustainable Building Cost Impacts | 1 |

| 0 | 0 | 0 | **Regional Priority Credits** | Possible Points: | **4** |
|---|---|---|---|---|---|
| Y | N | ? | | | |

| | | | Credit 1.1 | Regional Priority: Specific Credit | 1 |
|---|---|---|---|---|---|
| | | | Credit 1.2 | Regional Priority: Specific Credit | 1 |
| | | | Credit 1.3 | Regional Priority: Specific Credit | 1 |
| | | | Credit 1.4 | Regional Priority: Specific Credit | 1 |

| 0 | 0 | 0 | **Total** | Possible Points: | **110** |
|---|---|---|---|---|---|

Certified 40 to 49 points    Silver 50 to 59 points    Gold 60 to 79 points    Platinum 80 to 110

CASE STUDY

# ASHRAE Headquarters

**Owner**   ASHRAE Foundation

**Renovation Architect**   Richard Wittschiebe Hand

**Original Building Type**   Office

**Renovation Building Type**   Office, Assembly

**Original Construction Date**   1965

**Renovation Date**   2008

**Location**   Atlanta, GA

**Climate**   Humid Subtropical (Köppen Cfa)

**Area**   33,570 square feet

**Achievement**   LEED-NC 2.2 Platinum (67 points)

**Key Indicators**   Advanced Ventilation & Cooling Systems
   Dedicated Outdoor Air System (DOAS)
   Dual Stage Air-to-Air Heat Recovery Desiccant Wheels
   Variable Speed Outside Air
   Exhaust Air Fans, Direct Expansion (DX) Cooling
   MERV 13 Air Filters
   Geothermal Heat Pump
   Tightened Envelope
   Daylighting with Minimal Perimeter Offices
   Increased Ventilation Rates

**Energy Achievement**   31 percent less than comparable building

**Total Energy Use**   1,027 kBtu/year   (30.59 kWh/sf/year)   (329 kWh/m² year)

**Water Before**   253,000 gal/year   8.16 gal/sf/year

**Water After**   136,000 gal/year   4.35 gal/sf/year   46 percent less water

Renewables   20 kWh Photovoltaics (8 percent of electricity)

ASHRAE, the American Society of Heating Refrigeration and Air-Conditioning Engineers, an organization dedicated to the advancement of knowledge about the design of mechanical systems, decided in 2005 to direct their focus toward sustainability and transform their headquarters building into an exemplar of sustainable systems design. Located in Atlanta, the renovated 1965 two-story building provides a living laboratory of engineered techniques for building conditioning. Improvements to the building envelope and lighting set the ground for installation of several different reduced energy mechanical systems.

A roof-mounted Dedicated Outdoor Air System (DOAS) provides 6,000 cubic feet per minute (cfm) of outside air with heat recovery ventilation. The ground floor and learning center are conditioned with variable refrigerant flow inverter driven, two-stage outdoor DX heat pumps, and ducted fan coil units operating with a non-ozone-depleting refrigerant (R-410A). The second floor is conditioned with two-stage, 27 SEER variable-speed ground source heat pumps operating with a geothermal field of twelve 400-ft-deep wells. Lighting operates at 25 to 30 percent lower than comparable systems through use of daylight and occupancy sensors. A roof-mounted 20 kilowatt (kW) photovoltaic array provides 8 percent of the building's electrical power. Additionally, the plumbing system uses low-flow toilets, waterless urinals, and solar preheat of domestic water to reduce overall use by 46 percent. Around the site, stormwater bioswales are used for stormwater runoff reduction through soil infiltration–aquifer recharge.

Constructed in 1965, the 2005 renovation of the ASHRAE headquarters added 4,500 square feet while applying sophisticated heating and cooling systems in order to achieve a LEED-NC 2.2 Platinum rating. While providing 30 percent higher ventilation than required by indoor air standards, it achieves an energy use 31 percent less than comparable buildings. *Fred S. Gerlich Photography.*

▲ A roof-mounted 20 kilowatt (kW) photovoltaic array provides 8 percent of the building's electrical power. *Noel Thomas Tyler.*

▶High-efficiency lighting operates at 25 to 30 percent greater efficiency than typical systems. A tight building envelope reduces infiltration, reducing the size of the heating, ventilation system and allowing it to work at higher efficiency. *Fred S. Gerlich Photography.*

CASE STUDY

# Herman Miller Building C1

**Owner**  Herman Miller, Inc., Corporation, for-profit

**Renovation Architect**  Krueck & Sexton Architects

**Original Building Type**  Office

**Renovation Building Type**  Office

**Original Construction Date**  1977

**Renovation Date**  2002

**Location**  Zeeland, MI

**Climate**  Humid Continental (Köppen Dfa)

**Area**  19,000 square feet

**Achievement**  LEED v2/v2.1 Gold (41 points)

**Key Indicators**  Daylighting

  Retained 57 percent open space on site

  31 percent reduction water use, nonstructured stormwater management

  29 percent less energy

  On-site Energy Production—Biomass CHP Plant (69 percent)

  Locally Sourced Material

  Recycled Products

  Daylighting

**Energy Achievement**  29 percent less than comparable building

**Total Energy Use**  481,000 kWh/year   (25.31 kWh/sf year)   (272.5 kWh/m$^2$ year)

**Electricity After**  166,000 kWh/year   (8.74 kWh/sf year)   (94.1 kWh/m$^2$ year)

**Heating/Cooling After**  56.6 kBtu/sf year   (16.58 kWh/sf/year)   (178 kW/m$^2$ year)

**Water After**  31 percent reduction

**Renewables**  69 percent of electricity from shared biomass central plant

An early pilot project for the LEED certification, the renovations of the 1977 Herman Miller Building C1 continue Herman Miller's commitment to environmental issues. Aiming to determine what was possible in sustainable renovation, the entire building shell was reused, saving its embodied energy.

The original building included a sturdy, flexible building shell, operable windows, and solar shading, which were all used and improved throughout the renovation. High-efficiency low-emissivity glazing replaced original windows; reflective, perforated blinds were installed for user control. T-5 direct/indirect light fixtures were tied to daylight and occupancy sensors to further reduce electricity use while taking advantage of the building's abundant natural light.

Mechanical systems were changed to use variable-speed drives, while a 100 percent outside air economizer was added to the HVAC system to provide ventilation with minimal energy when weather was appropriate. Fresh air supply is optimized by a direct digital control (DDC) building management system that employs humidistats and

▲ Lighting controls and daylight harvesting combine with operable windows at top and bottom of two-story façade to permit 75 percent of the building to continue operating even during a power outage while providing everyday energy savings. *Mariusz Mizera.*

▶ Supplementing existing shading fins with newly planted trees, designers inserted new low-emissivity glazing to optimize existing façades. Fifty-seven percent of the immediate site area was retained for planting and preserving bird habitat while buffering the building from temperature extremes. *Mariusz Mizera.*

▶ Daylighting, supplemented by efficient electric lighting, combines with low-emitting materials to produce high indoor environmental quality. *Mariusz Mizera.*

▼ Durable materials combine with high-recycled-content furniture to lower the building's environmental impact. Seventy-five percent of construction debris was diverted from landfill. T-5 lamps in modular ceilings combine with a 100 percent open plan to allow easier modifications in the future. *Mariusz Mizera.*

carbon dioxide sensors to monitor indoor air quality. An on-site biomass-powered central plant provides steam, chilled water, and electricity, reducing dependence on grid-supplied electricity while using wood scraps from Herman Miller's furniture manufacturing process.

Outside the building a native-planted bioswale and sedimentation basin stormwater management system was developed while a parking area was compacted to maximize open space. Transportation associated with the renovation was minimized by using 57 percent of construction resources from within 500 miles. Lastly, materials used in the renovation prioritized recycled content and minimized use of products containing volatile organic compounds (VOCs).

## ENDNOTES

1. James Thurber, *My Life and Hard Times*, New York: HarperCollins Publishers, Inc, 1933, p. 16.

2. www.drinktap.org/consumerdnn/Home/WaterInformation/ Conservation/WaterUseStatistics/tabid/85/Default.aspx, accessed November 14, 2010.

3. LEED 2009 for Existing Buildings: Operations & Maintenance Rating System, USGBC Member Approved November 2008 (Updated October 2010), p. xvi.

4. *The Ingenious Dr. Franklin. Selected Scientific Letters*, edited by Nathan G. Goodman. Philadelphia: University of Pennsylvania Press, 1931, p. 20.

5. http://enconcorp.com/ecs/index.php?option=com_content&task=view&id=38&Itemid=77, accessed September 19, 2010.

6. www.noresco.com/behavior/ku/index.html, accessed September 19, 2010.

7. www.energystar.gov/ia/business/EPA_BUM_Full.pdf, pp.4–5, accessed September 19, 2010.

8. www.energystar.gov/ia/business/small_business/restaurants_guide.pdf, accessed October 16, 2010.

9. *Ibid.*, p. 1, accessed December 20, 2010.

10. "Energy-Efficient Operations and Maintenance Strategies for Packaged HVAC Systems," copyright © May 1997, Pacific Gas and Electric Company, all rights reserved.

11. *Ibid.*, PG+E.

12. *Ibid.*, PG+E.

13. www.drinktap.org/consumerdnn/Home/WaterInformation/ Conservation/Water UseStatistics/tabid/85/Default.aspx.

14. Kats, Greg, Capital E, "The Costs and Financial Benefits of Green Buildings: A Report to California's Sustainable Building Task Force," October 2003, p. 84.

15. www.epa.gov/iaq/largebldgs/i-beam/pdfs/text_modules_iaq_maintenance.pdf, accessed November 14, 2010.

16. www.carpet-rug.org/commercial-customers/cleaning-and-maintenance/seal-of-approval-products/vacuums.cfm, accessed November 14, 2010.

17. http://wsppn.org/Janitorial/jp4.cfm, accessed November 14, 2010.

18. www.epa.gov/pesticides/controlling/mgr-roles.htm, accessed November 14, 2010.

19. LEED 2009 for Existing Buildings: Operations & Maintenance Rating System, USGBC Member Approved November 2008 (Updated October 2010), pp. vi–vii.

# chapter 4

# BUILDING ENVELOPE DESIGN

A famous architect reached such a level of enthusiasm (...) that he asserted: "In the future one will build in the far North exactly as along the Mediterranean Sea." In a few years his demand has been fulfilled; Architecture has suffered such a defeat, that she will recover only very slowly. Had this been just an aesthetic mistake, then it would probably not have been fatal to a similar degree. But Nature—in this case the climate—will not withhold its revenge, for the fact that she has been so badly ignored.[1]

—Bruno Taut, 1936

## INTRODUCTION

Modern electricity and heating and cooling systems have produced an illusion that comfort can be provided with ease inside a building in any climate. However, this is only marginally true, and in most climates a building envelope (roof and exterior walls, with doors and windows) requires a tremendous amount of energy for electrical and mechanical systems to achieve interior comfort. To reduce this energy demand the building's walls and roof must interrupt the transfer of energy that acts through convection, conduction, or radiation.

The building envelope has a thermal function: to make sure the building does not conduct or radiate heat, or leak air, unless desired. It also functions to keep out water, and to manage condensation due to differential temperatures, pressures, and relative humidity. The envelope is required to admit daylight and views, while controlling glare and heat transfer. It manages the replenishment of fresh air for inhabitants and processes inside a building.

Heat, moisture protection, light, and air: renovation of a building's envelope can affect a building's functional performance more than any other aspect of sustainable renovation. With a well-designed envelope, the energy requirements for external sources of heating, cooling, ventilating, or lighting can be greatly reduced. And it is only after reducing demand through envelope improvements that the much more limited systems gains can be achieved (for example, a 10 percent gain from 80 to 90 percent machinery efficiency). This chapter considers the performance issues for roofs, walls, doors, and windows when redesigning existing buildings.

## AIR INFILTRATION LOSSES

For small buildings such as single-family homes, building weatherization can make huge improvements to the performance of an existing building envelope. Weatherization consists of sealing the gaps that allow the infiltration or leaking of air across a building envelope. Usually this is done with caulk or other flexible sealant. Depending on pressure, air can go either way. For houses, existing systems such as whole-house exhaust fans, bathroom exhaust fans, and kitchen hoods may be more likely to create negative pressure than positive pressure. In that case unconditioned air is sucked in from outside the building, bringing with it the outside temperature and humidity. Sealing gaps in small building envelopes is much more effective than increasing insulation.

Larger buildings have some important differences. They may have a larger ratio of enclosed space to building skin. They are typically kept at a slightly positive pressure, preventing infiltration from outside from being a big concern. The concern typically is losing conditioned air to the outside. Areas adjacent to the building skin will be most affected with problem areas quite concentrated. Energy use that varies with the weather within the heating or cooling season is a good indicator that outside energy loads dominate the building performance. Many office buildings and other commercial structures are more affected by their internal loads (lighting, plug loads, people). In that case building system improvements will make more of a difference in performance than envelope improvements.

However, particularly tall buildings are subjected to high winds and will often require attention to seal gaps. Such gaps, either between different materials such as walls and ceilings, walls and floor slabs, or between windows and walls, require sealant. Sometimes original windows were also of poor quality and constitute a major source of infiltration.

Commercial buildings and other buildings with intensive public use also lose energy through their doors. Installing a vestibule prevents doors opening and closing from changing all the air in the lobby. Revolving doors were also invented for that purpose.

## INSULATION STRATEGIES

Beyond infiltration the primary component affecting energy use of a building envelope is insulation value. Generally, existing buildings benefit from added insulation. Anywhere maintaining a temperature differential between inside and outside is desired, insulation helps save the energy necessary to set and maintain that difference. However, insulation benefits can vary greatly depending on a building's climate zone, solar configuration, humidity controls, and construction method. When looking at heating energy in cold or cool climate zones, four of the ten most cost-effective building modifications involve adding insulation.[2] Another pair of modifications involve sealing gaps to prevent air leakage. Thus, the majority of cost-effective energy-saving strategies address modifications to the building envelope.

Analysis of energy transfer helps to indicate where insulation would benefit most. In buildings where heated air escapes through the roof or attic, or where heat gain is intense through solar radiation on a flat roof, attic insulation and gap sealing will create the biggest benefits. Adding insulation *outside* a masonry wall may trade a durable wall surface for one with much less longevity; however, insulating inside the masonry may be counterproductive and negate the benefits of the existing thermal mass. A renovation that exposes the *inside* of a brick wall as an interior finish could

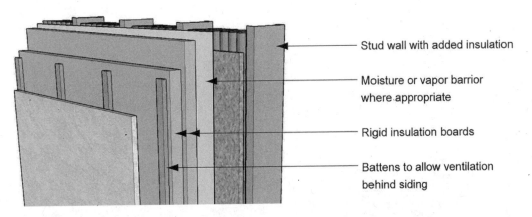

Stud wall with added insulation

Moisture or vapor barrier where appropriate

Rigid insulation boards

Battens to allow ventilation behind siding

Existing buildings with little or no insulation in a cavity wall can usually accommodate blow-in cellulose or expanded foam insulation. Expanded foam can double as an air infiltration barrier since it expands to fill small cracks and gaps. *Gelfand Partners Architects.*

ameliorate some conductive heat loss with good attic insulation and careful control of heat loss through air infiltration. It is rarely possible to insulate floor slabs and foundations unless significant reconstruction is undertaken. Thus, the thermal behavior of a renovated building must be *specifically* considered rather than predicted through generic models based on modern standards of practice.

## Cold Climate

Especially in cold climates, sealing and insulating provide remarkable benefits during the heating season. During the cooling season, load-dominated buildings such as offices (buildings in which interior heat sources such as lighting, equipment, and occupants outweigh heat losses through the exterior wall) can be harmed by increased insulation if not combined with a reduction in interior loads and with improve-

ments in solar shading and ventilation strategies. If insulation and building infiltration improvements are planned, new ventilation strategies must be applied in order to avoid buildup of even more inside heat, and to provide enough makeup air to prevent carbon dioxide buildup.

A common insulation strategy in cold climates is to add insulation to the interior walls, above the ceiling, and at the bottom of the attic.

Wall insulation strategy depends on the existing wall type and extent of renovation. Designers should investigate existing conditions throughout buildings to be renovated, to identify particularly egregious paths for heat loss. For example, many larger buildings have radiators placed directly against uninsulated exterior walls. Very large energy savings may be obtained by providing a thin radiant barrier insulation board behind the radiators, to reduce the energy wasted heating the exterior wall and the outside air.[3]

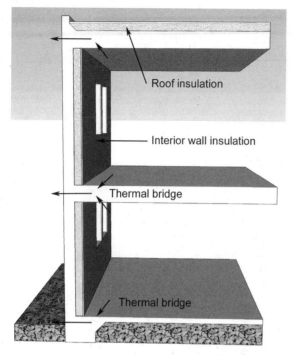

Roof insulation

Interior wall insulation

Thermal bridge

Thermal bridge

Often when new insulation is added inside a building, each floor level provides a structural pathway for cold to enter the building. Exterior insulation systems can eliminate thermal bridging, but are not appropriate for all buildings or all renovation programs. *Gelfand Partners Architects.*

Where basements or crawlspaces are exposed to weather, underfloor insulation and exterior insulation below grade are very important. Depending on the building's configuration and use, insulation added at the underside of the first floor or rigid board insulation outside the foundation can prevent thermal bridging into the heated space. *Gelfand Partners Architects.*

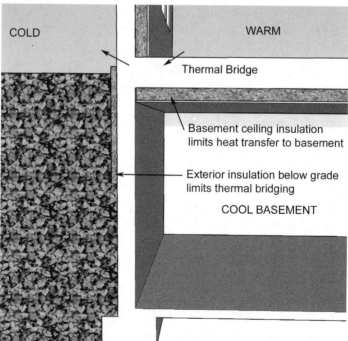

COLD

WARM

Thermal Bridge

Basement ceiling insulation limits heat transfer to basement

Exterior insulation below grade limits thermal bridging

COOL BASEMENT

## Humid Middle Latitude Climate

Within the Temperate Climate, strategies introducing insulation into existing wall, roof, and floor cavities can be very successful at reducing energy use without wholesale modification to the envelope. With smaller buildings of metal or wood stud frame construction, it is often possible to introduce blown or expanded insulation into existing wall cavities. Products popular in the residential market are appropriate for introduction in framed wall construction of larger buildings.

Spray-in-place foam insulation, whether icynene, urethane, or soy-based, is often preferable to the less expensive fiberglass batt insulation, because it does not require removal of interior finishes. Installed through holes in finishes in each frame bay, liquid insulation is sprayed into a wall cavity. A foaming agent causes the insulation to expand, filling the cavity and all the gaps and holes adjacent. Because of its ability to fill both large and small cavities, sprayed-in-place foam insulation also acts as an excellent air barrier, addressing both insulation and air infiltration issues. Care should be taken to evaluate water migration issues to ensure that condensation will not form on adjacent surfaces due to prevention of water vapor migration.

Although not as effective as exterior insulation systems in preventing heat migration, sprayed-in-place foam insulation can provide a very significant improvement to a wall assembly. High R-value (about twice per inch as batt insulation), combined with air barrier properties, leaves only thermal bridging as a weak point in a wall assembly. Finally, when choosing a sprayed-in-place foam insulation, avoid products that use HCFCs as foaming agents, or that off-gas formaldehyde or other toxic chemicals.

Another option for improving existing wall assembly insulation without removal of finishes is sprayed

While sprayed-in-place foam insulation can be used for attic or sealed ceiling joist space, commercial and institutional buildings generally have either an accessible attic area more suitable for blown-in cellulose insulation or a thin roof assembly more amenable to an exterior rigid insulation. © 2007, Cheri L. Wallace.

fiber insulation. Fibers can be cellulose, fiberglass, or mineral wool. Cellulose has the advantage of being made of natural materials with a high recycled content.[4] Generally, sprayed fiber insulation performs better than batt insulation because it more completely fills cavities, because it limits air infiltration (although not as well

## Insulation Types

| Type | Made of | Appropriate Use | Sustainability Issues |
|---|---|---|---|
| Fiberglass Batt | Fiberglass fibers and binder | Walls, ceilings, ventilated attics, basements, and crawlspaces | Can contain binders with added formaldehyde |
| Mineral Fiber | Mineral fibers and binder | Fire-stopping | Can contain binders with added formaldehyde |
| Cotton Batt | Recycled cotton fabric (jeans) | Walls, ceilings, ventilated attics, basements, and crawlspaces | Fire-retardant additives may contain harmful substances |
| Cellulose | Recycled newspaper | Walls, attics | Can promote mold growth if moisture is present; may contain fungicide |
| Spray-Foam | Urethane or soy-based foam | Walls, attics, ceilings | Loses R-value if water present |
| Rigid Board | Polyisocyanurate | Roof, walls where high insulation value per inch and compressive strength are required | Often made with blowing agents using CFC or HCFC |
| | XPS—extruded Polystyrene | Roof, walls where high insulation value per inch and compressive strength are required | Often made with HCFC blowing agents |
| | EPS—expanded polystyrene | Walls, ceilings, ventilated attics, basements, and crawlspaces | Often made with blowing agents using CFC or HCFC (pentane) |
| Vacuum Insulated Panel | Evacuated composite panel | Walls, ceilings | Loses insulation value if punctured |

as sprayed-in-place foam), and because of its higher R-value. Care must be taken to ensure that cavities are completely filled, or thermal bridging effects will remain pronounced. Material used should be evaluated for components that off-gas toxic substances.

## Hot Humid Climate

Affected by hot humid summers and cool humid winters, buildings in the southeast United States are dominated by cooling loads. Central Florida has about 3,000 Cooling Degree Days (CDD) and only 1,000 Heating Degree Days (HDD).[5] Approximately 50 percent of houses in Florida, and a significant portion of small commercial and institutional buildings, are constructed of concrete masonry units with concrete slab-on-grade foundations. A Florida Solar Energy Center/ Oak Ridge National Laboratory study from the 1990s concluded that exterior wall insulation (approximately R10) resulted in cooling energy savings of 5 to 9 percent.[6] Installation of R30 rigid board insulation (6 in.) complies with Passive House[7] goals and results in significantly greater savings. The study did not investigate winter heating savings or overall yearly savings, but exterior insulation combined with thermal mass within the insulation and heat exchange ventilation should produce significant heating savings as well.

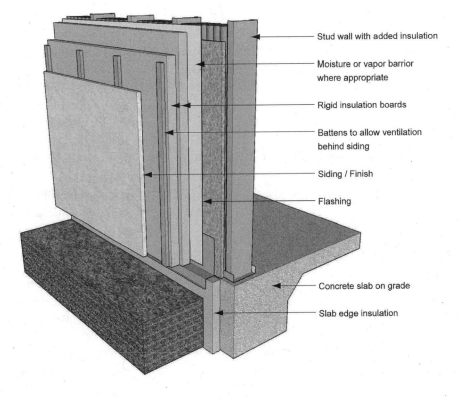

Stud wall with added insulation

Moisture or vapor barrier where appropriate

Rigid insulation boards

Battens to allow ventilation behind siding

Siding / Finish

Flashing

Concrete slab on grade

Slab edge insulation

Existing concrete masonry unit or concrete buildings can easily be retrofitted with exterior rigid insulation so long as moisture control is addressed. Extruded polystyrene boards, either with the application of battens to allow mechanical fasteners, or adhered directly to a cleaned wall surface, make an effective insulation barrier with a continuous R-value of approximately R3 to R5 per inch of thickness. *Gelfand Partners Architects.*

## Hot Dry Climate

The same Florida/Oak Ridge study also looked at adding exterior insulation to buildings in Arizona. Phoenix has a climate with about 3,000 CDD and 2,000 HDD. The study concluded:

> Exterior wall insulation [R10] installed on masonry-constructed houses produces the greatest air conditioning electricity savings and peak demand reductions in hot, dry climates similar to Phoenix, Arizona. Modeling estimated savings of 10% to 14% and demand reductions of 8% to 12% are possible in these climates, which were confirmed by measured data from eight test houses in Phoenix.[8]

This study looked at only moderate addition of insulation. Increased energy savings track directly with increased exterior insulation values, particularly because areas in the desert Southwest, such as Phoenix, have significantly higher heating loads along with the cooling loads. Developing summer night flushing and pre-cooling strategies may result in tremendous cooling energy savings in high-mass buildings. Low-mass buildings need to rely more on passive or low-energy heat exchange ventilation to reduce the waste heat/cool from the exhaust of tempered air.

## Continental Climate

Continental climates have both heating and cooling seasons. Calculations of energy demand should help determine which scenario dominates. In most larger buildings, cooling will dominate and insulation is more likely to be optimized to reduce heat gain from outside than heat loss from inside. That may amount to the same thing—making sure that walls and building assemblies do not provide a direct transfer path for energy to come in or out.

# PREWAR BUILDINGS

## Thermal Mass and Climate Zones

Larger prewar buildings generally were built in the relatively dense centers of towns and cities. They were built close together, or with multiple stories, and fire was a major concern. Exterior walls are usually masonry, and may be either load bearing or at least carry their own substantial weight. This robustness also means that the walls are slow to heat up and slow to cool down. This property of the wall to retain heat is called *thermal mass.*

Massive exterior walls exposed to the sun heat up during the day and take all night to cool down. Some of this heat is reradiated to the exterior, some to the interior. This can be an advantage in climates with hot days and cold nights; building systems can be timed to retain some of the cool from the night as the sun heats up the building in the morning. In addition to the sun and weather outside, other heat or cold sources are the building's heating or cooling system and the heat from people, machines, and lights. Because massive walls warm up or cool down slowly, building heating and cooling systems must be timed to go on and off with an appropriate lag. Overall, thermally massive buildings dampen the effects of weather, particularly in climates with large temperature swings between night and day. The benefit of dampening the diurnal temperature swings is that the interior of the building stays at a more even temperature, allowing heating and

cooling systems to work more efficiently. They can run at a lower rate and control lesser swings in temperature by taking advantage of the lag time between the peak heating or cooling time and the start of the next heating or cooling cycle.

Other than serving as part of passive solar design, thermal mass is most useful when it is on the interior of insulation. This assumes that the insulation is a significant weather barrier. In traditional buildings, the thermal mass consists of masonry, concrete, or adobe that encloses the building or forms floor construction. On occasion, insulation has been added on the interior to buffer the spaces from the exterior wall temperature when it rises during long, hot summers or when it cools during winter. Ideally, a building has a significant amount of insulation outside the thermal mass. As long as the interior mass is not overloaded by solar radiation or by internal heat sources, the interior mass dampens the swings in exterior temperature, keeping the building at a nearly constant temperature.

In cold climates, thermal mass is ideally suited for seasonal heating by solar radiation. As we learned with the early passive houses of the 1970s, this mass needs to be carefully coordinated with sun-shading in order to avoid the building overheating in the summer. It is relatively easy to solar-heat a space through most of a long cold winter (except for extended periods of cloudy weather). During periods of high temperatures, the sun must be blocked, and this depends on the proper building exposure to the sun and adjustable shades to accommodate unusual weather. Strategies used by vernacular buildings such as the cliff dwellings in Arizona and New Mexico provide useful examples of how the properties of the materials, orientation, and sun exposure create more comfortable environments without using additional energy.

In Mediterranean climates, thermal mass can be coupled with solar heating and sun shading to effectively heat and cool a building by taking advan-

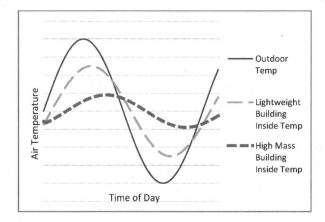

Cold climate heating season—Proper insulation and thermal mass can dampen the effects of temperature changes. *Gelfand Partners Architects.*

tage of the short periods of the day when the outside temperature is nearly the same as the desired indoor temperature.

In hot dry climates, traditionally massive buildings (adobe, brick, or concrete) typically buffer the interior space from hot temperatures during the afternoons. Since heat transfer is slow through the massive exterior walls, heat flows toward the interior during the afternoon, but then reverses after the sun goes down, working its way back out through the walls. So long as the material is thick enough, the excessive heat remains outside while the interior mass tends to keep the spaces at a more constant temperature. Like other climates, if all the thermal mass can be brought within a highly insulated exterior, and as long as excess heat from the sun or internal sources is excluded, the mass will do even more to stabilize interior temperatures and to lower heating and cooling energy requirements.

In hot humid climates, small buildings tend to be built of lighter materials. However, many larger buildings were built of masonry for durability or to prevent fire. Here, as in the hot dry climate, avoiding solar gains is vital. Thermal mass is not as effective, relative to the small diurnal swings outside the building. However, it is important for the management of interior heat sources.

## Masonry Wall Design

In addition to their thermal properties, masonry walls are durable and perform structural and waterproofing roles. In renovation of a masonry building, repair or major maintenance of the masonry itself is a common scope of work. With care, brick could well last 200 years or more. It might need cleaning every ten years or so with a major re-pointing after fifty years. This compares very well to cement plaster, which requires repainting every five to seven years, and which may likely need replacement of its water barrier after thirty to fifty years, plus associated dry-rot repairs to the wood substrate. Masonry walls were meant to last and have proved a success. They do, however, require significant attention at periodic points of major renovation.

The most common issues to be addressed with brick and stone masonry are deterioration of grout and steel supports or ties. Any building movement tends to develop cracks that can then lead to water infiltration. Water intrusion, whether from cracked grout or improper flashing, leads to rusting of steel members behind or within the masonry structure. When steel members rust, they expand, further cracking masonry work and allowing even more water into the system. In systems where bricks are tied back across an air gap to the structure, rusting of ties can lead to severe weakening of the brick facing, even to collapse of the surface.

Water infiltration through grout can leach chemicals, weakening the grout or causing efflorescence on the surface. Weakened grout requires re-pointing and in severe cases can require reconstruction of masonry walls. In re-pointing, the exterior portion of mortar is removed back to sound material, then new mortar is

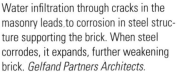

Water infiltration through cracks in the masonry leads to corrosion in steel structure supporting the brick. When steel corrodes, it expands, further weakening brick. *Gelfand Partners Architects.*

installed. Care must be taken to match the strength of the new mortar with the existing mortar and masonry in order to avoid problems with differential expansion. During re-pointing, damaged brick or stone can be replaced and masonry cleaned. Cleaners should test masonry before using powerful water jets, since some softer bricks can have their finish layers blown away during power-washing. Often, only low-pressure wash can be used, especially in cold weather when powerful water jets can force water deep into any cracks, ruining a wall during a freeze cycle.

Because of their age, prewar buildings have generally reached a point where they need a major renovation if they haven't already received one. Investigations should include testing of grout, opening of wall assemblies to determine if ties are corroded, and careful testing of steel structure incorporated in the brick.

## Window Replacement and Shading

Window replacement is one of the most heavily marketed means of producing energy savings. Yet it is third down the list of cost-effective energy saving methods to be pursued within sustainable renovation. In cold climates, much more energy is lost by air infiltration through poorly insulated walls than through the window frame or glass, yet loose and leaky windows *are* a large contributor to infiltration.

When considering renovation to windows, the first priority is to prevent air infiltration. Many windows can be sealed effectively with new gaskets and weatherstripping—usually in combination with refurbishment of hardware. Prewar window systems, like so many components of prewar buildings, were often designed for easy maintenance. So if lead paint or asbestos glazing compound is present, prewar windows can often be removed for off-site abatement and refurbishment. Off-site refurbishment allows greater control over quality, removing the difficulties of working outside from scaffolding. However, with a huge project, like the 6,500-unit window retrofit for the Empire State building in New York City, an on-site factory was created.

Where windows are beyond the possibility of refurbishment, or where inappropriate replacement windows have been installed, designers need to investigate a full window replacement. New windows often can be installed within existing frames. After removing the sashes or glazing, sealing and refurbishing the frame, new windows are mounted within the frame. As long as the existing frame does not have leakage problems, this avoids the difficulties that attend setting a new window into the waterproofing system of an existing wall.

All 6,500 windows in the Empire State Building were retrofit on-site. *Courtesy of Serious Materials, Inc.*

## Empire State Building

The Empire State Building, located in New York City, was completed in 1931 as the world's tallest building, with its 102 stories. Through the help of The Clinton Climate Initiative, Johnson Controls Inc., Jones Lang LaSalle, and the Rocky Mountain Institute, it is now in the midst of a $120 million renovation that is specific to becoming "greener" and more sustainable.[9] Improvements to the envelope are a major part of the retrofit:

All 6,500 double-pane windows are being removed and refurbished with new mylar sheaths between the panes and resealed with krypton-argon gas inside. Windows remain operable.

Sixty-five hundred insulated reflective barriers are also being installed behind the radiators.[10]

A window replacement project can introduce new shading or sunshelf elements to help control daylighting and better balance solar heat gain. Lower solar gains reduce cooling loads, allowing downsizing of cooling system equipment. *Gelfand Partners Architects.*

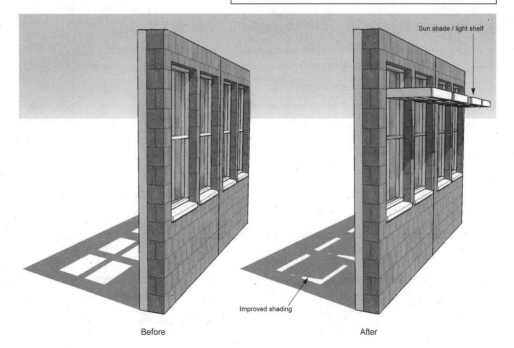

Sun shade / light shelf

Improved shading

Before                    After

Where sun-shading elements cannot be added, more appropriate glazing can be introduced to better control solar gains and glare.[11]

| REPRESENTATIVE GLAZING TYPES | Glass thickness (inches) | Visible light transmittance (VT) | Thermal transmission (U-value) | Solar heat gain coefficient (SHGC) |
|---|---|---|---|---|
| Single-Pane glass (standard clear) | 0.250 | 89 | 1.09 | 0.81 |
| Single White Laminated w/ Heat Rejecting Coating (*Southwall California Series®*) | 0.250 | 73 | 1.06 | 0.46 |
| Double-Pane Insulated Glass (standard clear) | 0.250 | 79 | 0.48 | 0.70 |
| Double Bronze Reflective Glass (*LOF Eclipse®*) | 0.250 | 21 | 0.48 | 0.35 |
| Triple-Pane Insulated Glass (standard clear) | 0.125 | 74 | 0.36 | 0.67 |
| Pyrolitic Low-e Double Glass (*LOF Clear Low-e®*) | 0.125 | 75 | 0.33 | 0.71 |
| Soft-coat Low-e Double Glass w/ Argon gas fill (*PPG Sungate® 100 Clear*) | 0.250 | 73 | 0.26 | 0.57 |
| High Efficiency Low-e (*Solarscreen 2000 VEI-2M™*) | 0.250 | 70 | 0.29 | 0.37 |
| Suspended Coated Film (*Heat Mirror™ 66 Clear*) | 0.125 | 55 | 0.25 | 0.35 |
| Suspended Coated Film w/ Argon gas fill (*Azurlite® Heat Mirror SC75*) | 0.125 | 53 | 0.19 | 0.27 |
| Double Suspended Coated Films w/ Krypton (*Heat Mirror™ 77 Superglass*) | 0.125 | 55 | 0.10 | 0.34 |

Even though prewar buildings often relied on large windows to provide ample daylight and ventilation, they were frequently designed without consideration of solar orientation. Problems arise from too much uncontrolled daylight. North façades are often well lit while south- and west-facing rooms can become scorching from too much sun and glare during the day.

## Roof Structure and Insulation

Prewar buildings often function better in rain and snow than newer buildings. Drainage is often less of an issue with the older buildings because of high-pitched, or at least well-sloped, flat roofs. However, older roof structures, particularly secondary structures added to create slopes, tend to be very minimal, and walking on them can feel like stumbling across a trampoline. Where attics are present, a structure can be braced in order to limit the movement that tends to speed degradation of the roofing and flashing.

Usually sloped at more than a half inch per foot, so-called flat roofs of prewar buildings can perform admirably, except at the actual drainage catchment. Internal drains are often undersized, both at the inlet and at the piping. Some roofs can be easily resloped to allow water to drain through scuppers over the side of the building, rather than down through the building itself. Wherever possible, it is always preferable to develop a strategy where water flows freely outside the envelope. Then when a component (drain, downspout, catch box) becomes clogged or corroded, the water remains outside the building rather than flowing inside the walls. Where drainage cannot be rerouted outside the building, the addition of a secondary overflow drain adjacent to an existing drain can prevent catastrophic ponding from an errant plastic bag or leaves over a drain inlet. Finally, internal piping can be replaced and resized for better performance.

## Roofing

High sloped roofs are often made of extremely durable materials—slate, tile, or sheet metal. While stone or tile can endure over 100 years, sheet metal tends to last 30 to 50 years. Renovation of slate or tile roofs requires significant expertise and especially careful management to prevent damage to the underlying water barrier. Sheet metal of the prewar age has generally been patched to death and usually warrants a complete replacement. At this point, the substrate can be inspected, repaired, and a new underlayment and sheet metal roof applied.

Low sloped roofs tend to be variations of tar and gravel or built-up roofs (BUR). While these are generally expected to last twenty to thirty years, some have been in place since the prewar years. Major renovation projects can usually assume a full replacement with newer materials.

When designing new roofing systems, the project team should carefully assess the underlying substrate for faults that may cause movement and failure of a new membrane. Prewar concrete is often of lower strength with minimal steel reinforcing; cracks can vary seasonally and degraded areas can allow significant movement, tearing new roofing membranes. Framed roofs also exhibit troubling amounts of movement necessitating careful detailing of joints and edges to allow a new membrane to move without failure. Finally, roof edge openings, parapets, and overhangs often require modification to accept new roofing materials.

Because of the prevalence of light secondary structures for creating slope at the roof level, use of roofs for terraces or green roofs could require total restructuring in prewar buildings. If such a restructuring is contemplated as part of the overall job it could be cost effective to think about these other uses. Be alert to the likelihood that the structural diaphragm may be at the ceiling level of the top floor, and several feet below the apparent roof surface.

Of the high-performance roofing systems available, cool roofs are probably the most generally applicable to prewar buildings. Such roofs are defined by their solar reflectance and thermal emittance rates. The objective is to reflect the sun's radiation back to the sky, and reduce heat gain. Cool roofing types or cool roof coatings provide surfaces that combine to allow the roof to reduce the amount of heat transmitted into the building below, while leaving the immediate area around a building significantly cooler. Where cooling the building is the major energy demand, cool roofs can make striking

Contemporary flat roofing materials include variations of multiple sheets of asphalt, single-layer synthetic membranes, and vegetated roof systems.

| Roofing Types | | | | | |
|---|---|---|---|---|---|
| Type | Composition | Common Name | Material | Substrates | Common Issues |
| Built-Up Roof | Sheets welded together with hot asphalt | BUR | Layers of organic felt impregnated with asphalt | Low slope (1:4 to 1:12) to steep slope (>2:12) | Loses plasticity over time—cracks, layering can cause dams at low slopes, seams inconsistently adhered |
| Thermoset | Sheets welded together with heat | EPDM, CSPE | Synthetic rubber sheet— Ethylene Propylene Diene Monomer, Chlorosulfonated Polyethylene | Low slope (1:4 to 1:12) | Build-up of moisture below membrane due to water vapor movement, improper sealing of joints |
| Modified Bitumen | Sheets welded together with heat | Torch down; SBR-, SBS-, APP-modified | Layers of polyester or fiberglass sheet impregnated with modified (added plasticizers) asphalt | Low slope (1:4 to 1:12) | Improper sealing of joints, migration of moisture from below causes bubbles |
| Thermoplastic Built-Up Roof | Sheets welded together with chemical process | PVC | Polyvinyl Chloride | Low slope (1:4 to 1:12) | Improper sealing of joints, migration of moisture from below causes bubbles |
| | | CPE | Chlorinated Polyethylene | | |
| | | EIP | Ethylene Interpolymer | | |
| | | NBP | Nitrile Butadiene Polymer | | |
| | | PIB | Polyisobutylene | | |
| | | TPO | Thermoplastic Polyolefin | | |

improvements. With the improvement of building insulation the transfer of heat from the roof can be reduced, but cool roofs still help reduce urban heat island effects, and may also extend the life of the roofing membrane.

An amazing array of materials and colors are available with cool roof ratings. Many darker colors comply because they reflect radiation in the infrared part of the spectrum that we cannot see, but that contributes greatly to heat build-up.

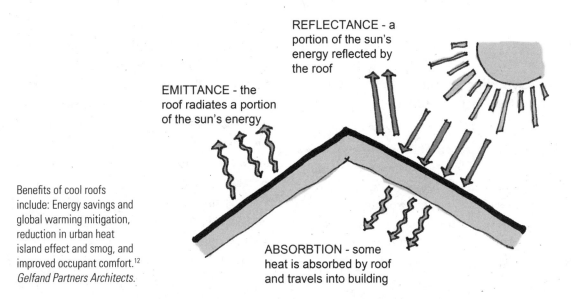

REFLECTANCE - a portion of the sun's energy reflected by the roof

EMITTANCE - the roof radiates a portion of the sun's energy

ABSORBTION - some heat is absorbed by roof and travels into building

Benefits of cool roofs include: Energy savings and global warming mitigation, reduction in urban heat island effect and smog, and improved occupant comfort.[12] *Gelfand Partners Architects.*

## Table 6: Making an Existing Roof Cool, Approximate Price Premiums*

| Roof | Maintenance Option | Cool Alternative | Price Premium ($/ft$^2$) |
|------|--------------------|------------------|-----------------------------|
| **Smooth Dark Surface** | Leave roof as-is | Apply cool coating | 1.25-2.40 |
| | Apply restorative dark coating (asphalt, bitumen, colored coating, etc.) | Apply cool coating instead | 0.00-1.70 |
| **Rough Dark Surface** | Leave roof as-is | Apply cool coating | 1.45-2.75 |
| | Apply restorative dark coating (asphalt, bitumen, colored coating, etc.) | Apply cool coating instead | 0.00-1.90 |
| **Old Light or Cool Surface** | Leave roof as-is | Apply maintenance coat (single coat) | 0.80-2.00 |
| | Apply restorative dark maintenance coating (asphalt, bitumen, colored coating, etc.) | Apply cool maintenance coating (single coat) | 0.00-1.45 |
| **Any Roof** | Replace roof | Replace with cool roof | See Table 5 |

*Premiums are the extra cost, per square foot of roof area, of installing the cool roof option as compared with the corresponding non-cool option. Premiums are based on achieving the minimum cool roof characteristics described in Table 1. Values are approximate, and are based on discussions with roofing contractors, manufacturers, wholesalers, and RSMeans cost data.

Cool roof coatings can be applied in conjunction with normal roof maintenance for minimal cost premium. *U.S. Department of Energy.*

# MID-CENTURY MODERN BUILDINGS

## Curtain Wall Replacement, Modification, and Shading

Although curtain wall buildings were originally conceived in the 1920s as part of the promise of a new technological century, they caught on in large numbers in the rebuilding and expansion of cities after World War II. The curtain wall was hung on internal frames and walls that provided the structure of buildings and allowed the exterior wall to be entirely glass or metal panel, reducing weight and allowing complete freedom for the architect to provide open views as desired from anywhere in the building. The excitement of this technological revolution is an expressive and aesthetic driver of early modern movement buildings. Simultaneously allowing the exterior wall to float free of the ground and the structural frame, curtain walls produced a revolutionary relationship between the inside and outside. Such architectural concepts are part of the logic of these buildings and may have considerable aesthetic and cultural value. However, changing standards in environmental controls, fire safety, acoustics, and daylighting along with the usual ravages of time have made many early curtain walls dysfunctional.

Attributed to Le Corbusier and Oscar Neimeyer, the United Nations Headquarters in New York City includes the iconic Secretariat building, a thirty-nine story curtain-walled slab. Less elegant versions of the curtain wall became the dominant cladding for mid-century multi-story office buildings. *Gelfand Partners Architects*.

Although they can be beautiful, the uninsulated steel frames and single glazing of many curtain walls unremittingly let in the winter cold, leading to a daily accumulation of rivers of condensation beneath the window and a small industry involving condensation collection. Part of an intern's job at the Yale University Art Gallery was to wet-vacuum the condensation troughs below each floor of a curtain wall originally designed by Louis Kahn (1953).[13] A 2006 renovation by Polshek Partnership Architects remedied the condensation problems by providing a new curtain wall with thermally broken frames and double glazing. Because of the historical significance of the building, they developed new profiles that matched the existing visually, but provided a thermal break to eliminate the condensation and thermal bridging problems.[14]

While the lions of early twentieth-century Modernism relied on the thinness of steel for their curtain wall designs, postwar curtain walls are most often made with aluminum frames, a byproduct of a wartime increase in aluminum production. Built during a time of increased standardization and a "systems" approach to building components, curtain walls of mid-century buildings were often experiments in factory processes for the extrusion of aluminum and advances in glazing technology. As such, mid-century curtain walls are often leaky, energy inefficient, prone to interior condensation, and inadequately braced against building movement. In most cases they do not contribute to building structural systems and can be completely replaced by a system of similar weight without affecting building structural behavior.

Designed during the rise of air-conditioning systems, these curtain walls had no operable windows. Engineers introduced outside air as part of the mix of conditioned air and sized their systems to overcome the radical heat gains brought on by expanding the glass wall to provide unimpeded view of the outside,

no matter what the exposure was to the sun. Concerns about spread of fires from floor to floor were dealt with by adding bands of spandrel glass and insulation.

Where modest historical issues are concerned, simple thermally broken curtain walls can be specified, so long as existing structure can take the weight of added double glazing. Where preserving the original building fabric or appearance is not a concern at all, it is usually prudent to add sun-shading on the exterior of mid-century curtain walls to help control thermal loads. Combined with improved glazing and thermal breaks, replacement curtain walls can form part of a sustainable envelope.

## Insulation Options

While many leaders in the modern movement took great care and investigated novel building methods to achieve successful building physics, others ignored the affects of nature in favor of an aesthetic or purely ideological approach. The early Modern Movement was also designing to an indoor environment standard that is lower than today's expectations. Where they understood that building occupants would wear sweaters or layered suits in the winter, we now expect to be in short sleeves throughout the year.

As mentioned earlier, insulation of mid-century modern buildings ties closely to infiltration issues as well as modernist construction techniques. As modern design filtered down from the movement's leaders to everyday designers, much of the attention to integrated building physics became lost. Because typical buildings relied on brawny mechanical systems to overcome the shortcomings of their envelopes, mid-century buildings often have little or no insulation. Like prewar buildings, a first step is to evaluate the existing wall assemblies to determine the path of renovation. Exterior insulation systems are likely to be

In buildings where an aggressive renovation is planned, interior wall surfaces can be stripped down to the masonry or framing, then a more extensive insulation of fiberglass or cotton batts, rigid board, or sprayed foam can be overlain with new light framing and interior finish. Wherever insulation is added, opening perimeters and any penetrations should be caulked against air infiltration. *Celbar Spray-On Systems, celbar.com.*

more palatable for mid-century buildings because of their simple geometries and uniform parts. Unless the building's visual heritage is important, the overlaying of walls with exterior insulation can both provide the needed buffer from temperature and a new wearing surface exposed to the weather. As mid-century buildings were often constructed with exteriors that are not as durable as prewar buildings, the opportunity to re-clad the building is also likely to be welcome. Instead of replacing the exterior finish just because of its lack of durability, an exterior insulation can double as a re-placement finish.

If the exterior is in good shape and insulation is still desired, insulation can be injected into wall cavities or placed at the interior with techniques similar to those of prewar buildings. With mid-century buildings, interior surfaces are more often gypsum board panels, so re-moval and replacement is not as laborious as with lath and plaster. However, because mid-century buildings were often built with minimal framing, filling wall cavi-

ties might not amount to much. Where an early build-ing would have massive walls with a thin finish and a current building might have thick framed walls, mid-century buildings tend to have very thin framed walls, accommodating only minimal insulation.

Flat roofed areas of mid-century buildings can be more difficult to insulate. Because flat roof construc-tion techniques were relatively new, many of their problems had not been fully resolved. In particular, flat-framed roofs or ceilings were often insulated with fiberglass batts, but without any ventilation. Over the years, moisture has migrated into the unvented roof space and mold may have developed on the interior of the ceiling surface or on the underside of the roof substrate. Mold needs to be properly abated, a task to be coordinated by an industrial hygienist. When reno-vating, it is often advisable to remove the ceiling sur-face, verify that framing is in good shape, install rigid board insulation (verifying its susceptibility to water), then provide a vapor barrier (where appropriate) and new finish. Where metal framing or a concrete slab is involved, investigation of corrosion is obviously in order as well. Generally, it is not possible to provide adequate ventilation to unvented flat roof spaces, and avoidance of batt insulation with possible water vapor is advised.

Crawlspaces and perimeter slabs are another common avenue for heat leakage from mid-century buildings. While walls and roofs of mid-century buildings are usually under-insulated, crawlspaces and perimeter slabs are almost never insulated. Uninsulated crawlspaces are relatively easy to remedy as long as insulation and moisture issues are coordinated. Batts, sprayfoam, and rigid insulations can all be used effectively, paying particular attention to minimizing thermal bridging at the perimeter and openings. Except in the mildest climates, perimeters of slab-on-grade buildings create a significant thermal bridge. They allow heat and cold to flow directly to and from the indoors through the slab edge. Provision of rigid insulation outside the foundation can cut this thermal bridge. In areas where termites are an issue and the building has wood framing components, a termite shield should be provided at the insulation.

## Window Replacement

Mid-century windows can sometimes follow the refurbishment and weatherization path common for prewar windows. However, many mid-century windows lack the robustness and reparability that typifies prewar windows. Transitioning from wood double-hung to monumental steel or aluminum frame casement windows tended to lower the energy efficiency and longevity of mid-century windows. Experiments with the slimming of molding profiles and sashes led to inadequately framed windows or fixed lites that can only be replaced through partial destruction of the frames. Therefore, window replacement is more likely

to be a priority for mid-century buildings, compared to prewar buildings.

Particularly in the case of mid-century buildings that already have had a poorly conceived window replacement project, window replacement can be an important part of envelope renovation. Because of the initial problems with lightly built, experimentally detailed windows, many mid-century buildings already have had a window replacement project. Unfortunately, these projects often resulted in an even worse situation than the original. Retrofit windows are a class of windows meant to be inserted into or overlaid on original window frames. They are designed for insertion in prewar window types and often do not fit easily into the specialized frame details of modern windows. We sometimes encounter newish windows that have been forced into a frame in a way that requires extra moldings or trim or reliance on large, irregular sealant joints. Also, because mid-century modern buildings suffer from a thin detailing of waterproofing around window openings, insertion of retrofit windows in original frames often leaves behind the inherent issues with water intrusion at the edges of the original frame. For mid-century buildings with high cooling loads, glazing replacement tuned to solar orientation relieves pressure on cooling systems and even allows downsizing of chillers and pumps.

## Roofing

The saying that all flat roofs leak has been borne out. Mid-century buildings are typified by flat roofs; therefore the typical mid-century building has a history of leaks. Since a primary function of a roof is to protect the interior from rain and sun, the most sustainable renovation is one in which the roof is renovated so that it actually keeps the water out. This is easier said than done. Mid-century designers often had unreasonable faith in modern "miracle" materials. Because many products

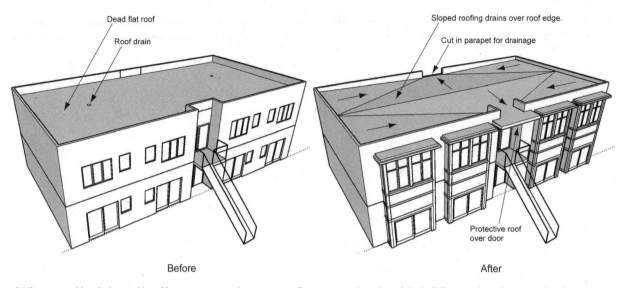

Adding tapered insulation and breaking parapets, so that water can flow out over the edge of the building envelope, improves the chances that a flat roof will not leak. *Gelfand Partners Architects.*

had not been field-tested for any length of time, overblown advertising often led to unhappy results. We once worked on a project in which the original drawings actually called out the roof as "dead flat." The architect believed that the roofing material (built-up asphalt roofing) would be impervious to water. Not surprisingly, the flat roof, surrounded by parapets, was a constant maintenance nightmare. Our sustainable options were to erect new sloped framing to provide a pitched roof that cast the water over the edges of the building, or to add tapered rigid insulation to give the roof enough slope to at least channel the water to new roof overhangs—moving the water over the edge of the building rather than collecting it at internal drains. Because the building could not support the weight of a new pitched roof structure, we opted for the next best option. Luckily, this second option also provided the added benefit of adding insulation to the entire roof area.

The lesson is that wherever possible, we should renovate flat roofs in such a way as to add as much slope as possible and to change roof edges to shed water outside the building envelope. While a slope of ¼ in 12 is common, this is generally considered a minimum and results in some ponding if the roof plies are thick or the building settles. A slope of ½ in 12 is preferable and even greater slopes afford more secure drainage. Wherever possible, change internal drains to systems that occur outside the building envelope—gutters and downspouts at the façade rather than pipes within the walls.

## LATE MODERN BUILDINGS

### Introducing Daylight

Many late modern buildings did away with the glazed expanses of the Mid-Century Modern movement in reaction to the energy crisis of the 1970s. As architects searched for ways to make buildings more energy efficient, the pendulum swung the other way; large expanses of single-glazed windows were replaced with

◀ "Gun-slit" buildings benefit from the introduction of significant daylighting; the saw is our best friend. The wall may be constructed of solid or heavy materials but is still likely to be irrelevant to the structural performance of the building. *Gelfand Partners Architects.*

▼ New atria can be used for daylighting and passive ventilation schemes, although larger, multilevel buildings will require sophisticated fire protection devices to prevent fire from using new atria as chimneys. *Gelfand Partners Architects.*

blank walls and slit windows. Gun-slit buildings and windowless big box stores dot our landscape, tributes to an era affected by an unsophisticated response to environmental concerns.

New openings can be sliced in walls or ceilings to provide controlled daylight. The operative word here is "controlled." Properly designed overhangs or sun shelves modulate daylighting and can reflect it deep into a space; unshaded windows or skylights can lead to yet another round of problems searching for a fix. As a rule of thumb, we can expect to provide daylighting two times a window's head height into a building. A maximum of 5 percent of the floor area is a good estimate of roof area to be opened for skylighting. In areas where neither is appropriate or available, a building might require a more radical solution, such as the introduction of an atrium or courtyard. Atria also can be used for passive ventilation schemes, although larger, multilevel buildings will require sophisticated fire protection devices to prevent fire from using new atria as chimneys.

Many late century modern buildings are restrained in their use of shading devices. Most rely on tinted glazing to reduce the amount of sunlight that windows provide. While proper specification of glazing can aid in adequately controlling sunlight, a single glazing type will never work optimally for both winter and summer sunlight. Provision of sunshades or light shelves at south façades and shading fins at

▶ A number of manufacturers now provide sunshade outriggers as part of their window framing systems. As long as the window substructure is strong enough to accommodate the additional loads, building skin type should not affect the ability to add sun shading. *E-Shade™ Sunshade, Courtesy of EFCO® Corporation.*

◀ While external blinds are available and can be effective, they are generally seen as requiring significant ongoing maintenance. *Gelfand Partners Architects.*

east and west faces can control excess sunlight and allow the glazing to be tuned more for temperature differential, using low-emissivity coatings to prevent heat escape in cold climates, or prevent entrance of heat in hot climates. Of course, building construction methods and program will affect whether sunshades can be added easily. Precast panel buildings or curtain wall façades do not lend themselves to modifications unless sun shades can become part of the window systems.

## Correcting Roof Structures and Slope

Late modern buildings continue mid-century modern's love affair with the flat roof. It seems that most moderate and large buildings built in the latter third of the twentieth century have at least some portion that is flat-roofed. Through better awareness of roof drainage standards, these roofs were at least originally designed to slope between ¼ inch per foot and ½ inch per foot. However, interruption by patches and the myriad mechanical and electrical machines

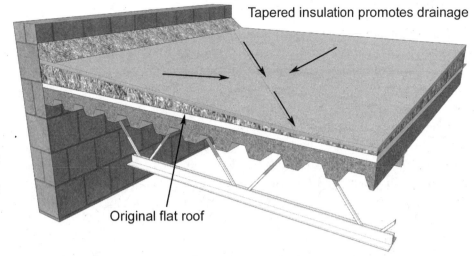

Tapered insulation promotes drainage

Tapered insulation improves flat roof drainage, increasing longevity of roofing while providing increased insulation value.
*Gelfand Partners Architects.*

Original flat roof

common to the late modern result in "flat" roofs that are as problematic as mid-century roofs. If there is any good news, it is that underlying roof structures of this era are usually stronger than mid-century roofs. As a result, late modern roofs are generally easier to remedy through addition of tapered rigid insulation. Although the addition of insulation requires a complete reroofing project, the benefits of increased roof slope and better drainage can pay back in the avoidance of just one rainy season's leak repair budget.

Tapered rigid insulation is produced in two main materials, XPS and "polyiso." XPS is *extruded* polystyrene—the actual "*Styrofoam*" patented by the Dow Chemical Corporation. (The "styrofoam" we see in coffee cups is actually *expanded* polystyrene, or EPS, a weaker and less insulating material.) XPS is a closed-cell insulation, meaning that it resists moisture. The other main roof insulation is polyisocyanurate board insulation. Polyiso is a thermoset (heat cured), closed-cell polymer formed into rigid boards. It has a higher insulating value per inch of thickness, but is slightly susceptible to water and has a higher coefficient of thermal expansion, so polyiso can be

difficult to use as a vapor barrier; a separate vapor barrier needs to be provided. Both insulation types are successfully used for low slope roof renovations. They can be applied to wood, concrete, or metal pan structures and can accommodate many kinds of roofing materials.

## Insulation Options

Architects' tendency in the mid-century to use minimal insulation continued into many late-century modern buildings. In a way, it is unfortunate that many late-century buildings added any insulation at all, because so many of them still have inadequate thermal properties. The presence of batt insulation in the wall cavity can make adding more insulation an even greater challenge. While walls without insulation in their cavity can be retrofit with blown-in or expanded foam insulation, walls with poorly insulated cavities must either be opened completely or avoided all together. Expanded foam insulation should always be coordinated with wiring and piping. A need for future access to these services will make injected insulation undesirable.

## Window Replacement

Late modern buildings tend to either have very skimpy windows (before the 1970s' energy crisis) or very heavy-framed, insulated windows (after the 1970s). Aluminum windows with very narrow frames tend to appear in buildings before the 1970s, especially in low-income housing, production apartments, and smaller commercial buildings with design driven by first costs. While these do not have the problems that appear in the "experimental" aluminum windows of mid-century modern buildings, they were developed to be cheap. Cheap they are, with very minimal internal weeps, corner reinforcement, and frames so light that racking and twisting are constant issues. Further, they are often installed in walls without adequate waterproofing flashing, leading to leakage both around the frame and within the window itself. Given that a full window replacement is almost inevitable, each project should be assessed to determine how the windows were originally installed.

Aluminum windows installed after the 1970s tend to be better constructed and often include double glazing. This glazing sometimes has deteriorated, the thin films have degraded, and the seals have broken, causing condensation within the double-glazed component. If these windows were installed correctly originally, and the surrounding walls are in good repair, they can be re-glazed with new insulated glazing with coatings tuned for each exposure. Sometimes, especially in cold regions, buildings have had large areas of

Narrow band aluminum sliders provide very little thermal protection, allow significant air infiltration, and do little to control condensation. Most often, it is best to remove some or all of the surrounding finish in order to provide a new waterproofing membrane, while taking opportunities to install better wall insulation and provide new windows. *Gelfand Partners Architects.*

This "extensive" green roof has been in place for ten years. *Gelfand Partners Architects.*

glazing filled with opaque insulated panels. In many cases, these panels were introduced during a panicked attempt at energy savings during the energy crisis of the 1970s. Through better understanding of the local climate and an integrated approach to thermal management of the building envelope, these insulated panels can be replaced with high-efficiency insulated glazing, combined with approaches to sun shading, passive heating, insulation, and infiltration, in order to bring back the original intent for daylighting.

## Roofing

Roofing types vary greatly in late modern buildings. Larger commercial, residential, and institutional buildings continued the trend in flat roof slopes, while the materials provided to surface these roofs expanded in variety. Built-up roofing continued to be installed, but many buildings turned to modified bitumen, thermoplastic membrane, or thermoset membrane roofing. These existing types of roofing do not affect the type of renovated roofing so much as they do the substrate and the project intention. Also, with late modern buildings it is likely that the roofing has reached

the end of its warranty if not its service life, so full roofing replacement is a strong possibility. As with earlier modern buildings, roof slope is key to providing sustainable roofing. Flat and very low-slope roofs should be modified if possible to have greater slope. Where roofing can be extended to shed water over the edge of the building, rather than down through central roof drains, there is a better chance of avoiding leaks. Wherever it is not already required by law, roofing should be provided with a cool roof rating.[15]

Green roofs are another option that may be possible to retrofit on a robust late modern building. Green roofs establish a planted area on the unused portion of roof. The plants are established in a thin medium that is installed above the waterproofing membrane. The weight of the planting medium can be reduced, but all plants require water, and that can add up to a substantial load. The benefits of green roofs include reducing the speed of water runoff, reducing the heat island effect of emittance from dark roofs, and reducing heat gain into the building. The area represented by roofs is extensive and the appeal of covering it all in greenery is intense. An established green roof can also provide a piece of the local habitat.

Green roofs are a complex sandwich of materials. *Image courtesy of CETCO*

Green roof systems may be modular, with drainage layers, filter cloth, growing media, and plants already prepared in movable, interlocking grids, or each component of the system may be installed separately. This green space could be below, at, or above grade, but in all cases the plants are not planted in the "ground." Planting may be extensive, as in the grasses shown, or intensive as in trees or large shrubs.

Plant selection for green roofs depends on a variety of factors, including climate, type and depth of growing medium, loading capacity, height and slope of the roof, maintenance expectations, and the presence or absence of an irrigation system. Preparing for maintenance needs to be a part of the selection of green roof system. With conventional low-slope roofs, when a leak occurs, roofing contractors can usually go up onto the roof, find the leak, and repair it. With a green roof, a leak may be more difficult to find if the membrane cannot be examined or if water has migrated through the green roof assembly. Visual inspection and repairs can be done only after removing vegetation, soil, and the assorted drainage and filter layers present with most green roofs. At least one green roof system addresses this concern through a modular design that allows planting areas to be lifted like tiles to access the roofing membrane.

Environmentally friendly roofs can serve other functions besides supporting vegetation, and some of these other uses may be incompatible with plantings. For example, a roof can support a photovoltaic or solar-thermal array, producing electricity or hot water for a building. Or a roof can serve as a rainwater harvesting system to serve the water needs of the building and surrounding site. Green roofs in Seattle were found to produce very limited amounts of runoff—the plants were using all the rain that fell on them!

Most low-profile (extensive) green roofs are not designed to be walked on. For applications in which rooftop gardens and patio space is desired, providing the most cost-effective and most environmentally attractive low-profile green roof may not make sense—or the area for such a roof may be limited. So-called "garden roofs" tend to be designed for much more intensive human use.

## CASE STUDY

# Home on the Range .

**Owner**   Northern Plains Resource Council, Corporation (nonprofit)

**Architect**   High Plains Architects

**Original Building Type**   Grocery Store

**Renovation Building Type**   Office

**Original Construction Date**   1941

**Renovation Date**   2006

**Location**   Billings, MT

**Climate**   Steppe (Köppen BSk)

**Area**   8,500 square feet

**Achievement**   LEED NC v2.1 Platinum (57 points)

**Key Indicators**   Daylighting and Light Shelves

       Radiant Floor Heating

       Evaporative Cooling

       Solar Thermal

       Photovoltaics

       Composting Toilets

**Energy Achievement**   79 percent less than comparable building (ASHRAE 90.1-1999)

**Total Energy Use**   95,600 kWh/year   11.26 kWh/sf year   (121 kW/m$^2$ year)

**Electricity After**   29,900 kWh/year   3.52 kWh/sf   (38 kW/m$^2$ year)

**Heating After**   49.9 kBtu/sf/yr   14.62 kWh/sf/year   (157 kWh/m$^2$ year)

**Water After**   0.57 gal/sf   872.8 gal/occupant

**Renewables**   9.9 kW Photovoltaics (37% of electricity)

Home on the Range, located in Billings, Montana, was originally built in 1940 as a grocery store. In 2003, Northern Plains and Western Organization of Resource Councils acquired it to make a permanent home by renovating it following green building strategies. The renovation emphasizes daylighting, using roof monitors to admit daylight to the middle of the building, and windows with light shelves around the perimeter of the building, it uses only 35 percent as much electricity for lighting as before. In addition, new insulation on the roof, walls, and windows help stabilize the interior temperature. The cooling

New exterior insulation brings the existing thermal mass (concrete block and roof structure) within the envelope—damping temperature swings and allowing more efficient heating and cooling. Light shelves inserted in new openings cut in the exterior walls reflect daylight deep into the offices, reducing lighting energy. *High Plains Architects.*

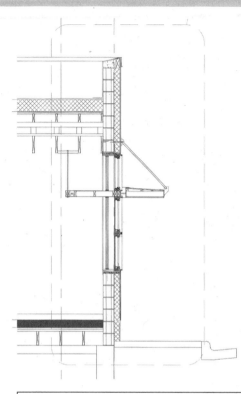

system is evaporative, calculated to use 25 percent as much energy as standard air conditioning. Finally, a 9.9 photovoltaic system on the roof faces south and provides 37 percent of the annual energy used.

In order to reduce the water consumption, on the inside, there are waterless urinals and microflush composting toilets that use 61 percent less water than standard appliances. Outside, native plants were selected in order to reduce the irrigation demand. Finally, the parking lot, which uses a plastic mat system with recycled glass cullet on the top, eliminates stormwater and therefore, runoff. Through the installation of all these features, the building has earned LEED Platinum.

While modeling proved slightly more optimistic than actual performance, the building performs with less than half the energy costs of a comparable baseline building. *High Plains Architects.*

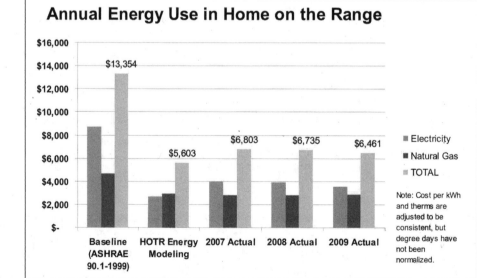

**Annual Energy Use in Home on the Range**

Baseline (ASHRAE 90.1-1999): $13,354
HOTR Energy Modeling: $5,603
2007 Actual: $6,803
2008 Actual: $6,735
2009 Actual: $6,461

■ Electricity
■ Natural Gas
▨ TOTAL

Note: Cost per kWh and therms are adjusted to be consistent, but degree days have not been normalized.

# Apartment Building on Makartstrasse

**Owner**   GIWOG (social housing association)

**Renovation Architect**   ARCH + MORE ZT GmbH
Arch. DI Ingrid Domenig-Meisinger

**Original Building Type**   Multifamily Housing

**Renovation Building Type**   Multifamily Housing

**Original Construction Date**   1957

**Renovation Date**   2005

**Location**   Linz, Austria

**Climate**   Humid Continental (Köppen Cfb)

**Area**   33,400 square feet

**Achievement**   None

**Key Indicators**   GAP Solar Façade
Winter Gardens
Efficient Insulation
Efficient Windows
Controlled Heat Recovery Ventilation

**Energy Achievement**   91 percent less than previous

**Total Energy Use**   6.4 kWh/sf year   (68.7 kWh/m$^2$ year)

**Electricity Before**   19.5 kWh/year   (210 kWh/m$^2$ year)

**Electricity After**   2.8 kWh/sf year   (30 kWh/m$^2$ year)

**Heating/Hot Water Before**   16.0 kWh/sf year   (172.5 kWh/m$^2$ year)

**Heating/Hot Water After**   3.6 kWh/sf year (38.7 kWh/m$^2$ year)

**Renewables**   None

▼ ▶ Re-skinning of this uninsulated 1957 apartment building resulted in a 91 percent improvement in energy use. To counter growing traffic noise, balconies were enclosed, providing more usable space to residents while buffering the interior from temperature changes. *Arch. DI Ingrid Domenig-Meisinger.*

Built in 1957 with uninsulated poured concrete walls, the apartment building was generally in good condition at the start of renovations. However, in response to resident complaints about the usability of balconies (due to traffic noise) and high heating costs, the owners decided to apply the Passive House standard in order to reduce heating energy to a minimum while improving ventilation and enclosing balconies. They also explored the use of prefabrication to limit the effect of construction on the residents. The project provided impressive amounts of insulation to the outside of exterior walls, the uninsulated basement ceiling, and roof. Combined with triple-glazed windows and heat recovery ventilation, the envelope improvements allowed the existing heating system to remain, but be adjusted to run at much more efficient lower temperature.

Supplementing the new exterior insulation is a "Gap-Solar" façade. Prefabricated wall units, the full height and width of an apartment, were installed at the south elevation. The panels are formed of glass with a corrugated cellulose honeycomb sandwiched between. Low winter sun heats the honeycomb, raising the temperature of the exterior of the façade and thereby reducing heating energy necessary. In summer, a higher sun angle does not penetrate the cellulose honeycomb, preventing overheating.

Apartments were enlarged by enclosure of existing balconies within new prefabricated units. New individual ventilation units with heat recovery capability (70 percent efficient) improve ventilation while minimizing heating costs. Hydronic heating is supplied by a district heating system, shared with the neighborhood and partially fueled by biomass. With these improvements, a 91 percent heating energy savings was achieved.

## ENDNOTES

1. Bruno Taut, *Architekturlehre* (1936), cited from Tomlow, Jos: "Introduction, Building Science as Reflected in Modern Movement Literature" *in* Climate and Building Physics in the Modern Movement, Preservation Technology Dossier 9, Docomomo, September 2006.

2. Information on the cost benefit for $CO_2$ reduction by Treehugger.com: www.treehugger.com/files/2009/02/spend-weatherization-money-wisely.php. Accessed May 4, 2011.

3. *Preservation*, March/April 2010, "The Height of Sustainability, The owners of the Empire State Building are turning New York's legendary skyscraper into a model of energy efficiency."

4. www.toolbase.org/pdf/techinv/insulationalternatives_techspec.pdf.

5. CDD and HDD are used to calculate the amount of energy needed to heat or cool a building. Cooling Degree Days = the summation of the number of hours in which the mean temperature is below 65° F for each day of the year. Heating Degree Days = the summation of the number of hours in which the mean temperature is above 65° F for each day of the year. For example, if the mean temperature for a day is 78° F, that day would add 13 CDD to the sum, but would not add any HDD since it is too warm to need heating (e.g., Miami ≈ 300 HDD/5,000 CDD; Chicago ≈ 6,500 HDD/1,300 CDD.

6. Modeled and Metered Energy Savings from Exterior Wall Insulation, Oak Ridge National Laboratory and Florida Solar Energy Center, www.osti.gov/bridge/purl.cover.jsp;jsessionid=1772E6D244DEE8CE385DA08A9E54A9FD?purl=/279699-wdP0vx/webviewable/ & http://www.fsec.ucf.edu/en/publications/html/FSEC-CR-868-95/index.htm, accessed January 19, 2010.

7. Passive House: www.passivehouse.us/passiveHouse/PHIUSHome.html.

8. Modeled and Metered Energy Savings from Exterior Wall Insulation, Oak Ridge National Laboratory and Florida Solar Energy Center, www.osti.gov/bridge/purl.cover.jsp;jsessionid=1772E6D244DEE8CE385DA08A9E54A9FD?purl=/279699-wdP0vx/webviewable/, accessed January 19, 2010.

9. www.usgbc.org/News/USGBCInTheNewsDetails.aspx?ID=4143, accessed February 10, 2011.

10. www.preservationnation.org/magazine/2010/march-april/height-of-sustainability.html, accessed February 10, 2011.

11. Ander, Gregg D., Windows & Glazing, Whole Building Design Guide, www.wbdg.org/resources/windows.php, accessed August 22, 2010.

12. Cool Roof Rating Council, www.coolroofs.org/.

13. Personal recollection, Chris Duncan.

14. www.architectureweek.com/2007/0613/building_1-1.html, accessed March 3, 2010.

15. Cool Roof Rating Council, www.coolroofs.org/.

# chapter 5

# BUILDING SYSTEMS REPLACEMENTS

## BUILDING SYSTEM NEEDS

Building systems produce heat, provide light, supply water, and drain away our waste so that we don't have to be directly involved in these activities. Building systems work while we sleep, while we are busy, and while we are away. Over the centuries, these systems have become more and more sophisticated, to the point that we expect them to control our interior environment to within a very narrow band of operation. These systems are also likely to be a major part of any renovation that extends beyond fittings and finishes.

Interior environmental standards have changed significantly over time. Where a 1920s building had few outlets, scant lighting, and little insulation, buildings from the 1980s provide an overabundance of lighting, massive cooling and ventilation systems, and sometimes complex control systems. In order to effectively develop a renovation strategy it is necessary to understand how the building's systems were originally intended to work and what options are available for improvement. We will focus on the major building systems involving heating, cooling, and lighting since these generally account for over 50 to 75 percent of a building's energy use.

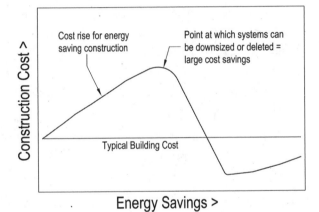

When renovating a building, costs for energy saving measures rise until the point at which they allow the reduction or elimination of basic systems through the use of passive strategies. A successful sustainable renovation can cost less than a "normal" renovation. *Gelfand Partners Architects.*

As mentioned elsewhere, improvements to a building's envelope are a high priority both in terms of protection from the elements and in terms of energy savings and general sustainability criteria. Load reduction through installation of efficient lighting, pumps, and equipment multiply savings by further reduction in size of cooling equipment. High-performance building envelopes reduce the amount of work that mechanical systems need to do to maintain comfort; with loads reduced, systems can often be downsized, saving energy and cost. As an example, the Empire State Building is receiving new windows, reducing the building cooling load to the point where a new chiller is no longer needed.

Finally, if a building's envelope can be improved and loads reduced enough, entire systems can be eliminated. The greatest monetary and sustainability savings are achieved when a building becomes passive—it heats, cools, and lights itself by harvesting the natural environment.

Adding more sophisticated control systems can also effect greater savings through careful modulation of system activities to smooth out spikes in use, provide heating or cooling at times of lower energy cost, or shut down systems when the building or individual spaces within are not occupied.

## Thermal Comfort

The definition of thermal comfort has evolved along with heating and cooling systems. Early investigators defined thermal comfort as:

"Conditions wherein the average person does not experience the feeling of discomfort"[1]

A more recent definition states:

"A condition of mind which expresses satisfaction with the thermal environment and is assessed by subjective evaluation"[2]

The move from expectation for an interior environment with a lack of discomfort toward a standard in which we express satisfaction followed the maturation of the heating, ventilation, and air-conditioning (HVAC) industry. Partly driven by bold advertising

▶ASHRAE 55, Thermal Comfort in Winter and Summer. Consensus acknowledges differences in perception between winter and summer and defines "comfortable" as lying in a very broad range between 0 and 85 percent relative humidity and 65° to 82°F. *2010 ASHRAE Standard—(55-2010). © American Society of Heating, Refrigerating, and Air-Conditioning Engineers, Inc., www.ashrae.org.*

▶Comfort can be affected by so many factors, not the least of which are recent outdoor temperature (the season), and controllability of thermal systems, that the industry has developed a different standard for naturally ventilated buildings. With a natural ventilation system, a larger range of temperatures is expected and accepted. *2010 ASHRAE Standard—(55-2010). © American Society of Heating, Refrigerating, and Air-Conditioning Engineers, Inc., www.ashrae.org.*

and partly by the mechanical techniques themselves, we have come to believe that the systems that control the interior of our buildings can provide "satisfaction" at all times. Of course, as the American Society of Heating, Refrigerating, and Air-Conditioning Engineers (ASHRAE) acknowledges, "satisfaction" is subjective. Thermal comfort varies depending on temperature, humidity, clothing, activity, convection, and conduction within a space, personal inclination, and a number of other lesser factors. A person wearing a heavy suit, having just run to a meeting, will be uncomfortably hot in a room where others have sat shivering because they are sitting still while wearing only thin clothing.

HVAC systems are expected to control the interior environment within tight bands of expectation. Complex interactions between temperature, humidity, and interior air movement must be orchestrated within the confines of existing buildings that were often designed to a completely different standard. Working with older buildings that provided a "lack of discomfort" when individuals wore heavier 1920s clothing, it can be very difficult to provide "satisfaction" to occupants wearing shorts and a T-shirt.

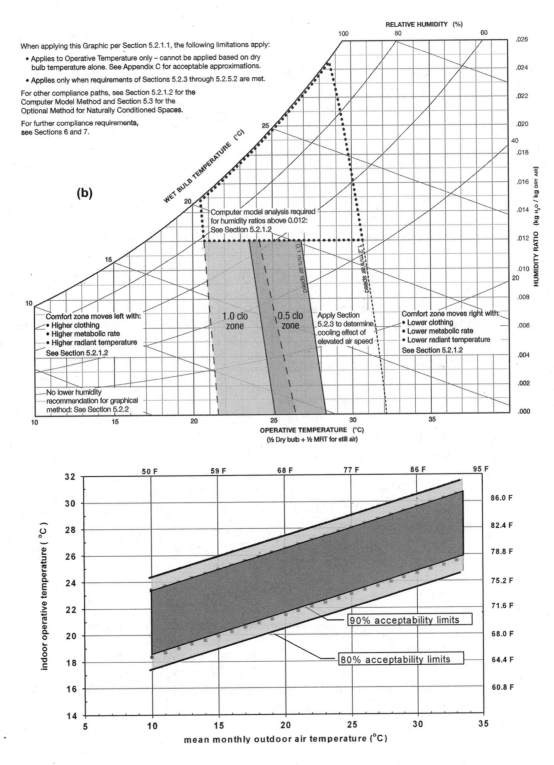

## Water Use

Since the heroics of the Roman aqueducts, we have developed myriad ways of providing water for human use. We and our buildings use water for drinking, hygiene, and mechanical systems. Piped potable water allows us to live in inhospitable deserts as well as on mountaintops. We and our buildings consume more and more water each year. The U.S. government subsidizes water use, and because we have been deferring maintenance on our water mains and sewers, the true cost of water escapes us. Recent talk of rate hikes to finance replacement of hundred-year-old pipes caused a furor in Washington, DC, and other places.[3] Because of this myopic view, we expect the water to flow unrestrained, cheap, and plentiful.

According to the American Water Works Association (AWWA), nearly 4 percent of our nation's electricity goes to moving and treating water and wastewater.[4] On an individual basis, Americans consume about 150 gallons of water per day while Europeans use about 75 gallons![5] On the supply side, every gallon of water consumed comes with the environmental price tag of the electricity used to pump it, the power used to treat it, as well as the embedded energy used to construct and maintain our distribution system. Further, to the detriment of the environment, many of our cities use combined sanitary and storm sewers, often dumping untreated sewage into our oceans and rivers during heavy rains.

Within the context of sustainable renovation, our task is to conserve water while wisely using the materials necessary to provide adequate water delivery and wastewater systems. On the delivery side, we usually encounter piping made of copper, ductile iron, or more recently polyvinyl chloride (PVC) or cross-linked polyester (PEX) within buildings. Older site-water distribution piping is sometimes made of transite (an asbestos-cement product). In the following sections

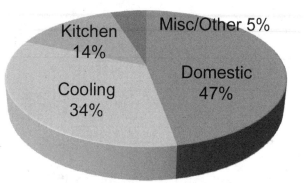

Nearly half of water use in commercial buildings comes from activities similar to residential applications. Replacement or retrofitting of fixtures and fittings produce tremendous savings while changes to cooling system water use can address a remaining third of use.[6] *Courtesy Massachusetts Water Resources Authority (MWRA).*

we will explore water conservation through the use of new fixtures and fittings, water reduction through landscaping strategies, HVAC system conservation, and water treatment and reuse for nonpotable activities. We will also discuss common issues encountered in the renovation of old water delivery systems.

## Light

Humans evolved to perceive electromagnetic radiation in only a small range of "light" emitted by the sun. Centered on the green wavelengths, our eyes see only a tiny fraction of the radiation around us, employing different parts of our eye for color rendition, low light conditions, and even for regulation of our biologic clock.[7] We need different amounts of light to perform different tasks, such as eating dinner versus reading the newspaper. As we age, our eyesight deteriorates, so careful consideration of the age of building occupants can also have a significant effect on the amount of electric light we want to supply.

Electric lighting has evolved from incandescent to fluorescent, to light emitting diode (LED). Incandescent lights, when analyzed for spectral energy output, are really heaters—they give off more infrared radiation than visible radiation. Each has its advantage, but at this time, fluorescent is the most mature technology, effective for most applications. Incandescent lighting provides a very "warm" light—giving off an overall yellow effect. While direct daylight (and especially diffuse daylight) is bluish in overall color, we perceive daylight as good because it also provides very good color rendition. Because daylight includes significant output at all visible wavelengths, objects reflect the colors we expect. Fluorescent light, however, gives off energy at discrete wavelengths—with little output at most wavelengths. Because of this, we perceive fluorescent light as "colored" due to the lack of some wavelengths in reflections off objects. In order to measure fluorescent lamp output, we have two main metrics: the correlated color temperature (CCT) and the color rendering index (CRI). Measured in degrees Kelvin (°K), CCT is bluer for higher temperatures and yellow or red for lower temperatures. Fluorescent lamps are rated by color temperature—from 2500° (very warm) to 5000° (very cool). Different color temperatures produce different effects, so fluorescent lamps should always be selected for appropriate color temperature as well as efficacy.

CRI is a critical measure allowing us to compare the ability of light bulbs to illuminate our interiors. While incandescent light has a CRI very close to 100 (the best rendition), many fluorescent lamps approach a CRI of 90 or better. While the CRI has been criticized because of our subjective perception, it remains the most common measure in the field. Combined with CCT, CRI allows a designer to select lighting for different uses and effects. ;

Daylighting, using the light from the sun and sky in a controlled manner that does not admit heat or glare, has remained the most energy efficient means of lighting buildings during the day. For any uses that happen during daylight hours and require light, it is obvious that the most sustainable strategy is to provide daylighting rather than electric light. Direct, intense light from the sun should be avoided in almost all cases. North windows and clerestories or shaded/reflected sunlight on other façades are most useful in replacing electric light. Typical buildings from different eras present different challenges for instituting or reinstituting daylighting.

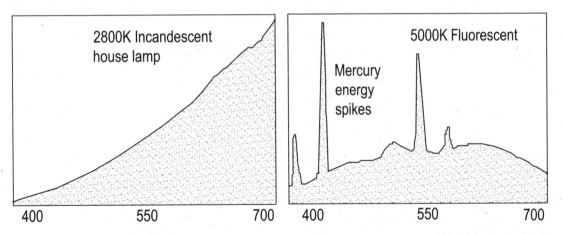

Spectral Power Distribution (SPD) indicates the amount of light given off by a lamp at specific wavelengths. SPD is closely related to Color Rendition Index (CRI) through the ability of a lamp to illuminate objects of different colors. The "cool white" fluorescent lamp has a CRI in the 60s while better fluorescent fixtures can achieve CRI in the 90s. *Gelfand Partners Architects.*

## Building Controls and Environmental Responsiveness

At the turn of the twentieth century, all building systems were controlled manually. Heating was on or off, the boiler was fired by a building superintendent and radiators controlled by the turn of a knob. Often, windows were used to control the heat—when a room got too hot, someone opened the window. Lighting was either on or off at the push of a button. That was about it—a few knobs or buttons that everyone knew how to operate. Today, we find ourselves at the mercy of fully automated systems, or under the control of a hodge-podge of manual and semi-automatic controls. While the installation of programmable thermostats is one of the cheapest ways to save a tremendous amount of energy in a small building, how many of us take the time to learn how to set it properly and adjust it seasonally? Improperly commissioned (set) automated controls lead to poor or even abysmal energy performance.

Our control of temperature through automated systems moved from knobs and valves to pneumatic or electric thermostats in the middle part of the century. While boilers were still controlled by a dedicated boiler operator, valves that controlled individual radiators became more sophisticated, employing pressurized lines connected to a thermostat to regulate heat. Later, thermostats were tied directly to the boiler, initiating startup and firing, then controlling the temperature in rooms containing a radiator. Finally, as thermostats evolved to electric models, they were tied to nascent air-conditioning systems, controlling both heating and cooling. Unfortunately, everyone prefers a different temperature, and everyone thinks everyone else is wrong. While we have never encountered purposely disabled thermostats, reports cite installation of fake thermostats in office buildings to placate all too frequent occupant complaints.[8] Today, we find thermostatic control systems with pneumatic control, line voltage (120V), or low voltage (24V). Whatever the

flavor, our goal is to provide a fully automatic control, usually with local override capability (within limits), and often tied to an overall Building Management System (BMS). BMS or EMS (energy management system) systems use a computer to control heating, lighting, and pumps in order to maximize efficiencies.

Electric lighting has gone through a similar evolution, from simple on/off buttons to multiple switches in a space, to dimming controls. Lights are often connected to occupancy and daylighting sensors, or a building management system, all designed to turn off or dim the lights when they are not needed. Daylighting controls come in two basic types—those connected to stepped ballasts and those that allow continuous dimming. Except in areas with generally cloudless days, we advocate continuous dimming systems. They allow the lights to get brighter or dimmer without occupants noticing the "jump" when a light switches from one level to another of a stepped ballast control system. Most of us find a sudden, unexplained jump in electric light levels disconcerting. In areas with cloudless skies, on/off daylight controls will generally turn off the lights in the morning when it gets light enough and turn them back on in the evening when daylight levels drop.

Both lighting and temperature control systems require proper installation and commissioning to work effectively. Further, building occupants need information about how and what they do so that the facilities staff does not end up waging an ongoing battle with individuals who want to override each new system installed.

## PREWAR BUILDINGS

Prewar buildings typically have very simple control systems or a variety of renovated add-ons. Frequently we find intact steam radiant heating with newer boilers and pumps, but essentially unchanged since the early twentieth century. Electrical systems are often nearly intact, but with incandescent fixtures replaced by fluorescents and added circuits for power in individual spaces. Because of their age, they often contain mixed and mismatched portions of systems including partial air-conditioning systems, package heating units, separate electrical subpanels, fire alarms, and security systems.

## Renovation or Replacement of Steam and Hydronic Systems

Most prewar buildings were heated by steam radiators and central boilers. While these systems can be fairly efficient, they come with inherent problems. There are two basic types: one-pipe systems and two-pipe systems. One-pipe systems employ a single pipe to deliver steam to each radiator, the condensate returns to the boiler via gravity. While two-pipe steam systems use a separate pipe for return of condensate, they also rely on gravity to return the condensate. Because of this reliance on gravity, changes to steam systems can be very problematic. Relocation of radiators can lead to sections of flat piping or to heroic routes for piping to avoid obstructions like beams and columns.

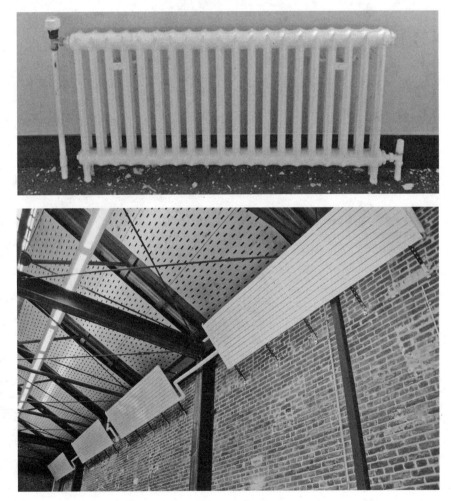

Cast-iron radiators and steam heating systems can be replaced with more efficient hydronic systems with radiant heat panels. Radiant panels can also be used for radiant cooling, if climate and equipment are appropriate. *Gelfand Partners Architects.*

Sometimes we find steam pipes cast into concrete structural systems without adequate separation. When the concrete comes in contact with the piping, the pipes corrode. In order to repair the system to prevent constant leaks, contractors will need to remove ceiling and wall finishes, repair pipes, sometimes reroute them around concrete, then patch surrounding dam-

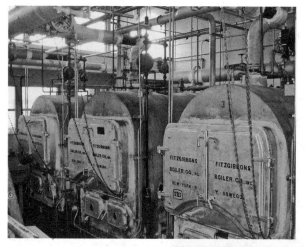

aged finishes. Lastly, steam piping, if it is insulated at all, is often protected with asbestos-containing insulation. Repairs often come with a need for hazardous materials containments to protect workers and prevent the spread of friable asbestos.

Steam boilers are no longer stoked with coal, but heating oil is common throughout many parts of the country even as natural gas heating is becoming the norm. In buildings with oil-fired boilers there may be an oil storage tank that requires hazardous material investigation and abatement. Conversion to natural gas is possible where the fuel is locally available; replacement by a hydronic system desirable. Hydronic systems run at a much lower temperature. They are more efficient and, because they rely on pumps to move heated water around, allow more freedom for routing of piping. Conversion to hydronic systems also allows greater freedom in choice of radiators. Stylish flat panel systems can be free-standing, wall-mounted, or ceiling-hung. While wall-mounted units below

With current hydronic systems, boilers are so much smaller than original steam boilers that additional space can be used for other purposes. *Gelfand Partners Architects.*

windows typically work most efficiently (through convection plus radiation), radiant ceiling panels have the advantage that they warm people's heads and bodies, particularly in renovations where furniture interferes with radiation of heat. Further, ceiling-mounted radiant panels can be used during the cooling season by routing cold water through them—not as effective as high-mass chilled beams, but still a system worth investigating.

Whatever the conventional heat source, hydronic boilers can be tied to geothermal or solar hot water heating systems to supplement or replace fossil fuels. In many areas of the country, waste stream biomass boilers have become the sustainable heating source of choice.

## Improving Ventilation and Fire Safety

Many prewar buildings were originally designed for natural ventilation. Through the years, this original design criterion has been thwarted by regulations intended to stop the spread of fire throughout a building. In many older buildings, exit stairs were open from floor to floor. Over the years, fire marshals have required that they be enclosed at each floor. The original "Sam Spade" hallways, with marble wainscot, dark woodwork, and transom windows above office doors combined with open stairwells and operable windows allowed old buildings to breathe through stack ventilation. Now, we often encounter hallways with transoms screwed shut or replaced with fire-rated panels.

With a returning desire for natural ventilation, we aim to re-create this passive system using stack ventilation. In most prewar buildings there will be a complicated interplay between the desire for hot air to rise freely through multiple floors and the requirement to limit air transfer from floor to floor in the event of fire. The typical solution is to provide a few controlled

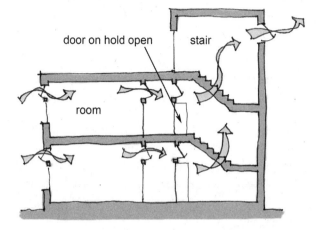

Each area to be ventilated requires opening control with tie-in to the fire alarm system plus the equipment for an automated fire damper or electromagnetic hold opens at doors. Windows or louvers can be motor-controlled by an EMS while doors can remain on magnetic hold-opens to allow stack ventilation. *Gelfand Partners Architects.*

openings between rooms and corridors, then either providing controlled openings to stair wells or new air shafts to the roof. At all the ventilation connection points between stairways/corridors and rooms, automatic fire/smoke dampers are usually required, allowing the various passages to be closed off from the rooms in the event of a fire. These dampers are usually tied to an automatic fire alarm system so that a fire anywhere in the building will activate them all to achieve high levels of fire protection.

As you can imagine, this is not an inexpensive system. However, once installed and tested, the energy to run the system is negligible—just a small amount of power to keep the fire alarm active and occasional power to close the dampers in an emergency and reset them after any danger has passed. For high-rise stairwells, the fire/smoke damper system or magnetic door hold opens must also be coordinated with stairwell pressurization.

## Restoring or Improving Daylighting

The original daylighting schemes of prewar buildings have often been obscured by one of two common renovation types. First is the introduction of suspended ceilings. Many older buildings had high ceilings—eleven to fourteen feet. Allowing room for air circulation and daylight to cast deep into the room, tall ceilings have often been transformed to low "pancake" space in order to install HVAC systems and suspended 2×4 prismatic fluorescent fixtures. The ubiquitous lay-in ceiling with squares of high-contrast downlight also tends to box in the upper third of older windows. Renovations can restore the windows to their original height if HVAC systems and other recent intrusions can be reconfigured. Often, replacement of typical ductwork with presentable spiral ducts and rerouting of exposed piping can clean up a room, reintroduce daylighting, and improve overall room ventilation.

## Water-Saving Strategies

Many prewar buildings still contain their original plumbing fixtures. Workhorses that have lasted decades, they also consume tremendous amounts of water. One of the easiest water-saving strategies for old buildings is the simple replacement of fixtures. Older toilets, while perhaps providing a sense of nostalgia, use between three and five gallons per flush, while new toilets can use less than 1.28 gallons. Two points are in order. First, new toilets can lead to great water savings—if they work. It is very important to look for data on how well they flush. The best source is testing by the Canadian Waste Water Association (CWWA). Their test method has become the standard by which to judge whether toilets flush well or not.[9] Second, old, high water–use toilets were connected to sewage systems that may have been designed for a large flow of liquid. We have found a few instances where install-

As discussed in Chapter 4, the other common intrusion on prewar daylighting is the introduction of insulated panels within the window frames. Replacement of insulated panels with new thermally broken insulated glazing systems can both reintroduce daylighting and provide enough insulation to achieve good energy consumption goals. *Gelfand Partners Architects.*

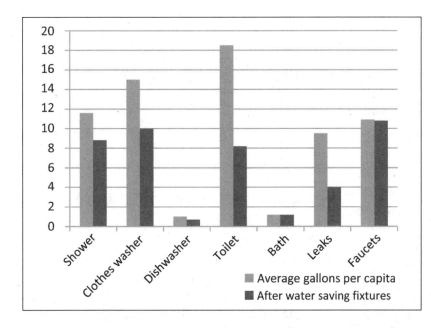

◀ Typical water savings per fixture for high-efficiency retrofit (gallons).[10] *Gelfand Partners Architects.*

▼ Urinals, in particular, can be replaced with zero-water fixtures. Becoming more common in many areas of the country, waterless urinals work well in facilities with robust maintenance programs. In buildings where maintenance is not consistent, waterless urinals have been criticized because of the smells that occur when liquid seals are not replenished on recommended schedules or where improper cleaners degrade the liquid. *Gelfand Partners Architects.*

ing low-flow fixtures has lead to frequent clogging of sanitary sewer lines within a few months of opening. Cleaning and inspection of existing sanitary lines is always a good policy when undertaking a renovation.

Faucets, shower heads, and other plumbing fittings can benefit greatly from addition of aerators or replacement with low-flow fittings. Metering and automatic faucets prevent water waste from improperly closed faucets.

Leaks in water supply lines account for about 10 percent of water use. A leaky faucet can consume 3,000 gallons a year while a leaky toilet can run through 200 gallons a day.[11] At number three on the Federal Energy Management Program's Water Efficiency Best Management Practices (BMPs), leak detection and repair, combined with an overall water management audit, can provide significant water savings. Additionally, many systems, especially irrigation, steam, or hydronic heating and cooling systems can benefit from wise management techniques—often set in motion by a significant renovation.[12] Finally, to prevent sys-

temic leaks, cured-in-place piping (CIPP) could be a solution appropriate for older piping systems. CIPP systems insert a synthetic liner into existing pipes and seal it in place with an epoxy curing agent.

## Electric Power and Controls Replacement

Sustainable renovation of prewar buildings' electrical power and controls systems often requires a large investigative component. Because of the advanced age and relative lack of power originally provided, prewar buildings are often filled with differing, overlapping systems that accrued over time. Electrical consumption was usually pretty minimal before the war, so we find few power receptacles in older buildings. Sometimes wired with knob and tube wiring, power receptacles were commonly set in series, sometimes stacked vertically in tall buildings or in loops in shorter buildings. We have found apartment buildings where three or four apartments are fed off one circuit, not necessarily in a logical order. Modifications to knob and tube wiring requires specialized knowledge, common among electricians who regularly work on older buildings. A significant allocation of time should be available for tracing existing circuits.

Also common in older buildings is a mixture of old and new fixtures with old and new wiring. While it is possible to connect new fixtures and even controls to old wiring, it is wise to confirm the circuiting to ensure that old wiring is sufficient for loads. Resistance testing will also help determine if old wiring has degraded. One important exception exists that prevents some new fixtures to be attached to old wiring. New receptacles require a ground; many old wiring systems did not include a third wire for ground. In particular, ground fault circuit interrupters (GFCI) for locations near water sources require grounding—their purpose is to cut the flow of electricity if a short circuit occurs in the line (appliance drops into a sink, and so forth).

Prewar buildings often have very simple controls—usually just on/off for power. While switches can be replaced easily, it may be difficult to provide more complex or automated controls. Most troubles occur because of unexpected circuiting routes or incompatibility of controls with voltage or line resistance. Again, thorough investigation at the start of a project can pay off in reduction in unexpected problems.

# MID-CENTURY MODERN BUILDINGS

Mid-century modern buildings tend to have slightly more complicated systems and controls. However, due to their age, they also tend to be obsolete or at least very limited when compared to today's expectations. Old clock/bell systems in schools, public address systems, and intercoms became common on the mid-century, adding to our expectations of how our buildings could ease our lives. While every generation seems to have its perception of which "modern conveniences" are important, an explosion of electrical devices and innovative components in the postwar period expanded the breadth of systems in our buildings to include automated fire alarms, fire suppression systems, environmental controls, and communications devices. While mid-century modern buildings tend to have more complicated systems than older buildings, they are often outdated and ready for replacement. Recent advances in wireless technology can provide systems that work as well as the old ones but without the expense and embedded energy of miles of wiring.

## Renovation or Replacement of Hydronic Systems

Many mid-century modern buildings used oversized forced air heating and air-conditioning systems, others were constructed with hydronic heating systems alone.

These systems used cooler water than older steam systems, relying on pumps to circulate hot water to heating elements. Sometimes the heating element was a series of pipes embedded in concrete floors. Unfortunately, these systems were often installed for uses that varied

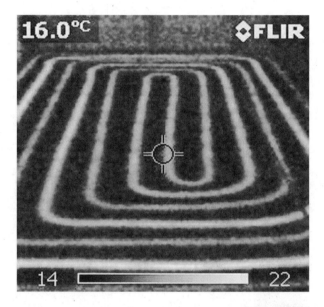

greatly throughout the week, losing efficiency through the effort required to heat the concrete floors in time to have them warm enough for morning arrival of occupants. While they provided comfortable environments for uses like schools and child care facilities, they spent a lot of excess energy heating in the pre-dawn hours for the arrival of students. Then, when twenty or thirty active bodies filled the space, classrooms overheated rapidly, requiring windows to be opened. Radiant floors end up running through large temperature swings in spaces that are periodically occupied, while they can be ideal in continuously occupied spaces.

Like many other mid-century systems, hydronic floor heating systems are usually at or beyond the end of their expected life span. Repairs tend to be very costly—requiring removal of concrete slab to get at piping. Usually, a complete replacement is justified—with a new radiant system if concrete replacement is possible—and sometimes with a new cementitious topping with embedded hydronic tubing, in more limited budget applications.

▲ Hydronic radiant heated floors can be extremely efficient, especially for buildings with consistent hours of use. Taking advantage of the thermal mass of concrete floors, hydronic boilers could run at very low rates, constantly pumping just a small amount of heat through the system to make up for losses to the cold outdoors. *Bay Hydronic, Inc.*

▶Above-slab hydronic systems from the mid-century tend to use fin tube radiators with fans to assist in movement of heated air. Many companies still make the old pressed-steel/baked enamel fin tube covers. Inside the covers, however, lurk inefficient fans and fin tubes that often leak and have almost no contact with air because of years of dust and grime. A thorough cleaning is the absolute bare minimum needed during a renovation, replacement of piping, radiators, and enclosures as well as pumps and boilers is a common scope of work. *Gelfand Partners Architects.*

## Creating New Passive Ventilation Options

While many mid-century modern buildings were originally designed for natural ventilation, others were conceived as sealed envelopes with an HVAC system controlling the interior environment. Because we aim to reduce the energy while improving indoor air quality, designers should investigate the possibilities for introduction of passive ventilation strategies. It can be particularly difficult to add ducts or piping to mid-century buildings, so added passive ventilation is often pursued by adding controllable openings between areas. As discussed above, this sometimes comes in conflict with requirements for fire safety—providing new openings might entail installation of fire/smoke dampers. Otherwise, the systems-built façades often lend themselves to introduction of operable openings. Even if the original curtain walls or large windows were designed to be fixed, fixed glazing can often be replaced with new operable sashes. In buildings with an energy management system (EMS), windows can be controlled by small motors attached to interior and exterior thermostats, allowing windows to opened and closed based on conditions—providing natural ventilation.

## Improving or Replacing Forced Air Heating, Ventilating, and Air-Conditioning

Heating, ventilation, and air-conditioning machinery and controls can almost always be improved over the models installed from the mid-century through the 1980s. Most mid-century buildings have had at least one round of equipment replacement, although controls are often still original. Both are ripe for sustainable upgrades. More efficient compressors and pumps are widely available since technological improvement has accelerated recently. Electronic controls, compressors, motors, fans, and pumps have all advanced recently with particular emphasis on reducing energy consumption. First, mid-century modern buildings should be assessed to see if integrated design strategies would result in changes to system types, reduction, or elimination of systems altogether. Reduction of mechanical system size can be achieved through coupling of decreased loads with increased insulation, better lighting, and solar control. It may even be possible to retrofit a geothermal heat exchange system in appropriate climates.

Given how much we rely on them, HVAC systems receive surprisingly little regular maintenance and

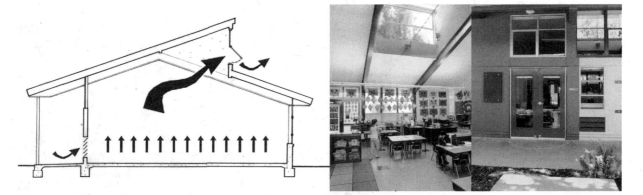

Provision of a low-side air intake grille with back-damper and filter, combined with an EMS-controlled clerestory window, can form a passive ventilation system that runs with little user input and almost no energy. *Gelfand Partners Architects.*

MERV (Minimum Efficiency Reporting Value) is a measure of the ability of a filter to remove particles from air. Higher MERV filters remove smaller particles. "Inhalable coarse particles" (such as those found near roadways and dusty industries) are larger than 2.5 microns but smaller than 10 microns; "fine particles" (such as those found in smoke and haze) less than 2.5 micrometers can be breathed deep into the lungs and may enter the bloodstream.[13] Moving from a typical MERV 8 filter to a MERV 12 will result in removal of 90 percent rather than 70 percent of particles down to 3 microns as well as filtering out 80 percent of particles down to 1 micron. A MERV 13 filter will remove 75 percent of particles down to 0.3 microns.[14]

| MERV (Std 52.2) | Average ASHRAE Dust Spot Efficiency Std 52.1 | Average ASHRAE Arrestance Std 52.1 | Particle Size Ranges | Typical Applications | Typical Filter Type |
|---|---|---|---|---|---|
| 1 – 4 | <20% | 60 to 80% | > 10.0 µm | Residential/Minimum Light/ Commercial Minimum/ Equipment Protection | Permanent/Self-Charging (passive) Washable/Metal, Foam/Synthetics Disposable Panels Fiberglass/Synthetics |
| 5 – 8 | <20 to 35% | 80 to 95% | 3.0 – 10.0 µm | Industrial Workplaces Commercial Better/ Residential Paint Booth/ Finishing | Pleated Filters Extended Surface Filters Media Panel Filters |
| 9 – 12 | 40 to 75% | >95 to 98% | 1.0 – 3.0 µm | Superior/Residential Better/ Industrial Workplaces Better/Commercial Buildings | Nonsupported/Bag/Rigid Box Rigid Cell/Cartridge |
| 13 – 16 | 80 to 95% + | >98 to 99% | 0.30 – 1.0 µm | Smoke Removal General Surgery Hospitals & Health Care Superior/Commercial Buildings | Rigid Cell/Cartridge Rigid Box Nonsupported/Bag |
| 17 – 20* | 99.97[†] 99.99[†] 99.999[†] | N/A | ≤ 0.30 µm | Clean Rooms High Risk Surgery Hazardous Materials | HEPA ULPA |

Note: This table is intended to be a general guide to filter use and does not address specific applications or individual filter performance in a given application. Refer to manufacturer test results for additional information.

*Reserved for future classifications.

[†]DOP Efficiency.

www.nafahq.org/LibaryFiles/Articles/Article006.htm.

cleaning. Beyond a reassessment of HVAC systems in relation to other building elements, simple cleaning of ductwork can both improve efficiency and remove environmental irritants or hazards. Additionally, re-fitting of better filters can improve indoor air quality tremendously. High MERV filters (see sidebar) will keep ductwork and equipment cleaner in the future—allowing them to run at higher efficiency.

Most HVAC systems were designed by conservative rule of thumb—oversized—with control valves used to adjust to the actual capacity needed. Careful recalculation and installation of more sophisticated controls and variable speed pumps can remove the inefficiencies of old systems. Efficient systems use only the energy required, rather than running at full speed then metering the flow of condensate and heated water. In a comprehensive HVAC replacement, straightening pipe runs and installation of Ys and 45-degree fittings rather than Ts and 90-degree fittings can reduce resistance to the flow of coolant, thereby minimizing pump size.

## Restoring or Improving Daylighting

While many mid-century modern buildings have large amounts of glazing, much of it is nearly uncontrolled. We recently renovated a 1950s school with two floors almost 650 feet long of windows extending from cabinet to ceiling for the entire length of each classroom—nearly 10,000 ft$^2$ of unprotected glazing facing almost due south. Needless to say, the blinds were drawn almost every day—hiding a tremendous view of the Pacific Ocean while doing little to protect the rooms from solar gain and glare. We proposed a replacement window system with integral sunshades to balance the light in the classrooms better while allowing the benefits of direct views to the outside and solar gain from the lower sun in winter.

Other mid-century buildings suffer from imbalanced daylighting or decades of retrofits that have attempted to address the failings of original designs. Often, glazing is covered with foil or paper, glass is replaced with opaque panels, or windows are filled in completely. Introduction of new sunshading devices outside the building envelope is likely to be most effective in eliminating the problem with over-daylighting. In many cases, replacement of glazing with properly tinted or coated glass can reduce heat gain and glare while allowing existing windows to remain. See Chapter 4 for more glazing information.

Unshaded windows of many modernist buildings lead to overheated interiors and, ironically, loss of views: occupants leave the shades down all the time to avoid the sun's heat. Added sunshading can alleviate overheating and return the intent of large window areas— unimpeded views of the outdoors. *Gelfand Partners Architects.*

## Water-Saving Strategies

In terms of water use, commercial and institutional buildings of the mid-century are similar to prewar

**Measures to reduce water waste in cooling towers include:** [15]

- Performing a lifecycle analysis, including all operating, capital, and personnel costs, to determine whether use of a cooling tower is more cost-effective than air cooling.

- Equipping cooling towers with conductivity controllers, makeup, and blow-down meters, and overflow alarms.

- Operating towers at a minimum of five cycles of concentration using potable water, depending upon the chemistry of the makeup water used, including considerations for reclaimed water or on-site sources.

- Avoiding once-through cooling with potable water.

- Using high-efficiency drift eliminators that reduce drift loss to less than 0.002 percent of circulating water volume for cross-flow towers and 0.001 percent for counter-flow towers.

- Evaluating the processes in the plant for maximum energy efficiency and waste-heat recovery, since a more efficient building will reject less heat to the cooling tower.

- Providing adequate training to cooling-tower operators.

buildings. Inefficient plumbing fixtures and fittings can be changed out readily. Because buildings from this era are that much younger, many more original plumbing components remain. In particular, mid-century buildings often contain rusted galvanized water piping that requires replacement. They often have perfectly serviceable copper piping.

Mid-century buildings sometimes use domestic water for direct cooling within air-conditioning systems. In these "once-through" systems, water cools HVAC condenser coils then drains away. While most of these simple systems have been replaced by more efficient types, remaining once-through systems can be converted to recirculating systems, conserving huge quantities of water, but requiring additional components to ensure that minerals and microbial contaminants do not build up in the system.

Similarly, evaporative cooling towers are often open systems that drain away water after one use, not closed loop systems where condensate is recir-

culated through the pipes. Closed loop systems rely on makeup water to replace moisture lost through evaporation. Eventually, the circulating water becomes saturated with minerals as the pure water is evaporated away. An important goal for sustainable design relies on treatment of blow-down water (the water removed to prevent build-up of minerals) to limit harm to equipment and minimize chemicals and biocides in waste water drawn off while increasing the percentage of water that can be recirculated.

Outside the building, mid-century landscapes sometimes used exotic planting, requiring larger irrigation systems. While most irrigation systems from this period have long since been replaced, the overall landscape scheme may still be fairly intact. An overabundance of turf grass, exotics not adapted to local climate, and reliance on petrochemical fertilizers and biocides makes many mid-century landscapes inherently unsustainable. As maintenance funds have diminished over the years, many

The EPA notes that up to 50 percent of irrigation water goes to waste because of evaporation, wind, improper system design, or overwatering.[18] "Smart" irrigation controllers that connect to weather data or soil condition sensors can adjust watering schedules to match conditions necessary for optimal plant health while conserving water. *Gelfand Partners Architects.*

of these landscapes have devolved into monocultures of grass with a few trees sprinkled about. One highly desirable water-saving strategy is a wholesale replacement of water-consuming landscaping with a planting scheme suited to the local climate and supplied by a water-conserving irrigation system

with smart controllers.[16] Further, introduction of organic landscaping methods can eliminate reliance on petrochemical fertilizers and toxic pest control methods.[17]

## Electric Power and Controls Replacement

As building systems and appliances became more complex during the postwar period, electrical power needs increased. We find additional wiring and controls throughout mid-century modern buildings, provided for more recent upgrades in technology. One interesting complication of 1960s buildings is the use of aluminum wiring, particularly for branch circuiting. Aluminum wiring is not a bad substitute for copper, per se, but it comes with some particular problems. First, aluminum requires larger wire size to conduct the same amount of electricity as copper. Secondly, and most importantly, aluminum wiring was often terminated at panels and devices with the same methods as copper wire. Two problems occur. First, since aluminum is not quite as good a conductor as copper, similar terminations will not allow as much current to flow through aluminum as copper. Secondly, aluminum wire is often terminated to dissimilar metals, resulting in electrolytic corrosion, causing a further degradation of conductor efficiency. Because these problems have been implicated in building fires, all buildings from the 1960s and 1970s should be investigated to see if they contain aluminum wiring and, if so, how the terminations and wire sizing match the intended use.

As mentioned earlier, pneumatic thermostatic control systems originated around the middle of the twentieth century. Accompanied by the electric thermostat not long after, many mid-century build-

Dielectric thermostat from the 1950s. Many of these units are still in operation—ready for replacement by programmable electronic thermostats. *Gelfand Partners Architects.*

ings are still operated by separate thermostats in each area. While many still work, newer programmable electronic thermostats allow more refined control of heating/cooling systems while eliminating the mechanical problems associated with pneumatic pumps and pipes.

# LATE MODERN BUILDINGS

As described throughout this book, late modern buildings are typified by materials and methods focused on quick production driven by first costs rather than by longevity or reparability. They tend to contain components that were made to be replaced on a fairly short time frame. However, building con-

trol systems in late modern buildings are noted for their increasing sophistication. From the advent of computer-operated building control systems in the 1970s, to addition of complex fire alarm, telecommunications, and data systems in more recent years, late modern buildings contain components whose complexity has often outstripped the flawed designs and environmental physics of the buildings themselves.

## Strategies for Deep Floor Plates

Especially in the commercial office sector, deep floor plates and wide expanses of undifferentiated space followed the economics of the bottom line. Unfortunately, these also result in buildings that rely heavily on overtaxed HVAC systems and electric lighting. Because of the tension between the need for privacy and the desire for open offices, often we see pancake spaces with high modular office furniture partitions, completely blocking any views and daylight from the exterior while doing little to provide acoustic separation.

In deep floor plate buildings where daylight cannot be introduced, it could be fruitful to investigate the possibilities of providing fluorescent lights that include a blue part of the spectrum associated with stimulation of the eye's ganglion cells. Recent research has indicated that certain wavelengths can be used to increase attention by adjusting the body's regulation of circadian rhythms through perception in the human eye.[20] While hopeful, this research has not yet tied together the complicated interplay between perception, circadian rhythms, and time, intensity, and length of exposure.[21] Alternatively, hybrid solar lighting (HSL—see Chapter 8) provides full spectrum lighting deep into large floor plate buildings.

When designing a renovation of a large floor plate building, it might be wise to investigate the provision of interior skylights, courtyards, or light wells in order to introduce daylight and ventilation deep into the building. While this reduces floor space, it can provide a much better and more productive interior environment.[19] *Gelfand Partners Architects.*

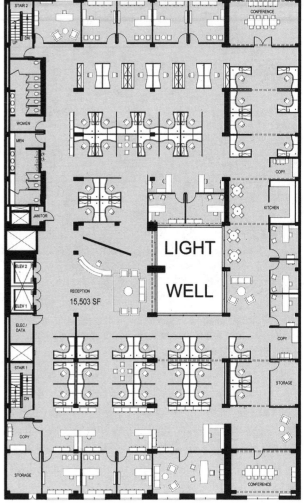

## Creating New Passive Ventilation Options

Like mid-century modern buildings, late modern buildings can often benefit from introduction of passive ventilation strategies. In passive ventilation, outdoor air is used directly. Outdoor air temperatures may often be comfortable enough to make heating or cooling unnecessary. It is very important to note that passive ventilation cannot normally overcome all the heat gains in typical buildings—internal gains must be reduced before attempting introduction of passive ventilation, or the system will be doomed to fail. As a rule of thumb, natural cross ventilation through windows can succeed in buildings/rooms where the depth of the room is less than five times the height of the window heads. Stack ventilation can be used in deeper buildings, although careful control of air flow is needed to avoid stagnant areas.

Passive methods take advantage of differing buoyancy of hot and cold air to move it without mechanical means. And, because people have a different level of expectations for naturally ventilated buildings, designers can employ a wider range of internal temperatures than allowed in a mechanically ventilated building.[22] The challenge with late modern buildings is to weave passive systems into buildings that were designed with mechanical ventilation systems. Addition of intake louvers, operable windows, transfer louvers, fire/smoke dampers, and exhaust louvers or windows plus control systems can provide natural ventilation.

The development of sufficient air intake grilles and paths for distribution remain a primary challenge. Because passive systems rely on temperature differentials to move air of different buoyancy, existing ductwork must often be abandoned and replaced with a series of louvers between rooms or larger ceiling plenum spaces acting at low pressure. Air intake and exhaust locations need added backdraft dampers to ensure that air does not enter the building during inappropriate periods. In humid climates, intake must be carefully controlled to avoid humidity condensing on cooled interior surfaces. Multistory buildings can accommodate both evaporative cooling and solar chimneys so long as prevention of fire spread is addressed.

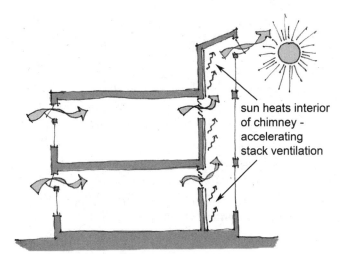

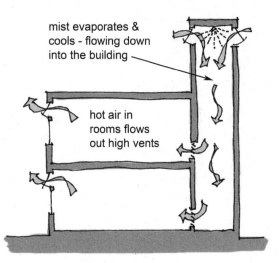

Solar chimneys can be added to the exhaust end of mechanical ventilation systems: If enough stack pressure is achieved, solar chimneys can take over the role of fans, pulling air through a building, leaving the mechanical system to run when needed. Sensors control intake of outdoor air, adjusting as needed. This method augments an economizer cycle, replacing the fan power with stack ventilation power. *Gelfand Partners Architects.*

Evaporative downdraft cooling tower: In many ways the opposite of a solar chimney, downdraft cooling towers work well in hot arid climates. Moist surfaces or mist sprayed into the air at the top of the tower evaporates, cool air then flows down into the building below. Cool air flow can be supplemented by the addition of a solar chimney at the other end of the ventilated area to increase natural ventilation. *Gelfand Partners Architects.*

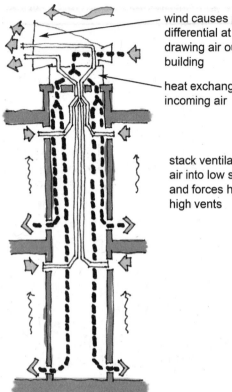

wind causes pressure differential at cowl - drawing air out of building

heat exchanger tempers incoming air

stack ventilation draws air into low supply grilles and forces hot air out high vents

Used in ZEDFactory's BedZED new construction project outside London, passive heat recovery ventilation systems provide energy-free fresh air to each apartment. Wind cowl uses pressure differentials to augment stack effect to draw air out of rooms below. Passive heat exchanger with 85 percent efficiency preheats or precools intake air flowing into the building. *Gelfand Partners Architects.*

Finally, passive heat recovery ventilation is perhaps the holy grail of ventilation design. Rotating wind cowls use local wind to power ventilation, ducts to channel stack ventilation through high and low grilles at each floor, and a passive heat recovery system to transfer heat from outgoing to incoming air. Retrofit systems are under development in England to be inserted in chimney flues, replacing the unused component of archaic heating systems.

## Improving or Replacing Forced Air Heating, Ventilating, and Air-Conditioning

Understanding basic physics, we know that using air to transfer heat is 1,000 times less efficient than using water. [23] Many late century buildings rely on forced air heating systems for climate control. While in the developed world we have become used to almost instant temperature control at the flip of a switch, these systems waste serious amounts of energy through the movement of vast quantities of air. Conversion of buildings from forced air to hydronic heating with natural ventilation or radiant panels for cooling can reap ongoing energy and monetary savings. However, the complete refit of a building heating/cooling system can be pursued only in the context of a substantial renovation.

## Restoring or Improving Daylighting

Once late modern buildings are improved to include as many daylit areas as possible, we are ready for the next, and sometimes forgotten, step. *Daylighting* has no sustainable energy benefit if the lights are left on. It is surprising to see how many buildings have good areas of daylighting but no automatic system for shutting off the lights in those areas. Integrated lighting control systems are readily available and easily retrofit onto existing lighting systems. In practice, daylighting controls consist of sensors that look down on work surfaces and detect when sufficient daylight exists. They then turn off or dim the lights in the area controlled. Important aspects include designation of areas to be controlled by each sensor and calibration of the sensors once installed. Since every area has differing daylight access and lighting requirements, sensors must located frequently enough to allow control of consistently lit areas.

Replacement of forced air systems by hydronics and natural ventilation will do little to affect energy use in a leaky and under-insulated building, but it will make the users more comfortable. While exploring the replacement of ductwork and bulky air-handing equipment with smaller radiant panels and insulated piping, ceilings can be raised, providing opportunities for better indirect lighting or even daylighting while refitting perimeter locations for radiant panels. *Gelfand Partners Architects.*

Radiant panel replaces suspended ceiling and forced air system

Many common light fixture systems come with integrated daylighting sensors. If fixtures are not being replaced, independent sensors can be provided. *Gelfand Partners Architects.*

If daylighting design is successful, spaces will have similar light levels, allowing wide spacing of sensors. However, many deep floor plate buildings will need sensors at the perimeter, then more at the interior—sometimes two or three rows to accurately control lighting. Daylighting controls then need to be coordinated with fluorescent lighting ballasts. Continuous dimming ballasts allow the light fixtures to smoothly dim and increase light, balancing with daylight to allow nearly constant light levels.

In big box stores, warehouses, and other high bay, single-story buildings, addition of daylighting through skylights is very desirable.[24] By harvesting an unlimited resource (the sun), we can avoid all the costs and energy associated with electric light. Coordinating lighting controls with daylight harvesting reduces energy loads while providing better overall lighting and connection with the outdoors. However, skylights must be baffled or diffused to reflect onto the ceiling and prevent direct sunlight creating irritating hot spots within a room.

## Water-Saving Strategies

Often, late modern buildings have numerous tenants or occupants, but only a single water meter. Studies show that users with metered water consume 15 to 20 percent less water than unmetered customers.[25] Some buildings allow an easy split into separate meters. Depending on the rules of the local water authority, individually metering tenants can provide significant water savings. If individual metering through the utility operator is not available, submetering can be provided through either of two methods. If individual tenant areas are supplied by single pipes (unlikely), submeters can be installed. More likely, submeters can be provided upstream of major water use components (water heaters, faucets, showers, toilets, and the like) with water use then estimated. In either case, the benefits of individual users knowing their consumption can be a driver of change.

Finally, many late modern buildings were provided with continuous flow trap primers. Intended to prevent floor drains in areas that rarely get wet from dry-

---

*Several water-efficiency choices are available:*[26]

- Recirculating hot-water systems for large buildings
- Steam boilers of 200 boiler horsepower (hp) or greater, equipped with conductivity controllers to regulate top blow-down
- For closed-loop systems, condensate-return meters on steam boilers of 200 boiler hp or greater
- Closed-loop steam systems operating at twenty cycles of concentration or greater (5 percent or less of makeup water)
- Steam-distribution lines and equipment with steam traps meeting all codes

- Makeup meters on feed-water lines:
  - to steam boilers and water boilers of more than 100,000 Btus per hour
  - to closed-loop hot-water systems for heating
- Boiler-temperature and makeup meters that are clearly visible to operators
- Discharge pipes that are easy to inspect for flow and visible indicators that will indicate whether the valve has activated, thereby reducing plumbing leaks due to repeated openings of water-temperature- and pressure-relief valves (TPRVs).

ing out and allowing sewer gases to leak into a building, trap primers periodically squirt water into the trap to replenish it. Unfortunately, continuous flow primers do just what they say. Using up to 360 gallons a day, each can drain away 130,000 gallons a year. Replacement of continuous flow trap primers with sensor-controlled trap primers or primers tied to nearby flush valves can reduce water use to between 3 and 30 gallons per year—a 4,000 percent savings!

## Electric Power and Controls Replacement

The renovation of many older buildings illustrates an energy paradox; while new systems introduced into buildings can be very energy efficient in and of themselves, the overall energy consumption of renovated buildings often increases because they simply didn't have the systems to begin with. This is less true with late modern buildings because they often come with all the bells and whistles, albeit very *inefficient* bells and whistles. Therefore, they are ripe for deep energy retrofits, including those associated with controls replacement.

Controls replacement alone can produce remarkable energy savings through elimination of system activity during inefficient or unneeded times. In many areas, commercial and industrial customers are required to pay for electricity on a time-of-usage basis. Smart meters record the usage and time of day, stepping electricity rates to match demand. In terms of money as well as energy, new controls systems that prioritize activity during cheap electricity hours and reduce activity during peak hours allow building owners to avoid excess charges on time-of-usage utility contracts. Many utilities are also instituting smart utilities programs in which customers agree to shut off some equipment during power emergencies in exchange for reduced utility rates.

Sophisticated controls systems also have the ability to predict energy use and modulate response, more subtly adjusting systems by planning for predicted temperature changes later in the day. Where an older "dumb" heating system might turn on a furnace and run at full speed to try to achieve a temperature increase, a sophisticated system might sense that outdoor temperature is rising and solar gains are increasing, predicting that increasing temperature quickly might result in overheating. By scaling back the heating response, a smart system can even out interior temperature swings during the day, resulting in a more comfortable interior environment while reducing energy consumption.

## SYSTEMS REPLACEMENT SUMMARY

Whenever possible within a sustainable renovation, priority should be placed on creating or augmenting passive systems. After interior loads have been reduced, daylighting, passive heating or cooling, and passive ventilation systems will reduce energy use both by replacing mechanical or electrical system energy and by allowing reduction in system or component sizing. Once passive systems have been optimized, changes to more efficient heating and cooling systems such as hydronic radiant panels or use of renewable fuels such as biomass heaters can minimize the environmental effect of the remaining mechanical systems. Replacement of inefficient fixtures and fittings and the addition of sophisticated controls for lighting, heating, and cooling will keep energy use to bare minimums. In sum, holistic design analysis carried through building systems should lead to sizeable reductions in energy use, thereby minimizing environmental effect.

# Normand Maurice Building

**Owner**   Public Works Governmental Services Canada (PWGSC)

**Architect**   PWGSC Architect ABCP, Beauchamp et Bourbeau   Busby Perkins+Will Architects Company

**Original Building Type**   Industrial

**Renovation Building Type**   Office, Warehouse, Classroom, Meeting, Gymnasium, Cafeteria

**Original Construction Date**   1851–1950

**Renovation Date**   2006

**Location**   Montreal, Quebec, Canada

**Climate**   Humid continental (Köppen Dfb)

**Area**   169,000 ft²

**Achievement**   LEED NC v2.1 Gold (57 points)

**Key Indicators**   Daylighting

> Radiant Heating and Cooling with Thermal Mass
> Energy Recovery Ventilation
> Underfloor Air Distribution
> Geothermal Heat Exchange with Thermal Storage
> Green Roof

**Energy Achievement**   54 percent less than reference building (Canadian energy code)

**Total Energy use**   4,244 kWh/year   25.11 kWh/ft² year   (270 kWh/m² year)

**Electricity After**   1673 MWh/year   9.9 kWh/ ft²   (107 kW/m² year)

**Heating After**   752 MWh/ ft²/yr   4.5 kWh/ ft²   (48 kW/m² year)

**Renewables**   None

With portions originally constructed from 1851 to 1950, the 168,900 ft² Normand Maurice Building in Montreal, Quebec, operates as an office headquarters, warehouse, and armory storage for several public bodies—the Department of National Defense and the Royal Canadian Mounted Police. Through sophisticated environmental systems, the building achieves approximately 54 percent energy savings, totaling $267,000 per year. Because of

A conversion and extension of a building complex originally constructed from 1851 to 1950, the Normand Maurice Building combines reuse of existing materials with sophisticated environmental control systems. A hybrid ventilation system with heat recovery enthalpy wheels combines with separate heating and cooling systems to achieve a 54 percent energy savings when compared to similar buildings. *Courtesy Busby Perkins+Will Architects Co*

the very humid summers and cold winters, a hybrid ventilation system was combined with a separate heating and cooling system, segregating ventilation needs from temperature control. An underfloor air system with pressurized plenum and floor diffusers distributes air to the occupied spaces, reducing horizontal ducts, and allowing less restricted air movement. Heating and cooling occurs via fluid-based radiant ceiling slabs. A system of energy recovery enthalpy wheels dehumidifies incoming air to prevent condensation on radiant cooling slabs in humid summers. A geothermal heat exchange system supplements gas-fired boilers and HFC-based chillers and is tied to a sand-based heat storage facility to dampen peak effects.

To reduce consumption, skylights provide multiple building levels with maximum natural lighting along with cold season solar heating. Rainwater is treated on-site, and then reused in dual-flush, efficient water closets and low-flow urinals. A green roof, which does not use an irrigation system, reduces potable water use further. Additionally, 100 percent of the steel materials, 82 percent of the wood materials, and 92 percent of the brick was reused from the original building. During construction 75 percent of construction debris was diverted from the landfills.

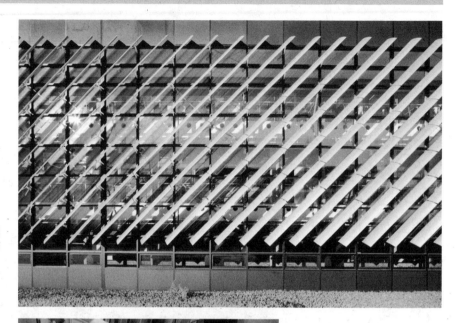

Engineers calculated the most efficient angle for application of shading fins to minimize energy use for cooling and heating. Since this façade faces southeast, the fins were angled west to prevent overheating. *Courtesy Busby Perkins+Will Architects Co.*

An atrium buffers interior spaces from exterior temperature shifts while still allowing daylight to penetrate the building. Combined with shading fins, exposed concrete on the interior captures sunlight to aid in winter heating. When the space begins to overheat in summer, natural ventilation systems cool exposed surfaces. Heating and cooling is provided mostly through radiant ceiling panels, although many spaces include radiant heating coils cast into new concrete floor slabs. *Courtesy Busby Perkins+Will Architects Co.*

## CASE STUDY

# Kansas City Power & Light Headquarters

**Owner**   Kansas City Power & Light

**Renovation Architect**   BNIM (Berkebile, Nelson, Immenschuh, McDowell Architects)

**Original Building Type**   Office

**Renovation Building Type**   Office

**Original Construction Date**   1980s

**Renovation Date**   2009

**Location**   Kansas City, MO

**Climate**   Humid continental (Köppen Dfa)

**Area**   230,000 ft$^2$

**Achievement**   LEED Gold, LEED CI v2.0 Gold (32 points)

**Key Indicators**   Efficient Lighting
Underfloor Displacement Ventilation
Water Efficient Fixtures
Indoor Air Quality

**Energy Achievement**   Projected 45 percent energy savings

**Total Water Use**   825,000 gallons/year

**Electricity Before**   3,629,542 kWh/year (estimated)   15.78 kWh/ft$^2$/year   (170 kWh/m$^2$ year)

**Electricity After**   1,905,046 kWh/year (projected)   8.28 kWh/ ft$^2$/year   (89 kWh/m$^2$ year)

**Heating After**   8.1 kBtu/ ft$^2$/yr (estimated)   2.37 kWh/ ft$^2$/yr (25.51 kWh/m$^2$ year)

**Water Before**   1,454,000 gallons/yr (6.32 gal/ ft$^2$)

**Water After**   825,000 gallons/yr (3.59 gal/ ft$^2$); 44 percent less than previous

Returning to renovate twelve floors of a building they originally designed in the 1980s, BNIM provides a showcase for sustainable interiors. Since the client, Kansas City Power & Light, made agreements with the Sierra Club to promote energy conservation and sustainable power production to its customers, the project also performs an important

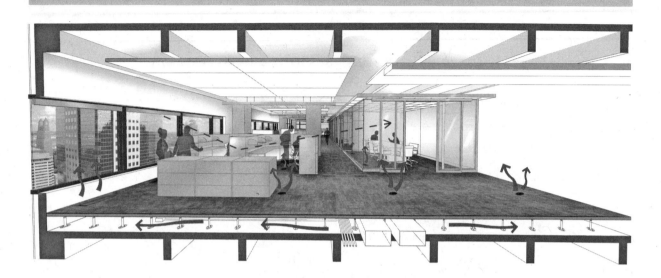

New raised floor provides high efficiency air distribution with increased user control while allowing easy access to future cabling and power changes. © *Berkebile, Nelson, Immen-schuh, McDowell (BNIM).*

role in illustrating the power of sustainable retrofit of a very common building type. Measures were taken to lower energy through efficient lighting and air distribution systems, water consuming systems, and sustainable materials. Typical office lighting was changed to high-efficient fluorescent fixtures controlled by daylight and occupancy sensors that dim or turn off lights when they are unnecessary.

The installation of heating, ventilation, and air-conditioning (HVAC) within a new raised floor system provides more efficient heating and cooling while giving better access to voice and data cabling. Future modifications to the office space will be achieved faster and easier while providing more user control of air supply at each workspace. Bathrooms were made water-efficient through installation of low-flow fixtures; by the end of the renovation water use was reduced by 44 percent. Throughout the office space, carpet, furniture, and materials were chosen to minimize the release of pollutants common in most offices. Low-emitting materials add to the renovation's focus on prov-en technologies that aid in employee productivity, including access to daylight and views, indoor air quality, and user control of lighting and temperature. The renovated office space is projected to reduce its energy consumption by 45 percent, and has received a LEED Gold certification.

Glass walled offices and conference rooms allow daylight to penetrate into areas deep within the floorplate. *© Assassi.*

By removing suspended ceilings the architects exposed concrete floor slab above, engaging its thermal mass to dampen temperature swings while increasing the height of the space. New suspended panels provide acoustical absorption while reflecting daylight deeper into the space while reducing resource use when compared to traditional hung ceilings. *© Assassi.*

## ENDNOTES

1. Olgyay, Victor, *Design with Climate, A Bioclimatic Approach to Architectural Regionalism,* Princeton University Press, Princeton, NJ, 1963.

2. ASHRAE Standard 55—2004, Thermal Environmental Conditions for Human Occupancy, American Society of Heating, Refrigerating, and Air-Conditioning Engineers.

3. *New York Times,* "Saving U.S. Water and Sewer Systems Would Be Costly," Charles Duhigg, March 14, 2010.

4. Electric Power Research Institute, Inc. (EPRI) (2002). *Water & Sustainability* (Volume 4): U.S. Electricity Consumption for Water Supply & Treatment—The Next Half Century.

5. United Nations Development Program—Human Development Report, 2006, from www.data360.org/dsg.aspx?Data_Set_Group_Id=757, accessed June 10, 2010.

6. Massachusetts Water Resources Authority, Water Efficiency and Management for Commercial Buildings, www.mwra.com/04water/html/bullet4.htm, accessed March 29, 2010.

7. Cone cells see colors, rod cells see in black and white in low light conditions, ganglion cells register "blue" light to reset our circadian clock (*Phototransduction by Retinal Ganglion Cells That Set the Circadian Clock,* Berson et al., Science February 8, 2002: 1070–1073).

8. *Wall Street Journal,* January 15, 2003, "Employees Only Think They Control Thermostat."

9. Canadian Waste Water Association performance testing of toilets—broken down by typical toilets and HETs, High Efficiency Toilets, www.cwwa.ca/freepub_e.asp.

10. www.drinktap.org/consumerdnn/Home/WaterInformation/Conservation/WaterUseStatistics/tabid/85/Default.aspx.

11. U.S. EPA, WaterSense, www.epa.gov/watersense/water_efficiency/what_you_can_do.html.

12. U.S. DOE, Federal Water Efficiency Best Management Practices, www1.eere.energy.gov/femp/program/waterefficiency_bmp.html.

13. U.S. EPA, Particulate Matter, Health and the Environment, www.epa.gov/pm/health.html.

14. NAFA User's Guide for ANSI/ASHRAE 52.2 – 1999; Method of Testing General Ventilation Air-Cleaning Devices for Removal Efficiency by Particle Size, www.nafahq.org/LibaryFiles/Articles/Article006.htm.

15. *Watersmart Guidebook,* A Water-Use Efficiency Plan Review Guide for New Businesses, East Bay Municipal Utility District, 2008.

16. "Smart Controller" is a timer-based irrigation controller with connection to weather data or soil condition sensors used to adjust watering schedules to better match conditions necessary for optimal plant health.

17. Organic Landscaping, Harvard University, www.uos.harvard.edu/fmo/landscape/organiclandscaping/, accessed June 10, 2010.

18. U.S. EPA WaterSense, Outdoor Water Use in the United States, www.epa.gov/watersense/pubs/outdoor.html.

19. www.h-m-g.com/projects/daylighting/summaries%20on%20daylighting.htm#. Windows and Offices: A Study of Office Worker Performance and the Indoor Environment—CEC PIER 2003—Accessed November 28, 2010.

20. Berson, et al., Melanopsin—Containing Retinal Ganglion Cells: Architecture, Projections, and Intrinsic Photosensitivity, *Science* 8, February 2002: Vol. 295. no. 5557, pp. 1065–1070.

21. Further information at Lighting and Research Center, Rensselaer Polytechnic Institute.

22. See ASHRAE standards for naturally ventilated buildings versus mechanically ventilated buildings, figure at the beginning of this chapter.

23. Specific heat of air is 1,000 J/Kkg, specific heat of water is 4,181 J/Kkg, therefore the volumetric heat transfer through water = 4,168 kJ/Km$^3$, heat transfer through air = 1.2 kJ/Km$^3$. It takes 3,473 times more volume of air to move the same heat as water.

24. See Warehouse Retrofit: Field Test DELTA: Integrated Skylight Luminaire, The Lighting Research Center at Rensselaer Polytechnic Institute, www.lrc.rpi.edu/researchAreas/daylighting.asp.

25. Alliance for Water Efficiency, Submetering, www.allianceforwaterefficiency.org/submetering.aspx.

26. *Watersmart Guidebook,* A Water-Use Efficiency Plan Review Guide for New Businesses, East Bay Municipal Utility District, 2008.

chapter **6**

# BUILDING MATERIALS

## ENVIRONMENTALLY BENEFICIAL PRODUCTS

Building materials range from the wood, concrete, steel, or masonry of the weight-bearing structure to finishes such as carpets and paints that produce the desired appearance and durability of the surface. Broadly speaking, the environmental impact attributable to materials derives from:

- The resources and energy required to extract, manufacture, and deliver the materials to the site
- The environmental effects such as toxicity that arise from their manufacture, installation, or volatility in the final building
- Their contribution to environmental goals such as energy conservation or acoustics in the building application
- The impact of the maintenance regimen required to keep the material attractive and useful
- The resources, energy demand, or toxicity that result when the material is removed from service

With all these potential contributions to either environmental improvement or environmental degradation, selecting beneficial materials is a complex process. A rapidly changing marketplace contains manufacturers and third-party testing and rating services that constantly adapt information and materials to meet demands for more sustainable choices. Our goal will be to provide a framework for assessing the attributes of materials, sources for up-to-date information, and an introduction to sustainability related to materials found in existing buildings of various eras.

In general, the U.S. EPA advises choosing products with the following characteristics: [1]

- Bio-based content
- Energy efficient
- Enhanced indoor environmental quality
- Low embodied energy
- Recyclable or reusable components
- Recycled content
- Reduced environmental impact over the lifecycle
- Reduced or eliminated toxic substances
- Reduced waste
- Responsible stormwater management
- Sustainable development, smart growth
- Uses renewable energy
- Water efficient
- Water reuse and recycling

## Ratings Systems and Lifecycle Assessment

The issues involved in selecting structural systems illustrate the complexity of making sustainable building material choices. The weight-bearing and wind- and earthquake-resisting structure of a building make up a major portion of material use. Structural elements chosen for a rehab will most often be based on their compatibility with the existing structure. Sustainability will be based on the details of recycled content and energy requirements for transport for steel, fly ash or other admixtures for concrete, and the management of the forests, milling process, and transport for wood.

It can be challenging to find reliable sources for such information. In addition, the data needs to be considered in the context of the overall project. A component of a building that is designed for disassembly can be reused more easily than a component that must be demolished to be removed, possibly providing a more sustainable choice despite higher initial energy.

Various ratings systems have been developed for specific products and industries to help inform specification of the material itself.[2] Such systems address the characteristics of the material before it arrives at a particular project. To address the rest of the life of the material, its use and maintenance in the building, and its eventual removal or reuse, lifecycle assessment (LCA) tools are necessary.

Traditional standards organizations such as the American National Standards Institute (ANSI) have joined pioneers such as the United States Green Build-

---

**Carpet and Rug Institute (CRI)**
- Green Label and Green Label Plus certification of carpets and rugs

**Collaborative for High Performance Schools (CHPS)**
- Database of environmentally preferable products related to schools

**Cradle-to-Cradle (C2C)**
- Certification of products and materials including ultimate recycling/reuse

**Forest Stewardship Council (FSC)**
- Sustainable forestry and forest products

**GREENGUARD Environmental Institute (GEI)**
- ANSI Accredited Standards Developer focused on reduced chemical exposure and improved indoor air quality

**Scientific Certification Systems (SCS)**
- Third-party certification of cradle-to-grave impacts including furnishings, carpets, finishes, and many other materials

Low-emitting materials can be found on the Websites of the organizations above. *Collaborative for High Performance Schools® and CHPS® are Registered, U.S. Patent and Trademark Office. Greenguard logo © 2011, The Greenguard Environmental Institute. CRI logo © The Carpet and Rug Institute. SCS logo © 2011, Scientific Certification Systems.*

ing Council (USGBC) in assessing the environmental attributes of building materials. Finding reliable information becomes easier every day.

Lifecycle assessment encompasses the information provided by various ratings systems while also attempting to provide a structure for a comprehensive analysis of the human health and environmental effect of a product, process, or activity over its entire service life. According to the U.S. Environmental Protection Agency, LCA consists of

"...a technique to assess the environmental aspects and potential impacts associated with a product, process, or service, by: compiling an inventory of relevant energy and material inputs and environmental releases; evaluating the potential environmental impacts associated with identified inputs and releases; interpreting the results to help make a more informed decision."[3]

This approach can be used to assess only the effect of a product's extraction and manufacture (excluding transportation to a site), installation, and life of a product. Such a snapshot is a baseline for comparing products of similar manufacture, installation methods, and service lives. Cradle-to-grave extends an LCA to include delivery, installation, service life, and demolition effects. Assumptions multiply as transportation and distribution are added, along with estimates of future maintenance and operations.

Rating systems such as Leadership in Energy & Environmental Design (LEED) prioritize the use of local materials, encouraging a short distribution chain to the project. Given equal energy used to manufacture a product, less transportation means less impact. However, the lifetime maintenance and repair effects can greatly outweigh benefits accrued in efficient manufacture. Finally, end-of-service costs often add up to

a significant portion of a product's lifetime environmental effect. The final extension of the LCA is beyond the end of the service life of a material and into the next form that material will take, either as waste or the component of a new use. This kind of thinking is called cradle-to-cradle (C2C), or *regenerative* design.

The ultimate goal of resource efficient and sustainable material design is a product with the lowest cradle-to-cradle LCA. A "perfect" product should be extracted and processed locally, with little energy and a benign effect on the environment during its manufacture. It would then require easy installation and little maintenance and be easily removed from a building for reuse or regeneration at the end of its service life. Within healthy ecosystems, plants and animals live and die and their minerals and molecules are the nutrition for the next generation. There is almost no waste in the sense of materials that leave the system. This is the model that is the goal of cradle-to-cradle systems. However, we are far from achieving it.

Materials such as bamboo derive from sustainably managed and rapidly renewable sources, wheatboard from nonfood parts of wheat plants, and soy-derived insulation, are part of the expansion of the bio-based sector of the construction material marketplace aiming at an efficient lifecycle. While beginning to close the loop, the complete environmental demands of such materials could include irrigation water, transportation, and antimicrobial treatments that do not yet have a closed cycle.

While our manufactured world is simpler than a biological ecosystem, it is still complex enough that a true LCA encompasses a daunting amount of information. A significant subclass of information used in constructing LCA is an LCI, a lifecycle inventory, a compilation of individual data points concerning a single product or process. Various software rely on LCIs to construct an LCA for a given item.[4]

Athena Environmental Impact Estimator (EIE)[6]: an LCA-based decision support tool focused at the level of whole buildings, or complete building assemblies (e.g., walls, floors, and roofs). The Estimator takes into account the environmental impacts of:

- Material manufacturing, resource extraction, and recycled content
- Related transportation
- On-site construction
- Regional variation in energy use, transportation, and other factors
- Building type and assumed life span
- Maintenance, repair, and replacement effects
- Demolition and disposal
- Operating energy emissions and precombustion effects

Athena® EcoCalculator for Assemblies (EC):[7] Calculator for full building assemblies from one of the following categories:

- Exterior walls
- Roofs
- Intermediate floors
- Interior walls
- Windows
- Columns and beams

The number of assemblies in each category varies widely depending on the possible combinations of layers and materials. Within the exterior wall category, for example, there are eight basic wall types, seven cladding types, three sheathing types, five insulation types, and two interior finish options. The results take into account:

- Resource extraction and processing
- Product manufacturing
- On-site construction of assemblies
- All related transportation
- Maintenance and replacement cycles over an assumed building service life
- Structural system demolition and transportation to landfill

**Athena Institute Reports:** The Athena Institute has also developed LCA-based reports investigating other aspects of the construction industry, including:

- Service life conditions in relation to green building rating systems
- Demolition energy analysis
- LCA for existing historic buildings
- Maintenance, repair, and replacement effects for building envelope materials

## Other life cycle assessment tools:[8]

- BEES 3.0® (Building for Environmental and Economic Sustainability) software
- SimaPro—PRé Consultants: Lifecycle tools to improve environmental performance and sustainability
- GABI 4 LCA software
- Umberto LCA software
- ECOBILAN: Tool for Environmental Analysis and Management—Team™ software
- Eco-Quantum: Tool for the environmental impact of buildings
- Pharos Project: Nonprofit organization that provides information on sixteen attributes under three broad categories: Environment & Resources, Health & Pollution, and Social & Community.

## LCA Tools

Among the most useful LCAs are those produced by the Athena Sustainable Materials Institute. A non-profit institution, Athena provides LCA-based tools that incorporate LCI information and are adaptable to regional conditions while assessing complete building assemblies. Athena also provides investigative reports about various lifecycle issues.[5]

Selection of new materials for a building can be based on available sources of testing and analysis within an LCA framework. Within this process, recycled content is clearly one of the attributes that affects a material's environmental impact. As an example, aluminum cans are used as beverage containers, then they are reconstituted as aluminum stock for window fabrication. While each step includes a certain amount of energy use, the recycling process saves energy when compared to extracting bauxite and smelting aluminum.

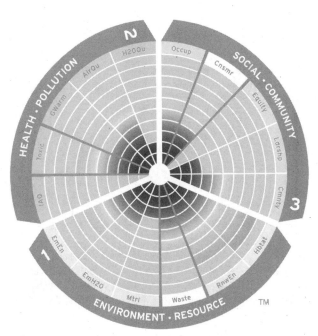

▲ The Pharos Project environmental rosette illustrates the relative environmental impact of a particular material. Divided into three main areas, Health-Pollution, Environment-Resource, and Social-Community, the Pharos framework provides a quick visual representation of a product's impact. Users can delve deeper into the individual properties to understand those issues most important to their project. *Healthy Building Network/Pharos Project.*

◀ This image depicts entire carpet tiles being recycled into new products. More typically, nylon fibers are mechanically separated from backing, then re-melted and used for new carpet yarn. Carpet is one of the most recycled of all building products; however, transportation of carpet to and from recycling centers remains a large environmental impact since most of the country's carpet mills remain concentrated in Georgia. *Tandus Flooring.*

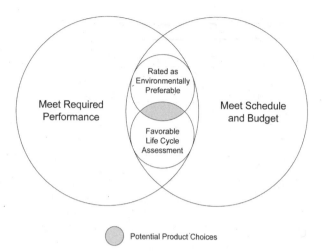

Potential Product Choices

Selection of materials involves a complex overlay of competing issues including performance, budget, schedule, and environmental attributes. The most sustainable materials combine a number of these attributes to find a successful place in a project. *Gelfand Partners Architects.*

Many recycled materials are widely available from manufacturers, competing with their standard line of products, often with very little monetary premium and very similar performance attributes. Especially finishes like gypsum wallboard, carpeting, and ceiling tiles are readily available with specified amounts of recycled content. The third-party certifications programs listed above help assure that manufacturer claims are reliable.

## Recycling, Salvage, and Reuse

The tools above assist in the selection of new materials for a project but any renovation project will also include management of materials that are either reused in or removed from the building. The energy embodied in an existing building or its components represents energy that need not be used to construct a completely new building or system.

The material already in an existing building represents between 10 and 20 percent of the lifetime energy of that building.[9] Retaining structural framing while replacing building systems and finishes can produce a building that performs as well as a new building while preserving much of the embodied energy of the old building. *Gelfand Partners Architects.*

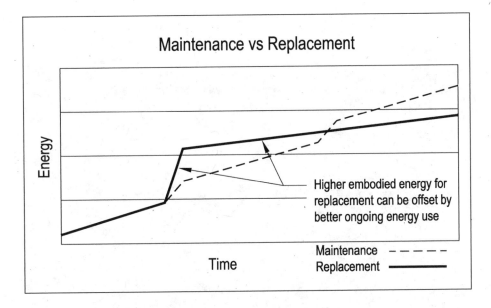

Maintenance vs Replacement

Energy

Higher embodied energy for replacement can be offset by better ongoing energy use

Time

Maintenance – – – – –
Replacement ——————

Designers must determine if the environmental cost of replacement will provide an assembly or component that has better performance than the original. If so, better performance can provide lower environmental impact over time. *Gelfand Partners Architects.*

Careful sustainable design can limit the amount of new products necessary for the goals at hand. So long as existing material is reparable, has remaining life, and can be a useful part of a renovated building, it is unlikely that a new material will be environmentally preferable.

At first glance, a material or system must either be very near the end of its useful life or must be so inefficient that a new material or system would be 10 to 20 percent better in order for replacement to be explored. On the one hand, the designer must determine if the environmental cost of providing a new product offsets the embodied energy of the original product plus the environmental detriment accrued through the continued use of the existing material. It may be that retaining an item, repairing it, then applying a more rigorous maintenance regime will result in a lower lifetime environmental effect than replacing it. On the other hand, full replacement of a material or system may lead to such good ongoing environmental performance that

a relatively high initial environmental cost can be justified.

Salvage does not involve reconstituting a material, but rather reusing it in its manufactured state. For example, salvaged doors can be reused again as doors or panels, perhaps with refurbished finishes and hardware rather than being sent off to landfill or to be turned into wood pulp for manufactured wood products. The economics of salvage decisions have a great deal to do with the condition, type, and amount of material to be salvaged, the type and cost of labor required to refurbish the material, and the inherent value of the material.

Often, salvaged material is unique—one door or one cabinet of each type. Such materials may become available from the project itself, or from stockpiles of materials removed from a variety of projects. In a larger project where repetition occurs, designers and contractors may spend time adapting salvaged assemblies to the building, or adapting the building design to the salvaged assembly.

Architectural salvage yards have increased in number in recent years, often in partnership with local waste management companies. *Gelfand Partners Architects.*

If design time and construction cost are malleable, tremendously interesting renovations are possible—combining the unique features of an existing building with the variable features of assemblies brought together from other deconstruction sites. Designers should be on the lookout for opportunities to turn someone else's waste into a surprising element in a renovation. *Gelfand Partners Architects.*

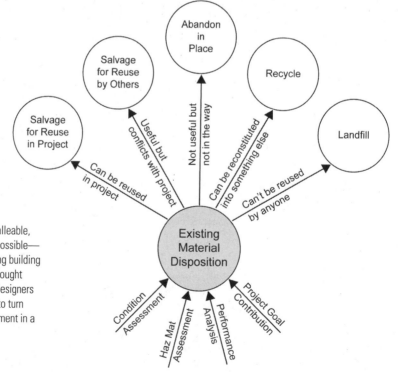

▲ Re-skinning the 1974 Edith Green—Wendell Wyatt federal office building in Portland, Oregon achieves energy savings both directly through reduction of heat gain, heat losses, and infiltration and indirectly through provision of daylighting to offset electrical use. SERA Architects, Cutler Anderson Associates. *Scott Baumberger.*

◆ The rooftop photovoltaic and solar thermal array on the Edith Green—Wendell Wyatt federal office building doubles as a rainwater collector. A former gun range in the basement has been converted to a 160,000 gallon tank that will store rainwater for reuse in toilet and urinal flushing, and for irrigation. SERA Architects, Cutler Anderson Associates. *Courtesy SERA Architects.*

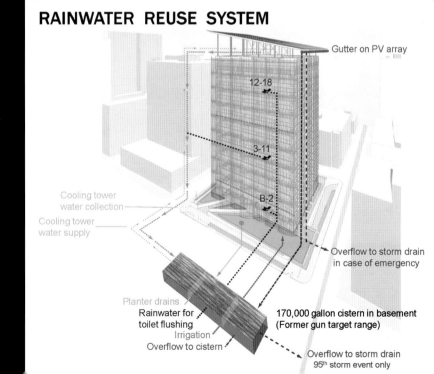

## RAINWATER REUSE SYSTEM

Gutter on PV array

12-18

3-11

B-2

Cooling tower water collection

Cooling tower water supply

Overflow to storm drain in case of emergency

Planter drains
Rainwater for toilet flushing
Irrigation
Overflow to cistern

170,000 gallon cistern in basement (Former gun target range)

Overflow to storm drain 95th storm event only

High Plains Architects transformed an uninsulated 1940s store in Billings, Montana into the daylit home for the Northern Plains Resource Council and the Western Organization of Resource Councils. The architect cut new openings in the perimeter and roof to allow daylight to penetrate deep into the space. Rooftop photovoltaics provide 37 percent of building energy, combining with new insulation to allow the organizations to save more than half of their energy bills. *High Plains Architects.*

◀ A conversion and extension of a building complex originally constructed from 1851 to 1950, the Normand Maurice Building in Montreal, Canada combines reuse of existing materials with sophisticated environmental control systems. PWGSC Architect ABCP, Beauchamp et Bourbeau, Busby Perkins+Will. *Courtesy Busby Perkins+Will Architects Co.*

▼ Normand Maurice Building, Montreal, Canada: A hybrid ventilation system with heat recovery enthalpy wheels combines with separate heating and cooling systems to achieve 54 percent energy savings when compared to similar buildings. Angled sunshades at the southeast façade prevent overheating. *Courtesy Busby Perkins+Will Architects Co.*

▲ Chicago Center for Green Technology, Chicago, Illinois: The Chicago Department of Environment won this 1952 building and grounds in a lawsuit over illegal dumping. After removal of 70-ft-high piles of construction debris they restored the site and transformed the complex into the first renovation in the country to achieve LEED Platinum (v1.0). The building uses 40 percent less energy than comparable structures. Stormwater is managed on-site with a green roof, a bioretention bioswale, four rainwater cisterns, and pervious pavers. FARR Associates. *Photography by Chris Kelly.*

◀ In 2005 ASHRAE added 4,500 ft$^2$ to their headquarters outside Atlanta, Georgia. Originally constructed in 1965, the building received a sophisticated heating and cooling system in order to achieve a LEED NC 2.2 Platinum rating. Around the site, bioswales reduce runoff through soil infiltration while recharging the aquifer. A closed loop of 400-ft-deep geothermal wells provides a heat sink to help heat and cool the building. Richard Wittschiebe Hand Architects. *Noel Thomas Tyler.*

In San Antonio, Texas Alamo Architects & OCO Architects transformed a 1940s/1950s trucking warehouse into a light-filled SOFLO office for themselves. Focusing on limiting construction waste and conserving water, they were able to retain all but 5 percent of existing materials while reducing irrigation needs by 80 percent. *Courtesy of Alamo Architects.*

SOFLO offices, San Antonio, Texas: Large new overhangs perform multiple tasks: they protect the interior from solar gains, reduce outdoor temperatures and their load on interior comfort systems, and protect the building walls from weather, extending their useful life. *Courtesy of Alamo Architects.*

Slicing through the existing 39 Hunter Street building in Sydney, Australia, then adding new floor area to the rear of the building, Jackson Teece Architects provided a new lightwell to daylight all floors while maximizing floor area. A gas generator couples with chillers and pumps to shave peak electrical loads, while the fire sprinkler water tank doubles as cold storage to further cut peak electrical demand by storing water from chillers that run during the night. *Jackson Teece Architecture—Sharrin Reese.*

At the 39 Hunter Street building in Sydney, Australia, new floor plate added at the rear contrasts with historic fabric; the lightwell cut through the center provides natural stack ventilation. Natural ventilation controlled by louvers at the upper right supplements the atrium's use as a return air plenum for the mechanical system. *Jackson Teece Architecture—Sharrin Reese.*

Architect Renzo Piano led the team that transformed the old California Academy of Sciences in San Francisco into a LEED Platinum rated building. Translucent solar panels at the new California Academy of Sciences provide 5 to 10 percent of the energy used in the building. The modern language of the new building juxtaposed with the historic façade preserves the story of the academy in its Golden Gate Park setting. *Gelfand Partners Architects.*

Brand + Allen Architects clad the historic building at 185 Post Street with a glass screen that creates a blend of transparency and reflection to preserve compatibility with its historic fabric and neighbors while creating a thoroughly contemporary image. The double skin preserves the thermal mass benefits of the masonry wall while mediating temperature swings and acoustic issues in this downtown location. *Gelfand Partners Architects.*

▲ Cathy Simon and her team at SMWM led a design effort including preservation architects Page and Turnbull at the San Francisco Ferry Building. The conversion of the concourse into a new food market takes advantage of the excellent daylighting that was integral to the existing historic building. *Gelfand Partners Architects.*

◀Gelfand Partners Architects transformed this daylit but uninsulated industrial space in San Francisco, California into a new office. High efficiency lighting with daylight sensors adjusts for outdoor light levels, hydronic heating panels replace unit space heaters, and a living wall takes advantage of abundant daylight. *Mark Luthringer.*

▲ As part of the massive international Euromediterranee urban renewal scheme, public subsidies allowed homeowners to improve their apartments by including energy saving features such as double glazing and low-consumption heating. *Gelfand Partners Architects.*

◀New windows and other envelope improvements do not significantly alter the appearance or function of the building envelope. Note the trickle vent at the top of this new window. New windows are significantly tighter than the windows they replace and must include deliberate accommodation for ventilation. *Gelfand Partners Architects*

▲ Kansas City Power & Light's new offices on the 5th floor of a thirty-one-story building in Kansas City, Missouri, renovated by BNIM (Berkebile, Nelson, Immenschuh, McDowell), combines underfloor air distribution with daylight harvesting and water savings techniques to reach a combined projected energy savings of 45 percent. An open stairway between floors encourages walking instead of elevator use while complementing the open office plan. Even lobbies and circulation spaces benefit from daylighting. © *Assassi*.

◀At KCPL in Kansas City, Missouri, high efficiency lighting reduces energy use throughout while low-emitting finish materials improve indoor environmental quality. © *Assassi*.

Re-skinning of this uninsulated 1957 apartment building
in Linz, Austria resulted in a
91 percent energy savings.
ARCH + MORE ZT GmbH,
Arch. DI Ingrid Domenig-
Meisinger applied a "GAP-
Solar" panel (a sandwich of
glass, insulation, and baffles
that harness low winter
sun to heat the skin of the
building) on top of exterior
insulation, designers re-
duced heating loads, thereby
downsizing hydronic heating
equipment. *Arch. DI Ingrid
Domenig-Meisinger.*

Enclosing balconies that
had fallen out of use due
to increased traffic noise
and dirt, the new panelized
exterior skin combined with
attic insulation and new
heating equipment to drastically reduce energy costs
for residents. The designers
in Linz also optimized a new
heat recovery ventilation
system to further minimize
energy use. *Arch. DI Ingrid
Domenig-Meisinger.*

SERA Architects transformed a 1970s office building in Portland, Oregon into the first LEED Gold Marriot in the country. Re-skinning the exterior with insulated panels and efficient double-glazed windows reduced energy use by 28 percent compared to similar hotels. While financial analysis showed a 1.2 percent soft and hard cost premium for pursuing LEED Gold, state of Oregon incentives eliminated these additional costs. Energy- and water-saving design saves the owner about $60,000 each year, realizing a 28.8 percent return on investment for sustainable features. *Michael Mathers*.

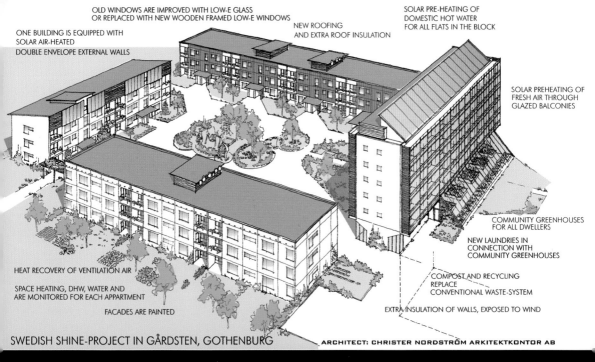

ONE BUILDING IS EQUIPPED WITH
SOLAR AIR-HEATED
DOUBLE ENVELOPE EXTERNAL WALLS

OLD WINDOWS ARE IMPROVED WITH LOW-E GLASS
OR REPLACED WITH NEW WOODEN FRAMED LOW-E WINDOWS

NEW ROOFING
AND EXTRA ROOF INSULATION

SOLAR PRE-HEATING OF
DOMESTIC HOT WATER
FOR ALL FLATS IN THE BLOCK

SOLAR PREHEATING OF
FRESH AIR THROUGH
GLAZED BALCONIES

COMMUNITY GREENHOUSES
FOR ALL DWELLERS

NEW LAUNDRIES IN
CONNECTION WITH
COMMUNITY GREENHOUSES

HEAT RECOVERY OF VENTILATION AIR

SPACE HEATING, DHW, WATER AND
ARE MONITORED FOR EACH APPARTMENT

FACADES ARE PAINTED

COMPOST AND RECYCLING
REPLACE
CONVENTIONAL WASTE-SYSTEM

EXTRA INSULATION OF WALLS, EXPOSED TO WIND

SWEDISH SHINE-PROJECT IN GÅRDSTEN, GOTHENBURG

ARCHITECT: CHRISTER NORDSTRÖM ARKITEKTKONTOR AB

This diagram of four of the ten buildings illustrates the techniques used to improve energy use by 44 percent in this Swedish apartment complex in Göteborg, Sweden. © CNA Christer Nordström Architects, www.cna.se.

Renovation of the ten-building Gårdstensbostäder apartment complex in Göteborg, Sweden cut energy use in half through introduction of integrated systems centered on reducing heating energy. Conventional exterior insulation clads all the buildings, and south façades are covered with a solar air-heated double envelope. Solar hot water panels preheat domestic water while new greenhouses at the base of the building preheat air circulated to the apartments. © CNA Christer Nordström Architects, www.cna.se.

New light monitors transform an oppressive corridor into a light-filled heart of this elementary school in Oakland, California. The modernization combined with the construction of a new building, providing a school with no dark classrooms.

Mark Luthringer

*Gelfand Partners Architects*

▶The two primary goals of the renovation of Omicron's own offices in Vancouver, British Columbia were to minimize negative environmental impacts, and to improve the work environment for employees. An open plan office encourages discussion across disciplines and facilitates the integrated design process. Employees are grouped into dedicated project teams rather than by discipline with four discreet pavilions throughout the floor created to house meeting rooms, a staff cafe (pictured), and other required support spaces. *Terry Guscott /ATN Visuals.*

◀ Originally designed in 1977 by A. Quincy Jones, the C1 Building in Zeeland, Michigan became a pilot project for LEED and for Herman Miller's continuing interest in sustainability. Capitalizing on original features like abundant daylighting, the renovations by Krueck & Sexton Architects developed a comprehensive sustainability approach resulting in LEED v2/v2.1 Gold certification. *Mariusz Mizera.*

▲ In the Omicron Offices in Vancouver, British Columbia, 61 percent of materials used in the renovation had high recycled content including a conference table made from Old Growth Douglas Fir salvaged from a decommissioned logging bridge. Radiant ceiling panels heat and cool the main board room. *Terry Guscott /ATN Visuals*

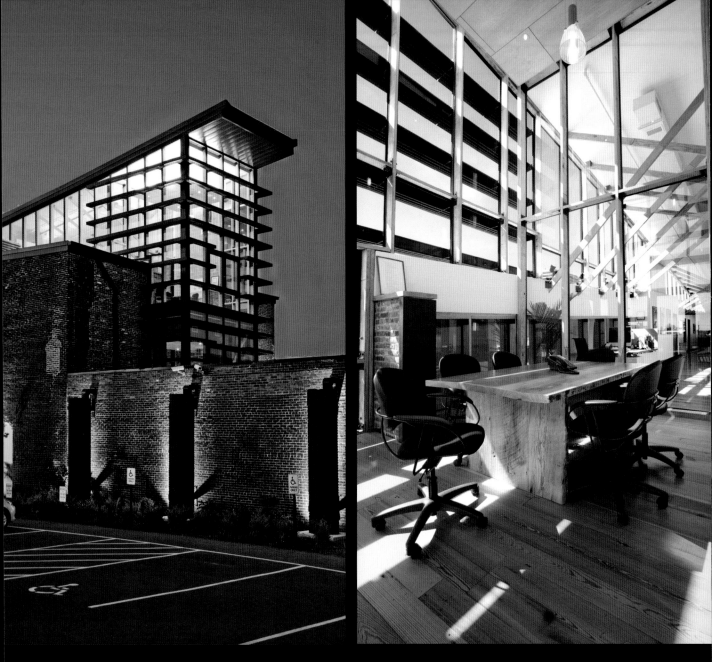

Introduction of a central daylit clerestory changes a sealed box dry goods warehouse to an inviting home for offices. The architects envisioned a new use and added a new element responding both to program and to environmental necessity. © Ted Wathen / Quadrant Studio, www.qphoto.com.

Reuse of materials is clearly the most energy efficient strategy when it does not replace the opportunity for a much more efficient replacement. An example is the reuse of existing single-glazed windows. These windows represent significant embodied energy. How does it compare to the energy saved by a new well-sealed insulated window over the life of the building? In mild climates the answer may be to forego the improved operational efficiency to save the energy embodied in the existing windows, while in a cold climate the ongoing efficiency could far outweigh the embodied energy.

## Resource Efficiency

There are two main drivers of resource efficiency in renovations:

- The reduction in the addition of new material through the reuse of existing building fabric.
- The reduction in ongoing operational energy and waste through the development of efficient building systems.

### Reduction in the Addition of New Material

In the 1970s, activists used the phrase Reduce, Reuse, Recycle (the three Rs) to highlight environmental awareness. However, in recent years it seems that the first two environmental Rs have been eclipsed by a focus on recycling, which is often a high-energy process. Reusing a material that is already in place consumes less energy and may produce additional environmental benefits.

"Reduce" is the first of the three Rs—we can simply make do with less. Inventive programming can avoid the trap of over-building. The most environmentally sustainable product is the one that is not used; the most environmentally sustainable building or addition may be the floor area that is not built. When we build or remodel what *is* necessary our goal is to attain the maximum lifecycle efficiency for the invested energy. We believe that renovated buildings should be better than new. By introducing appropriate new elements while retaining significant portions of old buildings, we can provide continuity with our past, while taking advantage of the technological benefits of our present.

Georgina Blach Middle School Library was built between existing classroom buildings. Windows were reused in place, providing needed supervision of computer classrooms from the library. Placement of a portion of the new library as infill between existing buildings capitalized on reuse of existing fabric without introduction of a complete new building. *Gelfand Partners Architects.*

Polished concrete flooring reduces recurring maintenance while also reducing the environmental effect of the work required to provide a finish in the first place. *Gelfand Partners Architects.*

## Reduction in Operational Energy and Waste

Reduction of operational energy use is the second driver of resource efficiency. The direct impact of materials on energy use in building envelopes is discussed in Chapter 4. But materials also carry energy implications through their required maintenance. This impact should be considered as part of the LCA of a building material.

Maintenance activities can have direct and indirect energy costs. Direct energy costs include the electricity that is used for floor buffing or the additional heating and ventilation necessary to dry a room after wet-carpet cleaning. These energy costs are generally small in comparison with typical operating energies, but within the scope of sustainability, they can become significant. More significant energy use is associated with products or assemblies that need to be replaced frequently or that consume maintenance material. Common examples are carpet and vinyl composition tile flooring. Carpet, while providing a better acoustical environment, must be replaced fairly frequently, and has been suspected in the diminishment of indoor air quality. Air quality concerns are particularly noted with carpet that does not receive frequent vacuuming and periodic deep cleaning.

Proper care *requires* a significant consumption of energy. Vinyl composition tile (VCT) is another common flooring material with significant maintenance component. VCT generally requires frequent sweeping but also requires periodic waxing, consuming both the energy for buffing and the energy embodied in the stripper and wax itself. When compared to its competitors—prefinished linoleum, locally quarried stone flooring, or polished concrete flooring—VCT appears a less sustainable choice.

# LOW-EMITTING MATERIALS

After World War II buildings were increasingly designed to rely upon powerful mechanical systems to control the indoor environment and seal it away from the changeable outdoors. Such buildings are susceptible to off-gassing of materials and "sick building syndrome." While designs have shifted toward climate control systems that introduce higher volumes of fresh air to avoid problems with buildup of toxins from building elements and furniture, the problems caused by off-gassing can be avoided by careful selection of materials in the first place.

Volatile organic compounds (VOCs) vaporize at room temperature. VOCs include a large number of compounds found in building materials, and cleaning materials and supplies. Some cause irritation, some cause neurological symptoms, some cause cancer. Indoor air typically contains concentrations of harmful substances many times higher than outdoor air. [10]

Indoor air quality problems may also include higher concentrations of molds and microbes and a less beneficial mix of gases than the air outside. VOCs can be produced by building materials, furnishings, finishes, adhesives, sealants, and maintenance and cleaning compounds. Molds and microbes find nourishment in building materials and moisture and can build up to concentrations leading to health problems in sensitive individuals. Lastly, when groups of people concentrate indoors without an adequate supply of fresh air, carbon dioxide ($CO_2$) gas builds up, causing headaches and sleepiness.

While employing methods to limit the toxicity and off-gassing of building materials, designers should also take into consideration the maintenance regimens they require. In many cases, construction materials are inherently safe, but require a maintenance cycle that includes application of toxic or volatile cleaners, strippers, or refinishers. Similarly, a material itself might be safe while its finish is toxic.

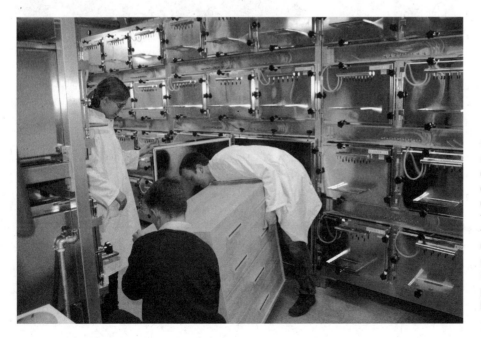

Materials testing chamber: Recent testing has helped define the classes of materials causing the greatest health concerns. Materials are tested for the amount of substances that are released into the air. Calculations of air volume, air movement, and relative toxicity of off-gassed substances provide a measure of potential hazard to indoor air quality. © *Eurofins Product Testing A/s.*

## "Natural" Materials

Inherently safe materials include many natural products such as glass, concrete, metals, and woods. However, these can all be installed and maintained under both low-emitting and highly toxic regimes. When considering installation methods, designers should use materials that are least toxic and release the least amount of VOCs. Thanks to California Environmental Protection Agency's pressure to reduce VOCs (managed through regional air quality management districts) in order to control air pollution, most major manufacturers provide VOC information. However, designers should also consult Material Safety Data Sheets (MSDS) to determine if products also contain other toxic materials of concern. The State of California provides a useful list of Chronic Reference Exposure Levels (CRELs) under their Section 01350 protocol for testing of low-emitting materials. [11]

## Concrete and Stone

Turning to particular examples highlights issues with low-emitting materials. Exposed concrete or stone surfaces can be left unfinished or can be sealed with chemical sealers or waxes. While cement dust and some natural stones can be harmful if breathed in quantity, Indoor Air Quality (IAQ) concerns in buildings generally arise from the substances *added* onto the surface of exposed materials. Sealers can range from water-soluble solutions that require minimal installer protection to highly toxic sealers with high concentrations of volatile compounds requiring respirator use by applicators. While some sealers complete their off-gassing cycle quickly, many sealers continue to give off gasses for very long durations. Combined with study of maintenance processes, designers should search for hard surface finishes that have the lowest initial emissions and that result in the lowest maintenance emissions.

Stone flooring can be sealed or covered with natural waxes, providing an easily maintained, nontoxic, and extremely durable surface. Stone flooring is especially appropriate for high-traffic areas such as lobbies and corridors. *Gelfand Partners Architects.*

## Metals

Similarly, metals can be finished with low-emitting paints or coatings that produce very little or no harmful material at the time of installation and emit very little over their lifetimes, or they can be coated with highly toxic finishes that not only give off terrific amounts of volatile components at the time of installation, but also emit toxic substances over their entire lifetimes. Of course, many metals can be left unfinished. Where a finish is required, designers should compare emissions from initial installation with durability and maintenance requirements. For building components like handrails that need to be very durable, it is often worth providing a higher-emitting finish that will last longer and require little maintenance, than a low-emitting paint that requires re-application every few years. Fortunately, as emissions standards have tightened, manufacturers have developed more products that combine low emissions with high durability.

## Wood

Wood finishes in existing buildings provide opportunities for physical and psychological benefits and can tap into our biophilic desires, leading to interiors that are often described as "warm" or "homey." While wood contains natural constituents that rank high on the "bad" list of emitted material (formaldehyde, xylene, and so forth), solid wood can be finished with low-emitting surfaces that reduce or eliminate concerns over natural off-gassing.

Finishes that leave wood visually exposed include oils, stains, waxes, and urethanes. Natural oils and waxes generally have the least toxic emissions. Take care to avoid waxes that contain synthetic or volatile carriers. Similarly, low-emitting stains and even urethanes can be formulated with toxic, highly volatile solvents or with just water. Finally, where existing or new wood requires an opaque finish, specify low-emitting paints. Required in a number of states, low-emitting paints (usually latex or acrylic formulations) are becoming more and more durable. *Gelfand Partners Architects.*

MDF, chipboard, and plywood can contain high levels of added formaldehyde that can off-gas inside buildings. MDF and plywood are becoming more available in no-added-formaldehyde formulations. Where low-emitting composite wood products cannot be obtained, designers should ensure that panels are thoroughly sealed with a non-toxic sealer that can prevent off-gassing. *Gelfand Partners Architects.*

Composite wood products (plywood, particle board, and medium density fiberboard—MDF) are traditionally manufactured with formaldehyde-based binders and adhesives. Formaldehyde used in composite wood materials can cause tremendous harm due to high emissions, leading to significant illness.

**Ingestion:**
- If swallowed, give two 12oz. glasses of water diluted with vinegar, or fruit juice.
- Consult a physician.
- Never give anything by mouth to an unconscious person.

## Fire Fighting Information:
**Unusual Hazards:**
- None.

**Extinguishing Agents:**
- Use extinguishing media appropriate for surrounding fire.

**Personal Protective Equipment:**
- Wear self-contained breathing apparatus (pressure-demand MSHA/NIOSH approved or equivalent).
- Use full protective gear.

## Hazard Information: Health Effects from Overexposure
**Primary Routes of Exposure:**
- Inhalation
- Skin Contact
- Ingestion

**Inhalation:**
*Prolonged and continuous inhalation of dust of any kind can cause the following:*
- Irritation of the respiratory tract
- Bronchitis
- Progressive Pulmonary Fibrosis (Silicosis)

**Skin Contact:**
*Prolonged or repeated skin contact can cause the following:*
- Contact Dermatitis
- Irritation to moist tissues
- Mucous with skin corrosion

**Eye Contact:**
- Eye irritation, intense watering of the eyes and possible lesions.
- May aggravate existing eye conditions when exposed for a prolonged period of time.

## Spill or Leak Handling Information:
**Personal Protection:**
- Appropriate protective equipment must be worn when handling a large spill or this material. Respiratory protection NIOSHA/MSHA approved Dust and Mist Respirator. If exposed to excessive material during clean up; see the FIRST AID PROCEDURES for action to follow.

**Procedures:**
- Contain spill and sweep up or vacuum. Do not generate dust. Use an industrial vacuum for large spills. Dispose of waste in accordance with Federal, State and Local regulations.

## Accident Exposure Information:  *Personal Protection Measures:*
**Respiratory Protection:**
- Use a NIOSH/MSHA approved dust and mist respirator (such as 3M #8710).
- A respiratory protection program meeting OSHA 1910.134 and ANSI Z88.2 requirements must be followed whenever workplace conditions warrant a respirator's use. None required if airborne concentrations are maintained below the TWA/TLV's listed in the COMPONENT EXPOSURE INFORMATION section.

Portion of an MSDS sheet for a paint product. MSDS sheets describe a product's ingredients, its potential hazards and health effects, as well as first aid measures for accidental exposure. *Courtesy of the Real Milk Paint Company.*

Unfortunately, while they may only give off small amounts of material, even low-emitting paints contain up to hundreds of ingredients, many of them toxic. For buildings where environmentally sensitive individuals are likely occupants, natural and nontoxic formulations using milk or other natural binders are also available, although they often require extra care for proper application. While applying low-emitting finishes will reduce concentrations of contaminants inside buildings, good preparation combined with premium quality low-emitting finishes is a key to greater durability.

## Carpet

While carpet has been criticized for both initial emissions (the "new car" smell) and troubles with dust or mold/mildew propagation, some studies indicate that a proper specification and an appropriate maintenance plan can reduce or eliminate these concerns. [12] Carpet varies widely in initial toxicity and emissions. A number of testing and certification programs can lead designers to carpets that minimize off-gassing while also providing recycled content benefits. Of course, wool carpets or natural fibers like sisal are available, but often at significant additional cost.

Vinyl composition tufted tile (VCTT) looks like carpet but is a short-tufted tile bonded to an impregnable vinyl backing. Sealed completely, liquids cannot penetrate the backing, so one of the mold growth factors is greatly diminished. Secondly, the tufts are very short so removal of "food" for mold is much easier. *Tandus Flooring ©2009.*

Concerns about mold growth during a carpet's lifetime can be addressed by eliminating moisture problems (never place near exterior doorways or sinks) and by frequent, thorough cleaning with high efficiency particulate air (HEPA) –filtered vacuums. If a carpet remains wet for any length of time and has not been completely vacuumed of dust and dirt, mold and mildew are likely to grow.

## Resilient Flooring

Resilient flooring is manufactured in sheets or tiles. While VCT is ubiquitous, many sustainable renovators are moving away from it because of the widely publicized problems with the toxicity of vinyl manufacture and because VCT is generally maintained in a very unhealthy manner. VCT, composed of limestone or other stone fragments in a vinyl binder, actually requires an applied wax as its wear surface. If left unfinished, VCT will absorb stains and wear significantly. Therefore, VCT requires frequent stripping, cleaning, and waxing to meet most facilities' management standards for appearance.

These strippers and waxes usually contain volatile solvents that linger in buildings after application. Further, VCT and other tile products do not completely seal a floor from liquid intrusion. If set over concrete and cleaned with a wet method or attacked by water from spills, the adhesive under the tiles can become the food for mold growth. Vinyl sheet eliminates worries about water intrusion, but manufacturing and disposal concerns remain. However, vinyl sheet is generally seen as a short-term finish, requiring significant lifecycle environmental cost because of its frequent replacement cycle.

As an alternative, rubber and linoleum sheet flooring have gained prominence in recent years. While vinyl sheet, rubber sheet, and linoleum sheet can all be manufactured in low-emitting formulations, rubber

Natural cork flooring can provide a sustainable alternative to other resilient flooring. Often found in schools and gymnasia, a fifty-year lifetime is not unusual for a cork floor. Composed of chips of natural cork bound together in tiles, cork provides a warm, resilient surface often compared to leather. Like linoleum, it can be prefinished to minimize the maintenance cycle, but, like other tile goods, it is susceptible to water damage and mold growth in its adhesive. Also, some cork flooring is made with formaldehyde-containing binders.

Finally, it should be noted that all types of flooring, including low-emitting materials, can be installed with both good and bad adhesives. It is true that adhesives in "the good old days" held the flooring better than current low-emitting water-based adhesives. However, with proper preparation, especially the control of moisture in any flooring substrate, low-emitting adhesives can perform as well as the highly volatile adhesives of the past without endangering building occupants with continuing emissions.

## Wall Finishes

Wall surfaces are commonly covered with gypsum plaster, wood, or gypsum wallboard. Gypsum plaster remains very durable so long as its substrate does not exhibit much movement and water is not present. Easily cracked, plaster can become a continuing maintenance headache when building movement or leaks occur frequently. Beginning in the 1940s, gypsum wallboard became the material of choice for many building interiors. Minimizing the labor-intensive methods required for lathing and three-step plaster for interior walls, gypsum was formed into sheets with paper surfaces, making easy-to-handle and very easily installed wall panels. Gypsum board, while better at crack resistance than plaster, is also susceptible to moisture failure. Whether gypsum board is entirely covered with a skim coat of plaster

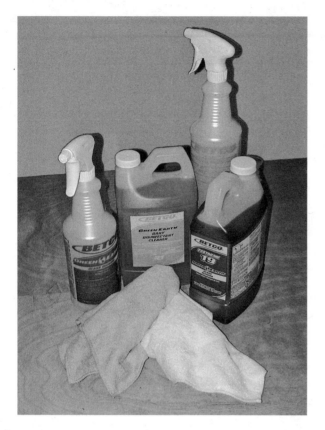

Unlike VCT, linoleum and rubber floors can be cleaned without toxic strippers and waxes. Many finish companies have developed nontoxic and low-emitting cleaners, improving indoor air quality (IAQ) when compared to traditional methods. *Gelfand Partners Architects.*

and linoleum provide benefits in terms of lower environmental cost for a lifetime of use. Linoleum is produced from cork or wood flour (considered a rapidly renewable resource) mixed with linseed oil and placed on a jute backing, while rubber is made from natural and recycled rubber. There are some concerns about heavy metals in recycled rubber flooring and some rubber flooring contains polyvinyl chloride (PVC), plasticizers, or halogens. Both rubber and linoleum can be prefinished to eliminate the need for frequent stripping and waxing.

or not, it is finished similarly to gypsum plaster. Both accept a painted finish that is readily available in low-emitting paint formulations.

So long as it is well adhered to the substrate, gypsum plaster can be repaired indefinitely. Older buildings sometimes have plaster covered with burlap—a very durable finish unless it requires modification at renovated areas. New finishes can be separated from burlap plaster with a distinct joint to preserve the old material while making a clean connection to new smooth surface material.

Sometimes, plaster and gypsum board are finished with wallpaper or synthetic fabrics. Papers are relatively benign, but can contain toxic decorative surfaces (heavy metals in some printed colors). They can be installed with natural glues made of wheat flour which also allows them to be removed with steam. Like the plasters below them, they can develop mold and mildew when exposed to moisture.

New sheet wall finishes include vinyl wallpaper and other materials. Sheet wall goods come in both low- and high-emitting formulations. The vinyl component, if present, is a material of concern. Also, like sheet flooring, wall surfacing can be installed with low-emitting adhesives. It is important to combine low-emitting sheet goods with low-emitting adhesives to minimize off-gassing. Finally, many synthetic wall coverings can lead to an additional problem when combined with the presence of moisture. If an exterior wall is relatively breathable and the interior wall surface becomes colder than the wall cavity or the exterior, moisture can condense on the backside of an impermeable surface material. If placed over gypsum wallboard with a paper surface, or adhered with an organic adhesive, mold and mildew can appear. So, breathable wall surfacing is recommended; paperless gypsum board and nonorganic low-emitting adhesives complete a sustainable installation.

# PREWAR BUILDINGS

Materials used in buildings constructed before World War II tend to be more robust than those employed after the war. Particularly before 1930, builders constructed commercial and institutional buildings with an eye toward longevity and reparability. They also used locally available materials and local methods while still attempting to keep up with prevailing styles and functional needs. Therefore, buildings of this era vary in construction method while often showing great consistency in floor plan and decoration.

In the United States, smaller buildings tended to be constructed of wood or masonry exteriors with wood infill framing usually topped with lath and plaster. Larger buildings had steel frames, often encased in masonry or concrete, concrete floors, and masonry exterior walls. Interior partitions in larger buildings tended to be gypsum plaster finish over wood frame or terra cotta fire brick. The finished floors were often strip wood flooring over sleepers with occasional accents of terrazzo or stone. Sometimes, whole buildings were constructed of reinforced concrete with terrazzo finished floors as well as marble wainscots and bathrooms. More commonly, "battleship" linoleum lined public hallways, carpets dressed up wood floors, and restrooms had thickset ceramic tile with marble or wood partitions. Public areas were built of durable materials and sometimes decorated with significant artworks.

## Salvage of Masonry and Finishes

Masonry exteriors can last hundreds of years if properly built and maintained. They are often load-bearing, carrying the floors and roofs of the building. They are also part of the weather-proofing system, excluding rain and snow. The details by which the materials solved all these problems have long-term implications for the condition of the walls today. Masonry restoration is discussed in Chapter 4, Building Envelope Redesign.

If not being restored, masonry is very heavy and difficult to dispose of but can usually be stabilized and left in place, even if it is overclad on the outside or lined on the inside. Because of its longevity it is generally kept as the primary exterior surface. However, as we move toward the need for greater and greater energy efficiency, there will be more occasions (especially in cold climates) where it is best to overclad brick and stone.

In prewar buildings, fire stairs, boiler rooms, and demising walls between apartments or offices were often constructed of terra cotta tile, brick, or concrete. All are good insulators against fire, although terra cotta tile is a very poor performer in seismic zones. Terra cotta walls are often damaged by building movement because of their fragile nature. Where overlain with plaster, any of these substrates can last centuries with periodic finish repair. Where terra cotta tile is encountered, designers should carefully study seismic concerns and consider whether the thermal mass is beneficial enough to warrant the effort of secondary support.

Exterior concrete often suffers from poor initial quality control and insufficient reinforcing or reinforcing protection. Early concrete buildings are of uneven quality and exhibit inconsistent and often skimpy levels of reinforcing. Aggregates and sand originally used were often of poor quality or contaminated, particularly in areas near the ocean where beach sand was used without proper washing. Salts degrade the concrete and accelerate rusting of the reinforcing, leaving current designers with the problem of very low

A previous repointing project with hard modern mortar; sand blasting has contributed to widespread deterioration of this eighty-year-old brick. *Gelfand Partners Architects.*

Especially in suspended slabs, reinforcing often was set directly on the formwork with concrete poured over. As a result, reinforcing at the bottom of the slab has been exposed to atmospheric water vapor, rusting, and popping the minimal concrete off the bottom of the bars. It is not uncommon to find ceiling slabs with rusted lines of steel spanning their entire length. Unfortunately, this situation is usually only visible at the basement level, where decorative plaster ceilings have not obscured the problem. *Gelfand Partners Architects.*

Pencil stud walls are constructed with approximately ¾ in. folded steel studs, often connected like wire trusses. Steel "pencils" are connected to the studs, the whole frame is wired together, then lath and plaster applied to the pencils. This framework was then finished with metal lath and plaster on either side. The studs, pencil rods, and lath were all tied together with annealed wire. Wood doors are supported by wood blocking wired to the studs. *Gelfand Partners Architects.*

strength concrete. Additionally, in prewar buildings, routines for the embedment of steel reinforcing in concrete were inconsistent at best. Where high humidity has been consistent, reinforcing is often reduced to half its original diameter. So, like most structural issues, concrete condition should be referred to an experienced structural engineer for thorough investigation and remedy.

## Strategies for Obsolete Plaster and Partition Systems

The early twentieth century was replete with experiments in speeding and simplifying construction as well as responding to increasing understanding of fire spread in buildings. While interior partitions constructed prior to 1900 were most often wood stud with wood lath and plaster, turn-of-the-century buildings, especially larger buildings, show evolving methods of metal framing systems for support of gypsum plaster. Aimed primarily at preventing fires, use of steel framing went through a number of discrete stages.

First, walls were constructed out of rolled steel channels about 1½ in. across, spanned with metal lath, then covered on both sides with plaster, resulting in a solid wall about 2½ in. thick with a core of lath and steel. Next, metal studs formed like mini-trusses sandwiched between ¾ in. steel angles began appearing. This system allowed pipes or wires to be placed in the central void space with ¼ in. diameter rods (pencil rods) attached as a layer carrying metal lath.

Finally, around World War II, metal studs were formed of stamped and rolled sheet metal bent into the C shapes still used today. The legs of the rolled studs allowed gypsum board panels to be screwed directly to the studs, greatly simplifying and speeding installation.

Where new work abuts existing, a few techniques can resolve the conflict in materials. Perhaps the most costly but secure method is to install two new studs normally, in a position abutting pencil studs. Metal lath can then be added to the first new stud, overlapping the old lath. The lath is then wired together and to the stud similar to the historic method. Gypsum board can then be screwed to the second stud while the lath is overlain with gypsum plaster. On occasion, new studs will need to be welded to existing studs or pencil rods in order to brace the new or old work properly. *Gelfand Partners Architects.*

New metal studs
Existing pencil studs
Existing lath & plaster

New gypsum board flush with plaster
Patch plaster

A second method relies on a bit of luck. If the total thickness of the existing plaster wall matches closely the width of a new metal stud, the old plaster/pencil stud wall can be cut back to the next stud. Install a new C stud adjacent to the existing stud so that the gypsum board for the new wall can be lapped over the existing plaster. Ending the lapped gypsum board with a plaster bead and filling any voids between existing plaster and new gypsum board with sealant (sometimes fire sealant) leaves a bump in the wall, but avoids the labor-intensive wiring, welding, and plastering required of the other method. *Gelfand Partners Architects.*

New metal studs
Existing pencil studs
Existing lath & plaster

New gypsum board overlapping plaster
Plaster bead
Patch plaster

Modifying walls of any but the later C stud configurations brings complications that can derail project budgets if not identified prior to bidding or negotiation. Builders are flummoxed by pencil studs, unless they have experience working with prewar buildings. Early investigations can alert the designers to potential problems before the contractor arrives with screw gun in hand.

When introducing new doors to existing pencil stud walls, it is best to just cut out the existing wall from floor to ceiling and introduce a completely new section of metal C studs. Trying to provide a new header in the pencil studs is extremely difficult and time consuming.

We should note that we often encounter wood lath and plaster in older or smaller buildings. If the project

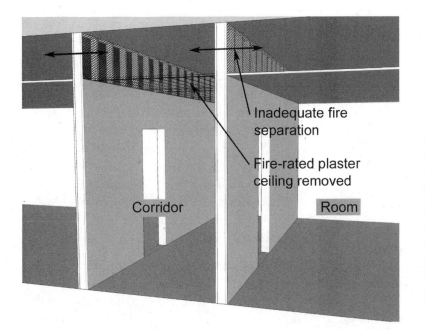

Inadequate fire separation

Fire-rated plaster ceiling removed

Corridor

Room

During comprehensive modernizations, ceilings are often removed to rework building utilities. New gypsum board or plaster may then be added to the upper portion of the remaining pencil studs, reestablishing a fire rating. In areas of tight access, or where acoustical tile ceilings cannot be removed, we have occasionally been allowed (through discussion with code officials) to install mineral fiber batts between the studs in order to improve the fire separation. Designers should investigate hidden fire separations to determine if they need to be improved. *Gelfand Partners Architects.*

involves significant pounding or demolition, fragile plaster loses its key. Plaster then drops off the lath in sheets, accompanied by the sound of the plaster key (the little blob of plaster forced behind the lath during installation) dropping into the wall cavity. Bulging plaster can be repaired by applying a fiberglass mesh to the surface, then drilling pilot holes through the plaster and underlying lath and using screws to pull the plaster back tight to the lath. The entire patch can then be overlain with a skim coat of plaster.

The last common problem encountered in pencil stud construction is presented by corridor fire containment systems. While this occurs mostly in buildings from the 1930s and 1940s, the problem extends to some mid-century buildings in regions where pencil studs were still used. In pencil-stud buildings, the fire separation between rooms and corridors was often formed by carrying the studs from the floor to slab above, but stopping the plaster at a hard lid ceiling over the corridor. The hard lid usually consists of

small heavy-gauge metal C channels wired to the concrete slab above with pencil rods tied across, then lath and plaster tied to the pencil studs. The plaster ceiling forms a tunnel corridor or a fully enclosed room.

Many projects will uncover areas where hard ceilings were removed to make way for above-ceiling services like heating, ventilating, and air-conditioning (HVAC) equipment, piping, and wiring. Ceiling removal leaves behind a weakened wall structure that is no longer tied across at the ceiling level. During the scoping phase of a project it is important to look above the ceilings to see what may have been done in previous renovations.

Masonry, plaster, and pencil studs of early buildings present a large disposal volume and weight. From a sustainability point of view, studs and plaster are best left in place if program permits. Masonry can be salvaged, but usually with a high input of labor. If the project requires removal, it is best to remove plaster completely instead of trying to cut and patch in small sections.

# MID-CENTURY MODERN BUILDINGS

Mid-century modern buildings exhibit all the advances in materials and building techniques that accrued during the war years. New materials like plywood, asbestos panels, and plastics developed for the war effort became the "wonder" materials of the early postwar years. Accelerating production of housing for the booming wartime and postwar suburbs drove the need for simplified building methods for commercial and institution buildings. Speed of erection supplanted durability of materials for mid-century buildings. New systems were devised, experiments undertaken, and belief in the heroic capabilities of air-conditioning systems drove a faith in technology to overcome nature. Even while the case-study modernism from California promoted at least the appearance of indoor-outdoor

living, buildings became increasingly unprepared for natural influences. "Modern" meant a floor-to-ceiling view framing a life where all the conveniences of technology were available at the flick of a switch.

Construction methods can often drive a need for removal of hazardous materials. Such remediation is tightly controlled by legal requirements that must be followed but it is no longer the major obstacle that it was when the issue was first recognized. However, it may be the deciding factor in whether a material or building component can be reused effectively.

## Disassembly Options

The designs for many mid-century buildings rely on repetition. Following on the heels of successful implementation of modern ideas of factory assembly and iterative construction, these buildings can lend themselves to disassembly and reuse. Some mid-

The Community Centre Pointe-Valaine by Smith Vigeant Architectes in Quebec, Canada, reused insulated precast concrete panels from a dismantled tire store to build 40 percent of the exterior walls.[14] *(left) © Smith Vigeant Architects; (right) © Yves Beaulieu Photographe*

century modern buildings can be greatly improved by selective demolition because their site plans often favored regimented layout over social interaction. While many mid-century modern buildings employ composite assemblies or traditional assembly methods designed to look modern, some actually provided an infrastructure that was simply assembled and relatively easy to remove. In these buildings there is an opportunity to keep the removed material out of landfill by spending a bit more effort on disassembly rather than using a traditional demolition method that would grind it to bits. By cutting, unscrewing, or unbolting assemblies, partitions, panels, or cabinets can be salvaged wholesale, for reuse or sale to the salvage industry. In East Germany where much of the social housing of the mid-century was built with concrete panels, one creative architect has disassembled the concrete panels and reconfigured them into a new building. [13]

Here in the United States precast concrete planks and tilt-up concrete panels are ripe for reuse since their lifespan exceeds one hundred years. Hotel, motel, apartment building, store, and office components can find new life in the reuse of precast panels.

Curtain wall systems can also find reuse in renovation projects. Since mid-century curtain wall systems have such poor insulation capacity, most designers would prefer to move them inside. Like reuse of precast concrete panels, reuse of curtain wall systems requires significant on-site measurement and cataloging of parts and careful planning for new installation. However, curtain wall mullions and frames are easily cut and reinstalled. So long as lengths exceeding the existing size are not needed, reuse is fairly easy. Also, once inside, curtain wall sticks can be in-filled with wood or metal panels, allowing greater design freedom than that permitted when they are used for exterior weather-proofing.

# LATE MODERN BUILDINGS

## Hazardous Material Issues

Late modern buildings have hazardous materials concerns similar to many mid-century buildings. Asbestos and lead are usually present, although lead was banned from use in paint in the United States after 1978.[15] While lead-containing paint lingered on the market or in repair stocks for some time, buildings constructed after the later 1970s generally do not contain it. Similarly, while asbestos has not been formally banned in the United States, litigation concerning asbestos-related health problems has drastically limited its use since the 1980s.

Late modern buildings are typified by even more reliance on air-conditioning, most often in combination with inoperable windows. Those built after the late 1970s oil crisis were also sealed very well to prevent leaking of heat during the winter. Because of this, many late century buildings suffer from various forms of "sick building syndrome." Problems with interior air quality can come from materials that off-gas or from the presence of moisture that can lead to growth of mold and mildew. Especially during the period right after a renovation, these buildings are particularly susceptible to high levels of off-gassed materials unless care is taken to avoid high-emitting materials and to increase fresh air intake.

Late century buildings also contain more components that are made with hazardous materials including carcinogens[16] (formaldehyde, asbestos), neurotoxins[17] (lead), and endocrine disrupters[18] (PCBs, PBBs, PBDEs, BPA, phthalates). These substances, particularly in plastics and sealants, are ubiquitous throughout late modern buildings; however, they are hard to identify since manufacturers did not publicize their use. Part of the problem is that data about various substances in our building materials is depicted only in terms of exposure to single constituents, not to the additive effect of multiple materials of similar properties.

While these substances may have stabilized and given off all the volatile particles that originally composed them, they could still be dangerous through slow decomposition, inadvertent heating, or at the time of demolition and disposal. Since some of these chemicals are accumulative in bodies over time, extra care should be taken with their handling. While removal and replacement is probably beneficial to indoor environmental quality, cutting, heating, or otherwise releasing them should be carefully monitored during any demolition activities. Moving away from traditional brute force methods, current demolition practice focuses on protection for workers and thorough cleanup prior to new construction. These materials may not be part of the industrial hygienist's scope of work and therefore the design team needs to identify areas where the contractor must control not only dust but also ensure that any suspected materials are not vaporized or spread around a renovation site.

In general, late century buildings were not designed for permanence. Their detailing required sealant replacement every five to ten years and major overhauls after fifteen to twenty years. Should a maintenance cycle be deferred, these buildings leak, drip, and weep their way toward self-destruction. Especially in later buildings where tight exterior envelopes were installed in order to provide better insulation and interior climate control, improperly installed or inadequate vapor barriers can exacerbate microbial contamination.

## Disposal Reduction

Like mid-century modern buildings, late century buildings can lend themselves to waste reduction. Because of their modular, factory-produced methods,

A 2004 study of California's waste found that construction and demolition (C&D) debris comprised 22 percent of the waste stream.[19] Many communities have instituted centralized waste separation in order to divert C&D waste to recyclers. Other communities require demolition contractors to separate waste on-site for separate transportation to recyclers or waste management facilities. Whichever method is used, recent experience shows that in communities with active recycling programs, 75 percent waste diversion is a readily achievable figure. *Gelfand Partners Architects.*

many components of late modern buildings can find a new home in a renovation or on the salvage market. From small components like doors and interior partition systems to larger components like bowling alley flooring, a bit of creative thinking can lead to significant waste diversion. Doors are often reused as workstation surfaces or partitions. Similarly, wood flooring can be reused as work surfaces or wall finishes if it is not appropriate for reuse in place. Cabinetry can be relocated or modified for new locations and interior partition systems can be reconfigured. Where significant site modifications are envisioned, demolition debris like brick and concrete can be crushed and reused for base materials for paving or cut in sections and reused for site walls or directly as paving.

For smaller components or products that are difficult to reuse on-site, sorting the waste stream can turn waste into new resources for industry. In San Francisco, local ordinance *requires* diversion of a *minimum* of 65 percent diversion of C&D waste. Many projects approach 90 percent diversion. In communities where recycling diversion is not as developed, designers should research major manufacturer recycling programs. For common materials like ceiling tile, carpet, and other flooring, many manufacturers will reclaim the available product.

Gypsum wallboard is one of the most commonly used materials in late modern interiors. While it is very difficult to reuse whole sheets (because of screws, nails, and tape), the gypsum recycling market is developing. For buildings constructed prior to the mid-1970s, asbestos could be present in taping compound. For those built before 1978, painted surfaces could contain lead. Both of these should be tested prior to recycling. If free of contaminants, recycled gypsum board can become a component of new gypsum board (up to 15 to 20 percent) or can find a home as soil amendment.[20]

Finally, new construction activities can be affected tremendously by design that is sensitive to managing waste products. By designing with standard dimensions or designing for disassembly, architects can minimize construction waste. During construction, contractors can segregate waste, often finding uses for cutoffs and scraps prior to sending materials to recyclers.

## CASE STUDY

# Omicron Office

**Owner**   Omicron AEC, Ltd., Corporation, for-profit

**Renovation Architect**   Kevin Hanvey, Principal, Omicron Architecture Engineering Construction Ltd.

**Original Building Type**   Office

**Renovation Building Type**   Office

**Original Construction Date**   1974

**Renovation Date**   2004

**Location**   Vancouver, BC, Canada

**Climate**   Oceanic (Köppen Cfb)

**Area**   15,400 ft$^2$

**Achievement**   LEED-CI Gold (35 points)

**Key Indicators**   Radiant Heating/Cooling

   Daylighting and Occupancy Sensors

   50 percent Less Water Use

   Salvaged Materials from Former Office

   61 percent recycled content, 15 percent rapidly renewable

   56 percent manufactured locally, 52 percent harvested locally

   98 percent FSC Certified Wood

   73 percent of construction waste diverted

**Energy Achievement**   15 percent reduction below baseline

   38 percent reduction in lighting power density

**Water After**   5.78 gallons/ ft$^2$ year; 1,060 gal/occupant year

Bentall Tower Three, located in Vancouver, British Columbia, was originally constructed in 1974. In November 2004, Omicron completed its sustainable renovation of its head office—located on the entire fifth floor—earning a United States Green Building Council (USGBC) LEED Gold for Commercial Interiors rating, the first tenant improvement in Canada to achieve this distinction.

The Omicron office renovation project in Vancouver, BC, Canada, was a pilot under the USGBC's LEED for Commercial Interiors program because an equivalent program did not exist in Canada at the time. *Terry Guscott/ATN Visuals.*

As an integrated design and construction firm, Omicron had a strong desire to outwardly express their commitment to sustainability in the renovation. In order to achieve the firm's sustainability goals, the project required a significant intervention with the existing building's architecture and systems. To reduce water consumption by 50 percent, waterless urinals and low-flow fixtures were added. Task lighting was eliminated and radiant ceiling panels heat and cool the main board room. Private offices gave way to an entirely open plan to increase access to daylight and views and to encourage discussion across disciplines and facilitate an integrated design process. Additionally, Energy Star appliances are used throughout.

Of the materials used in this renovation, 25 percent were reused from their previous office location and 61 percent of the new materials were recycled, including rubber flooring made from old car tires; exposed concrete panels made from plant material, recycled paper, and industrial waste; and wheat-straw fiber board for casework. Additionally, 56 percent of the materials were manufactured within 800 kilometers of the site and 73 percent of the construction waste was diverted from the landfill through reuse and recycling. The project used 98 percent FSC-certified wood, difficult to source in 2004/2005. Finally, all paints, carpets, composite woods, furniture, and insulation are low-emitting materials.

▲ Ninety-eight percent of wood used in the office is FSC-certified. In 2004/2005 sources of FSC-certified wood were difficult to source; Omicron's commitment to sustainable forestry is particularly noteworthy under the circumstances. *Terry Guscott/ATN Visuals.*

▶ Omicron considers their innovative office a sustainable design laboratory to educate and inform staff, clients, and visitors, who are welcome to walk the space with the help of a self-guided tour. *Terry Guscott/ATN Visuals.*

CASE STUDY

# SoFlo Office Studios

**Owner**   Magnificent So Flo Seven, LLC

**Renovation Architect**   Alamo Architects & O'Neill Conrad Oppelt (OCO) Architects

**Original Building Type**   Warehouse

**Renovation Building Type**   Office

**Original Construction Date**   1940s

**Renovation Date**   2007

**Location**   San Antonio, TX

**Climate**   Humid subtropical (Köppen Cfa)

**Area**   16,600 ft$^2$

**Achievement**   LEED 2.0 Silver (36 points)

**Key Indicators**   Daylighting and Sunshading
   Salvage
   Low Flow Fixtures
   Cistern for Condensate and Rainwater
   Natural Ventilation

**Energy Achievement**   19 percent less than comparable building (ASHRAE 90.1-2004)

**Total Energy Use**   47 Kbtu/year   2.83 kWh/ ft$^2$/year   (30.48 kWh/m$^2$ year)

**Water After**   80 percent less for irrigation, 32 percent less for interior uses

**Renewables**   None

When two firms, Alamo Architects and OCO Architects, teamed to transform a 1940s/1950s truck warehouse in San Antonio, Texas, into offices for themselves, they looked for ways to use the site's inherent qualities to inspire new work. Focusing on salvage and reuse, they managed to limit landfill to just 5 percent of construction waste. Existing building components were reused throughout: steel sash windows were glazed with expanded metal for new guardrails, pine flooring was reused as interior wall finish, and interior concrete slabs were left in place and polished, while exterior concrete was reused as stepping stones or tilted up for property line fencing. Components of a steel mezzanine were reconfigured as entry gates and garage doors were reused as interior partitions.

Interiors are formed from salvaged material—old pine flooring, garage doors, and even steel sash windows find new uses as walls and guardrails. Existing concrete floors are polished and left in place, providing a low-maintenance, low-emitting surface. *Courtesy of Alamo Architects.*

The team minimized water use through the installation of low-flow fixtures and sensible site strategies. Piping diverts roof water and cooling system condensate to a cistern that supplies water for irrigation of locally adapted planting. Energy use was similarly affected by response to existing conditions. Where one of the two buildings was oriented with mostly western glazed exposure, salvaged steel was used to build a planted trellis to cut afternoon heat. The team also added overhangs to existing clerestory windows, optimizing daylighting while limiting heat gain. Overall, the project uses 32 percent less water (80 percent less for irrigation) and 19 percent less energy than comparable buildings.

Water from air-conditioning equipment and the rooftop collects in outdoor cisterns to find a later reuse as irrigation supply. Locally adapted planting reduces the need for irrigation while covering trellises made from salvaged steel, shading the building to reduce cooling loads and providing a cooling sink for natural ventilation. *Courtesy of Alamo Architects*.

## ENDNOTES

1. www.epa.gov/epp/pubs/products/construction.htm

2. For more information, see *Guide to Green Building Rating Systems*, Linda Reader, 2010.

3. www.epa.gov/nrmrl/lcaccess/index.html.

4. NREL, The National Renewable Energy Laboratory has an extensive database. Its reference includes the Life-Cycle Inventory Database, www.nrel.gov/lci.

5. www.athenasmi.org/.

6. www.athenasmi.org/tools/impactEstimator/index.html.

7. www.athenasmi.org/tools/ecoCalculator/index.html.

8. www.nrel.gov/lci/related_links.html.

9. Buildings and Climate Change—Status, Challenges and Opportunities, United Nations Environment Programme (UNEP).

10. An Introduction to Indoor Air Quality (IAQ), Volatile Organic Compounds (VOCs), U.S. Environmental Protection Agency, www.epa.gov/iaq/voc.html, accessed November 28, 2010.

11. California Section 01350—Special Environmental Requirements Specification includes criteria for testing of materials emissions which includes the Chronic Reference Exposure Levels (CRELs) concentrations established by the California Office of Environmental Health Hazard Assessment and procedures developed by the U.S. EPA.

12. Carpets, cleaning, and allergies, various studies: www.flooringsciences.org/e-journal/title.cfm.

13. Wiewiorra Hopp Architekten, Berlin, www.wh-arch.de/, "plattenpalast" project.

14. www.cpci.ca/index.asp?sc=potm&pn=monthly72009 and www.sabmagazine.com/blog/2009/08/20/sab-awards-winner-pointe-valaine-community-centre/.

15. U.S. Environmental Protection Agency, www.epa.gov/lead/.

16. World Health Organization, http://monographs.iarc.fr/ENG/Classification/crthgr01.php.

17. U.S. EPA, www.atsdr.cdc.gov/toxprofiles/tp13.pdf.

18. The Endocrine Society, www.endo-society.org/journals/scientificstatements/upload/edc_scientific_statement.pdf.

19. www.calrecycle.ca.gov/Publications/LocalAsst/34004005.pdf.

20. www.calrecycle.ca.gov/ConDemo/Wallboard/ and www.drywallrecycling.org/.

chapter **7**

# CONSTRUCTION
# OPERATIONS

In renovation rough construction operations must occur right next to finished building components. *Gelfand Partners Architects.*

## INTRODUCTION

Old habits die hard. Sustainability, for all its exposure in the press, has yet to fully penetrate the world of hammers and saws. In order for a project to carry its sustainable intentions through to completion, those intentions must be clear and consistent, oversight and careful coordination must be continuous, and there must be one advocate who ensures that the construction team carries the project through to a sustainable conclusion.

Successful construction begins with clear goals and standards set early in the design process. The design team develops a written document that spells out the performance criteria for both the construction team and for the final building. During construction, this document then informs the process and allows team members to quickly check if the project meets sustainability goals. Criteria about materials qualities (recycled content, product constituents, and maintenance regimes) can be compared with those of proposed substitutions. Criteria about performance can be referenced to determine if proposed products will meet the project goals.

Major issues for all sustainable construction operations include:

- Maintaining indoor air quality during construction and occupancy
- Waste and debris recycling and disposal
- Protection of building materials and assemblies to remain
- Commissioning electrical and mechanical systems

Renovations add issues of safety for occupants if the building is not vacant. In occupied renovations systems must be phased so that HVAC, elevators, and power remain in operation while construction of new systems proceeds. Dust control within occupied buildings is also more challenging than in new construction projects.

Every successful project requires a sustainability advocate who spearheads the efforts to see that the project remains on track in terms of sustainability. While this advocate need not perform all the checks or calculations, the advocate steers conversations back to sustainability issues, reminding other team members that sustainability can be intertwined with many of the issues that commonly arise during design and construction. Further, the advocate makes sure that a qualified commissioning agent acts at appropriate points in the construction process to observe and co-ordinate sustainability measures that physically embody the project goals.

# INITIAL CONSTRUCTION ACTIVITIES

## Assembling the Team

The contractor who will perform the construction of a project may join the team at a variety of times. In much private construction the owner may hire a contractor before choosing a design team. It is often the contractor who lets the owner know that design is required to accomplish the owner's goals, to get a building permit, or to allow the contractor to give a firm price. Another point at which the contractor could join the team is at the end of a conceptual design phase when the owner already is working with the architects and engineers. The contractor is then available to start cost estimating and assisting in discovery of existing conditions as design decisions are made.

The third approach is to choose a contractor after the design is complete and building permits obtained. The choice at that point may be a competitive bid where the contractor wins the job by bidding the lowest price. This method, or some variant of it that breaks the project into smaller contracts coordinated by a separate general contractor or construction manager, is typically used for publicly funded work and some private work.

The ideal team for sustainable construction is formed during design and includes a contractor who is experienced and committed to sustainable construction. This allows the contractor to be part of decisions about construction methods that may have important sustainability implications. Where the traditional approach to contracting was to put drawings out to bid

## LEED Construction Phase Credits

TABLE 2: CONSTRUCTION CREDITS

**EAP1**  Fundamental Commissioning

**EAc2**  Enhanced Commissioning

**EAc3**  Energy Use, Measurement & Payment Accountability

**EAc4**  Green Power

**MRc1.2**  Building Reuse, Maintain 40% of Interior Non-Structural Components

**MRc1.3**  Building Reuse, Maintain 60% of Interior Non-Structural Components

**MRc2.1**  Construction Waste Management, Divert 50% from Landfill

**MRc2.2**  Construction Waste Management, Divert 75% from Landfill

**MRc3.1**  Resource Reuse, 5%

**MRc3.2**  Resource Reuse, 10%

**MRc3.3**  Resource Reuse, 30% Furniture and Furnishings

**MRc4.1**  Recycled Content, 10% (post-consumer + 1/2 pre-consumer)

**MRc4.2**  Recycled Content, 20% (post-consumer + ½ pre-consumer)

**MRc5.1**  Regional Materials, 20% Manufactured Regionally

**MRc5.2**  Regional Materials, 10% Extracted and Manufactured Regionally

**MRc6**  Rapidly Renewable Materials

**MRc7**  Certified Wood

**EQc3.1**  Construction IAQ Management Plan, During Construction

**EQc3.2**  Construction IAQ Management Plan, Before Occupancy

**EQc4.1**  Low-Emitting Materials, Adhesives and Sealants

**EQc4.2**  Low-Emitting Materials, Paints and Coatings

**EQc4.3**  Low-Emitting Materials, Carpet Systems

**EQc4.4**  Low-Emitting Materials, Composite Wood and Laminate Adhesives

**EQc4.5**  Low-Emitting Materials, Systems Furniture and Seating

**IDc1**  Innovation in Design[1]

and rely on contractor means and methods, sustainable construction practices need to be specified if they are to be included in a bid. That means specifications will cross into the contractor's logistics, site access, and practices. This is one reason a contractor's input is very helpful during the design process. It is also ideal if a commissioning agent is involved during design to verify that all designed systems are coordinated and documented properly to meet the design intent and that the contractor's coordination with the commissioning agent during construction is part of the contractual agreement.

At the beginning of construction the process reverses, and the contractor provides submittals of drawings, samples, and specifications back to the design team and commissioning agent to verify that the design intent is being met before fabrication or ordering. If the project will go through third-party verification as a Leadership in Energy and Environmental Design (LEED) or Collaborative for High Performance Schools (CHPS) project, the contractor's responsibilities include providing documentation for dust control, erosion control, stormwater pollution prevention, proper disposal/recycling, material choices and sources, and protection of mechanical equipment to remain, among others. These responsibilities create new tasks for a contractor and should be included in the bid documents.

In most older buildings some hazardous materials are present and must be properly removed or encapsulated both for the future health of the building occupants and the safety of workers during construction. Specialty contractors generally perform abatement of these materials. This is done in a negative pressure containment that only trained workers can enter and therefore needs to be carefully coordinated with general demolition or salvage work so that when the plastic comes down there are no nasty surprises.

The core sustainable construction team includes:

- Owner
- User group representative (if different from owner)
- Building management representative (in occupied building)
- Design team architect and engineers
- Hazardous material consultant (industrial hygienist)
- Hazardous material abatement contractor
- General contractor and subcontractors
- Commissioning agent
- Sustainability advocate (generally owner or design team member)

## Exploratory Demolition and Investigations

Exploratory demolition and investigation are part of a process aptly called *discovery*. Exploratory work uncovers hidden conditions, and finds and identifies the materials, systems, and condition of the building. Information can be found on existing drawings, old photographs, and most directly in the building itself. Exploratory demolition and investigations, while often disruptive to building occupants, are invaluable to the

Exploratory demolition can help confirm what lies "'behind the walls" when existing drawings are insufficient to determine how renovations should proceed. Actual connections of lintels to steel framing differed from details shown in drawings for this historic building. *Gelfand Partners Architects.*

design team. Few buildings come with complete or accurate "as-built" documents. In fact, the older the original building, the less likely a team will find complete drawings. Frequently, construction of a large prewar building required twenty or so drawings where a building of that size would require two hundred or more today. In older buildings, architects and engineers relied on contractors to follow accepted local standards, building on inference from the plans combined with a long tradition of accepted building practices.

Some areas of buildings simply do not appear on drawings at all. Void spaces can frequently be filled with a tangle of pipes and conduit, but occasionally they remain surprisingly empty—ripe for repurposing. Because renovations often introduce new elements into a building (elevators, stairs, mechanical systems, pipes), exploratory demolition can be the only way to have any assurance at all of the feasibility of these introductions. Whether trying to determine floor-to-floor heights in a warped and settled building or calculating the strength of existing concrete to determine seismic upgrade, every renovation project benefits from early explorations. A thorough discovery process carried out with the participation of the contractor is one of the strongest reasons for adopting a project delivery method that allows the contractor to be selected during design.

## Demolition Documents versus Site Discussions

The first physical phase of a project is often selective demolition, or the removal of deteriorated or undesirable building components. They are either demolished, which means that they are removed for off-site disposal to appropriate recycling or landfill facilities; abated, if they are hazardous; or salvaged for reuse by others or as part of the design. In renovation, it is critical to identify clearly what is supposed to be removed, what will be reused, and the amount of protection required for the materials, finishes, equipment, and fittings that remain.

Selective demolition encompasses a wide range of removal strategies necessary for successful renovations. Often initiated early in the design phase with exploratory demolition, selective demolition allows the design team to make the best use of existing building materials and assemblies that remain as integral components of renovated buildings.

Particularly in competitive bid projects owners and designers can find themselves with very different project goals and aspirations than the construction team. While contract documents describe the result that the whole team agrees to achieve, there are obviously conflicting interests at work. Selective demolition illustrates this separation all too often.

A common scope of work such as enlarging a bathroom runs into the whole gamut of hidden conditions—pipes that may connect restrooms on other floors, concrete bases that were often built to confine spills to the bathroom and raise sills above the floor, slab depressions cast in place for thickset ceramic tile floors. Drawings that describe demolishing

Even relatively new buildings have unexpected conditions in their walls such as concrete bases, criss-crossing pipes, or interrupted studs for recessed fixtures. *Gelfand Partners Architects.*

a wall need to indicate the concrete base if it exists (and could be found during discovery), relocation of pipes, or any other scope the design team expects the contractor to undertake. If the drawings don't include such descriptions, either the contractor bids high enough to absorb the risk of surprise extra work (and the owner pays for work that was not needed), or low and the surprises turn into change orders during construction.

Traditionally, architects and engineers simply provide drawings (plans) that show or note removal of certain building components. Too often, these plans develop schematically and include broad language like "…and other components required for the completion of new construction." Where the design team remains uncertain about hidden items or has not thought through the constructability of "new" details, the contractor's demolition team must guess at the dividing line between items to be demolished and items to remain.

Education is often required before owners can be persuaded that more fee needs to go into discovery work. Where this does not occur, many design teams are reluctant to spend time thoroughly investigating existing conditions. They may not develop both the limits of selective demolition and the final details of the interfaces with new construction. Newer project delivery methods such as design-build, general contractor/construction management, and integrated project delivery attempt to reduce risk through earlier involvement of the contractor in discovery and constructability decisions.

While drawings and written description provide the basis for information transfer from the design team to the construction team, sustainable renovation design adds pressure on the need to communicate intent. Where projects employ integrated design and construction teams, this transfer becomes easier—collaborative development of documents spurs discussions of intent and leads to better clarity in the field. Where design teams remain separated from the construction team through traditional bid-build project delivery, sustainable designers can short circuit this separation by including documents illustrating the sustainability intent and by requiring a site walk-through jointly held with the designers and builders.

Invaluable in communication, face-to-face interaction at the building site allows simple point-and-discuss methods that soon illuminate the various issues each team member brings to the renovation. Walking the project with the contractor and demolition team and physically marking the limits of selective demolition while discussing the intent of the new construction leads to better coordination and can highlight designers' concerns and lead to creative solutions from the construction team.

Most architects would see this as an added burden on top of their regular contract and perhaps an avenue for potential liability. However, even if a site walk uncovers designers' mistakes, the ultimate goal of the renovation will be made clearer. Further, there will likely be fewer problems down the road than if a demolition team must guess about intent or extent of selective demolition. It is easier to undo a mistake early in the process than to rebuild items removed by aggressive demolition or re-contain spaces already cleared from hazardous materials abatement.

## Hazardous Materials Abatement

### Asbestos

Unfortunately, the constituents of many "modern" materials had unforeseen effects on building occupants. Perhaps foremost among the wonder-materials of the immediate prewar and postwar years is asbestos. A natural mineral fiber, asbestos was easily mined and provided fibers with seemingly miraculous properties.

Fibers added strength to sheet materials and adhesives, and assisted in creating fire-resistant coatings and materials. In combination with cement it is found in "Transite" boards and pipes—thin, fireproof, durable, and easy to handle. When bonded to fabric, asbestos added extreme durability and fire-resistance to coatings for insulation on steam and hot water pipes and flues. Mixed with vinyl and pressed into thin tiles, asbestos gave strength to a polymer in order to provide a cheap floor covering for institutional applications— vinyl asbestos tile or VAT. It is also found in adhesives and window putty.

Unfortunately, some asbestos fibers are easily friable (caused to become airborne) and, when breathed or ingested have carcinogenic properties. Most renovations of mid-century modern buildings will encounter asbestos in at least one form. While some forms are inert if not disturbed, most become hazardous during normal renovation activities. Professional industrial hygienists (IH) are required to determine how materials should be handled during construction, how workers can be protected best, and how materials should be disposed.

While the project IH (or "hazmat consultants") may recommend leaving some asbestos-containing materials in place if they can be encapsulated and are likely to remain undisturbed in any future work, asbestos-containing materials must be removed or "abated" by specialized workers. These tainted materials will then be transported to a hazardous material disposal site.

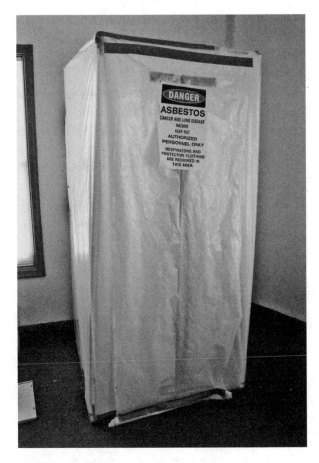

Asbestos containment enclosures have become a routine part of the demolition process in many areas of the country. Workers don protective clothing and respirators to enter the containment, remove hazardous material, then thoroughly clean the contained area before removal of the containment barrier. *Gelfand Partners Architects.*

### Lead[2]

An elemental metal, lead has a very low melting point, making it desirable as a material used to join other metals. It also lends brilliance to paints while increasing its durability. Unfortunately, lead is toxic when ingested or inhaled. Lead is present primarily in paints and in solders used in plumbing and electrical work. Particularly where lead-based paint is on wearing surfaces, lead may accumulate on the floor below the surface and later become airborne. Lead is also found in soils under walls that were repeatedly painted or next to highways where lead from car exhaust accumulated. Where lead is used in pipe solder—generally in copper pipe for water supply— lead will slowly leach into the water, especially when the water is hot. In older prewar plumbing fittings, lead packing is sometimes present in water taps, providing an especially easy route for lead to leach into our bodies.

Hazmat consultants can approach lead in paint in one of two ways. First, they can recommend encapsulation. If the existing paint surfaces are in good condition, or if loose and peeling paint can easily be removed, new paint can be applied over a primer over the lead-containing paint in order to seal it in place. While providing the least expensive method of dealing with lead paint, encapsulation has two problems. First, if the existing paint is not very well adhered to the original surface, it can continue loosening and be released into the atmosphere. Second, if lead is present on wearing surfaces, a new layer of paint can be worn away, again releasing lead. The alternative to encapsulation is full abatement of lead paint by chemically stripping it from its substrate, or abatement by removing the entire material that is covered by the paint.

Expensive and time consuming, chemical strippers remove the lead paint in a wet mass, preventing it from escaping into the air. Lead paint removal can happen off-site when building components (doors, windows, cabinets, and so forth) can be removed easily and taken to a controlled containment. However, lead paint is more often located on materials that cannot be removed or that present particular challenges for abatement. Lead paint is often present in the primer on steel structural members. Where steel members require welding, lead can be vaporized by the heat, providing a high danger to the adjacent steelworkers while leaving a lead vapor that easily moves throughout a construction site. Because of this, steel primers should always be tested before any welding takes place, then removed before welding commences.

Lead in pipe solder presents other challenges. Where drinking water is concerned, water can be tested to determine if lead leaching is present. If so, fixtures and fittings should be replaced as a first step. Sometimes, replacement of fixtures will remove the problem because as pipes age, an interior coating covers the soldered areas. Leaching of lead is more common from the moving parts of the plumbing fittings. Again, an industrial hygienist can advise on the appropriate steps to be taken to test for and remedy any drinking water contamination problems.

### PCBs (Polychlorinated Biphenyls)[3]

PCBs are commonly found in mid-century buildings. They often exist in transformers—ranging from the transformers in fluorescent lights (usually called "ballasts") to larger building transformers. They are also found in other electric equipment, hydraulic oils, some cable insulation, oil-based paints, caulk, and plastics. PCB use was banned in the United States in 1979. However, many products containing PCBs are still present in our buildings; there are no alternatives other than removal and proper disposal. Fortunately, the light fixtures and transformers that are of an age to contain PCBs typically require replacement as an energy-saving measure. So, other than the care needed to properly dispose of these devices, and the minimal cost to route them to a hazardous materials waste facility, removal of these items is routine.

Hazardous material abatement may occur throughout construction, particularly if materials such as asbestos-containing plaster remain in place and are only abated where disturbed (spot abatement). However, it is often one of the first activities on a job. While regulations and industry standards can vary from state to state, construction teams should use local industry

| Hazard | Found in | Hazard | Common Remediation Methods* |
|---|---|---|---|
| Arsenic, Copper | Treated Wood (CCA, ACA) Chromated copper arsenate, Ammoniacal copper arsenate | Toxic | Abate (remove) |
| Asbestos | Floor Tile (VAT) | Carcinogen | Abate (remove) or encapsulate |
| Asbestos | Pipe Insulation | Carcinogen | Abate (remove) |
| Asbestos | Window Glazing Putty | Carcinogen | Abate (remove) |
| Asbestos | Fireproof siding | Carcinogen | Abate (remove) |
| Formaldehyde | Plywood (cabinetry, panels) | Carcinogen | Abate (remove) or encapsulate |
| Formaldehyde | Composite Wood Products | Carcinogen | Abate (remove) or encapsulate |
| Lead | Paint | Toxic | Abate (remove) or encapsulate |
| Lead | Pipe Solder | Toxic | Larger pipes: CIPP—epoxy pipe lining Smaller pipes: abate (remove) |
| Lead | Plumbing Fixture/Fitting | Toxic | Replace with no-lead fixture/fitting |
| Lead | Soil | Toxic | Abate (remove) or encapsulate |
| Lead | Ceramic Tile Glaze | Toxic | Abate (remove) or encapsulate |
| Mercury | Fluorescent Lamps (bulbs) | Toxic | Replace |
| PCBs | Transformer Oil | Carcinogen | Abate (remove) |
| PCBs | Fluorescent Lighting Ballast | Carcinogen | Abate (remove) |
| Radon | Basement Air (from concrete aggregate or naturally occurring) | Carcinogen | Improve ventilation, provide subgrade ventilation |

*Consult Industrial Hygienist for Recommendation

standard processes for dealing with hazardous materials abatement. Most regulations and standards focus on containment, cleanup, worker protection, and proper disposal.

In construction, hazardous materials are either "abated" or "encapsulated." Simply put, abatement describes the complete removal and proper disposal of a hazardous material. Friable asbestos, PCBs, and lead paint on building components that have wear surfaces commonly require abatement. Encapsulation defines a process that "permanently" entombs a hazardous material in place. Teams often encapsulate rather than

◀Abatement commonly includes removal of 9 × 9 in. vinyl asbestos tile (VAT) flooring. After containing an area within a perimeter of plastic sheeting, personnel remove and bag the asbestos-containing floor tiles. Frequently the mastic also contains asbestos, so the entire floor requires chemical cleaning. Following removal of the hazardous materials, an industrial hygienist tests the space to determine if the containment can be removed safely. *Photo provided by Mitchell Edwards, Sensible Environmental Solutions, Inc.*

▶Encapsulating lead-containing paint commonly occurs in renovations. If the paint surfaces do not typically wear, well-adhered paint can be left in place. In order to complete a successful encapsulation, any loose or peeling paint must be removed by scraping, wet sanding, or chemical removal. Heat removal should never be used since the lead will vaporize, spreading throughout the building and causing an acute hazard to workers in the immediate area. To effect encapsulation, contractors completely remove loose paint, then prime and paint the entire surface, sealing in the lead paint. However, care must be taken throughout the remainder of the renovation to prevent disturbing the lead-containing paint. *Photo provided by Mitchell Edwards, Sensible Environmental Solutions, Inc.*

abate lead paint, asbestos-containing flooring and mastics, and asbestos-containing plasters. Encapsulation, while less expensive than abatement, depends first on whether the material will degrade over time, then on whether it can be covered effectively with a durable material, and third whether future renovations or minor activities such as hanging bookshelves will disturb it. Surfaces such as paint that require fairly frequent maintenance are also not as appropriate for encapsulation since future work can release the hazardous material if not properly handled. In general, a sustainable renovation protocol would recommend removal of hazardous materials to mitigate the risk of future harm.

In projects where encapsulation covers a significant portion of the work, complications during the normal construction activities can slow or even stop the work. While monitoring usually ends at the completion of abatement, it needs to continue sporadically throughout the main construction phases if encapsulated material remains on-site and must be disturbed occasionally. For example, a recent project had the option of abatement or encapsulation of asbestos-containing ceiling plaster. Complete removal (abatement) looked to be a very significant cost. However, in investigating the complications of working around the encapsulated material, it became obvious that the initial abatement cost would be less than the incremental cost of mini-containments and special procedures as literally hundreds of areas would be disturbed throughout the renovation work. The burden to the construction team to continuously monitor the encapsulation of the asbestos plaster far outweighed the initial cost to remove it

completely and provide a clear run at normal construction processes.

The skill and attention of a hazardous materials monitoring company is critical to the hazardous material abatement process. Usually consisting of registered industrial hygienists, hazmat monitoring companies typically join the team working for the owner during the development of demolition drawings. After reviewing the scope of demolition and construction activities planned, they review the site and take samples of suspected hazardous materials. They arrange testing of the materials then, working with the design team, they develop hazardous materials abatement plans including written descriptions of processes and procedures.

During the demolition and abatement process, they review the contractors' documentation, assess whether personnel received appropriate training,

In order to prevent harm during and after the abatement process, containment, cleanup, and monitoring processes have been developed to limit the chance of worker or building occupant exposure to hazardous materials. The careful monitoring of abatement can make the difference between a clean and healthy site and a hazardous waste disaster. *Photo provided by Mitchell Edwards, Sensible Environmental Solutions, Inc.*

whether health certifications comply with worker protection regulations, and then monitor the installation of containment areas and the work within and around the containment areas, enforcing procedures and ensuring proper disposal of hazardous material.

Hazmat containments consist of plastic sheeting completely enclosing an area requiring abatement or encapsulation. Containments include rooms for donning protective clothing (white jumpsuits, masks, and the like) as well as filtered, negative-pressure ventilation systems to prevent contaminated dust from escaping the containment. *Gelfand Partners Architects.*

The last part of the abatement process involves appropriate disposal. Throughout the country, designated landfills provide certified locations for proper management of hazardous wastes. Ranging from locations that will accept bulk construction debris with low concentrations of lead to specialized landfills that accept highly concentrated asbestos-containing material, the construction team must monitor proper bagging and delivery of hazardous materials to their final site. In most areas, the paperwork involved enables a legal structure in which the owner of the building that is the source of the hazardous material continues to be the "owner" of the hazardous material at the landfill.

Although the growth of specialized abatement contractors has led to a more routine ability to manage hazardous materials safely, the separation from the general demolition contractor can cause coordination problems. Abatement may be the first opportunity for extensive discovery, particularly if hazardous materials made exploratory work prohibitively expensive. But observation is difficult and quick adjustments in scope almost impossible because design team members remain excluded from the areas under containment.

All the workers who enter the containment must be properly trained and have recent medical records attesting to their state of health. These protections prevent hazardous materials from spreading outside the containment and protect the workers' health. Because of this highly regulated situation, contractors most often split the abatement work from traditional demolition so that skilled workers only perform the necessary abatement and lower-skilled workers carry out the remainder of demolition.

Understanding the economic necessities for separation of abatement and demolition, the design team can aid the process by providing both those teams with as much information as possible. In the best case, the same person acts as both the supervisor for the

Hazardous material and demolition contractors should coordinate their work. *Gelfand Partners Architects.*

structural steel joints that would become connection points for new seismic work, our structural engineer trained in hazmat procedures in order to enter the containment to assess each situation. This allowed abatement to be modified immediately to accommodate the undocumented existing connections. Because we had very poor documentation of the existing structure, we expected that the areas we selected to be abated would not be sufficient to account for varying conditions we might encounter. Rather than just order additional abatement everywhere, the design team and contractor decided that the cost of savings accrued by a limited abatement scope would outweigh the cost of training for observations by the structural engineer.

## CONSTRUCTION DEBRIS

As noted in Chapter 6, Building Materials, construction debris is a major contributor to landfills. While hazardous materials need special disposition, general construction debris makes up a large volume of trash. Where possible, reuse of materials on-site saves transport, space in landfills, and manufacture of new materials. For contractors this can be a significant task and expense and must be clearly specified in the contract documents. As the industry retools to work more sustainably, the scale of appropriate reuse will be a major factor. Today there are already mature markets for recycling common metals found on job sites. This may make more sense than trying to reuse such materials on-site.

abatement and the supervisor for general demolition. If not, the designers should plan to visit the project with both supervisors so that together they can view the circumstances and, while the designer indicates the material to be removed, the abatement and demolition contractors can decide among themselves how the work will be carried out.

In some cases it can make sense for members of the design team to be trained to enter hazardous material containment areas. On a recent project of ours in which abatement needed to occur around

Similarly it may be more cost effective to haul away framing lumber for processing (removal of nails and fasteners) by a salvage yard than to prep lumber on-site for reuse there. Concrete or asphalt may be ground up and reused off-site more efficiently than at individual job sites. Building contractors would usually need to subcontract such tasks anyway, and it may be more efficient to dispose of materials to businesses that focus on processing them.

On the other hand, some recognizable materials and building components such as marble restroom partitions, panel doors, and old windows may have additional value as a link to the building's history. That may justify more effort on-site. Each project requires attention to the waste stream that it will generate. One job's waste is another job's treasure.

## OCCUPIED REHABS

Frequently, renovations require work in buildings with active occupancies. Often the level of occupancy determines the scope of work possible. In an apartment building with 70 or 80 percent occupancy, work must be set up in many phases, extending the schedule for the project and increasing the costs. Where project cost drives scope, building occupancy naturally reduces the amount of money that can be spent on construction, tying dollars to organization and coordination, sometimes to overtime wages to allow work to proceed faster or during specific hours. Occasionally, full occupancy drives the scope of a project. Careful coordination of work and shifting of occupants to temporary locations within the facility allows construction to continue, but always at a premium. In a limited budget the more money spent on separation of work areas, cleanup, or overtime, the less spent on the work itself.

### Relocation

Renovation usually involves some level of building occupancy. Wherever possible, projects should explore off-site relocation of existing uses to allow the construction team a free hand in organizing and un-

dertaking the work. The efficiencies gained in free access to the site can often offset relocation costs. This depends on the local resources for similar facilities, the ability of the organization to stage and arrange relocation, and the particular needs of the relocated users. In residential buildings this can be as simple as locating nearby empty apartments and moving occupants' belongings. In business settings, complications with information technology infrastructure, telecommunications, proximity to business resources, and speed of relocation might drive the process.

Temporary partitions can provide a safe working environment away from building occupants while preventing dirt, dust, noise, and smells from reaching outside the work area. *Gelfand Partners Architects.*

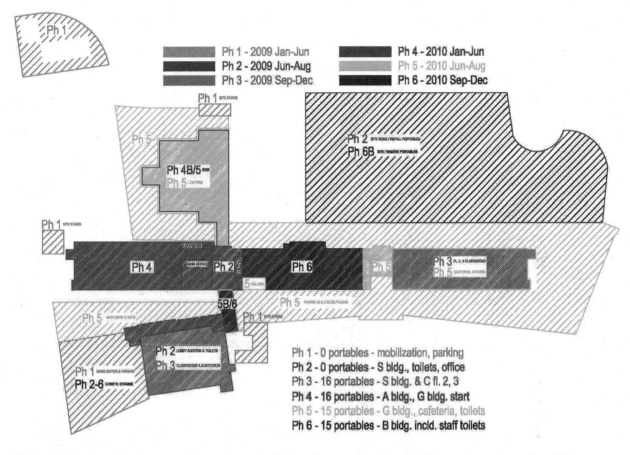

Whether dividing the project into two or thirteen phases, the design and construction teams should have a clear understanding of the sequence of work so that the relationship between the construction team and the occupants remains clear. *Gelfand Partners Architects.*

Whenever work adjacent to occupied areas takes place, careful separation of work areas from building occupants becomes paramount. It is ideal to work with the contractor to determine the most efficient phasing and sequence of work. However, in an open bid, the design team must include a phasing scheme as a basis for pricing. In analyzing the project in relation to building occupancy, the team should look at construction sequences to determine requirements such as delivery times, times of noisy work, times of smelly work (hopefully reduced through use of low-emitting materials), times of dusty work, access paths, and finally, separation of work areas from occupants.

## Phasing

Often, the techniques of construction will drive the physical layout of phasing plans. Multistory projects seem at first blush to be accomplished easily by floor-by-floor renovations. Control of building occupants and construction materials requires just a separation at existing floor-to-floor access points. Also, many

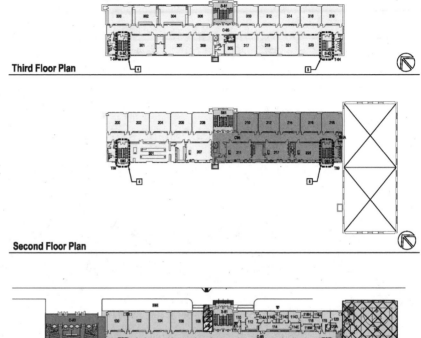

**Third Floor Plan**

**Second Floor Plan**

**First Floor Plan**

Since plumbing waste piping relies on gravity, multi-floor plumbing systems run vertically. Work on one floor ties directly to the floors above and below. Depending on the original techniques of plumbing connections, it can be difficult to modify plumbing without shutdown of other floors. Therefore, some multistory projects dominated by plumbing work (e.g., apartment renovations) can benefit from phasing that runs in stacks rather than floor by floor. *Gelfand Partners Architects.*

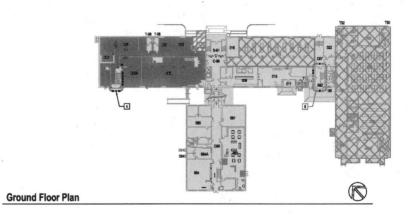

**Ground Floor Plan**

building services such as electricity, phones, IT, and HVAC commonly distribute in systems radiating within single floors. However, plumbing can throw a wrench into this scenario.

## Separation and Noise

Separation of building occupants from construction areas relies on partitions and air-handling machinery. Physically, construction zones can be separated from occupied areas with plastic sheeting. This plastic sheeting will help contain dust; however, it does nothing for noise and very little for odors. In occupancies that require better separation, plywood barriers with sound attenuation insulation combined with sealed plastic perimeters and negative air systems will separate work more effectively from occupants. In sensitive projects like schools or elderly housing, negative pressure exhaust systems can be fitted with high efficiency particulate air (HEPA) filtration at the outlet to prevent irritating or toxic particles from being spread from the work areas.

Preserving indoor air quality in renovation is even more challenging than in new construction. HVAC ducts connected to undisturbed parts of the building may traverse through construction areas. People are occupying parts of the building directly adjacent to construction activities. Many of the same measures applied in new construction are useful:

- Prevent construction debris and dust from being tracked out of work areas with walk-off mats.
- Control where workers eat and dispose of their food.
- Seal ducts by wrapping registers to prevent dust from entering occupied areas.
- Air out materials prior to installation.

Inherently noisy construction activities cannot be avoided completely, so relaying information about the expected noisy work to building occupants is essential. A wise construction team will provide information to occupants prior to construction, and help them understand the realities of living or working near a construction site. Design teams should not sugar coat this information—they should realistically portray the expected construction activities.

Importantly, construction management should focus on finding alternatives to the most disruptive activities or at least schedule them when they are likely to have least effect. Pile driving, jack hammering, steel installation, and roto-hammering all reverberate throughout a building structure. They cannot be separated completely from the rest of the building. If these can be scheduled for weekends or nights in occupied offices or schools or in the middle of the day for residential occupancies, the effect on occupants will be diminished.

## Notification

Of course, priority should be given to notification of occupants. People tend to react better when they understand what will happen. With knowledge of the particular times scheduled for loud noises, occupants can often reschedule sensitive activities, or arrange for off-site venues. Communication should be at least one way—the construction team should plan to provide some method of notification to occupants. Since construction occurs directly in a building site, simple notification boards can provide effective daily updates.

## Elevators

Many older buildings do not have adequate elevator access to allow both building occupant use and construction activities. In fact, some older buildings only have one elevator. If the elevator must be taken out of service, creative solutions for building occupants must be developed. On a recent project of ours, a six-story residential building with a single elevator required a

complete elevator overhaul. Residents, mostly elderly, faced the transformation of their building into a walk-up for three months. While the contractor pushed the elevator work on an overtime schedule, the building management provided assistance for residents. The frailest residents relocated to lower apartments and the owner hired attendants to help residents up the stairs and to carry packages up and down. A few residents decided to remain essentially home-bound for the duration, coordinating delivery of food and necessities with the construction support team.

While the situation described above lies at the extreme of occupied rehabs, providing safe and accessible routes for building occupants can be a challenge. In particular, fire egress must be rigorously maintained throughout construction. Many local fire officials will not grant permits without fully developed and approved temporary egress plans. Often these consist of the development of construction barriers (partitions, doors, enclosures, and so forth) with temporary signage and that allow emergency access to the normal egress routes, but

▲ Building occupants appreciate notifications about disruptive construction activities. While nothing can make the noise and odors of construction go away completely, timely and clear notifications prepare building occupants for upcoming work, allowing time for preparations and resulting in smoother relations between the construction team and building users. *Gelfand Partners Architects.*

▶ When emergency egress must occur through a construction area, contractors must implement procedures to ensure maintenance of egress pathways—constantly shifting personnel must keep tools, debris, and construction materials out of hallways, aisles, and corridors to allow egress through the construction to the exterior. *Gelfand Partners Architects.*

through the construction areas. The challenge here is to provide visually obvious, safe routes of egress for building occupants that are not too inviting. Construction sites are not safe places for casual visitors. Building occupants should not wander into the construction area.

# COMMISSIONING

Commissioning is a systematic process to determine if a building or its components perform as designed and work as efficiently as possible. As buildings become more and more complex an integrated approach that crosses disciplines and areas of expertise must be used in order to understand where optimization of one system affects the performance of another. The "commissioning agent" leads this cross-disciplinary process. Ideally, a commissioning agent joins the project during the design phase to assist in development of the design intent and verify if designed systems will meet that intent.

During the construction phase a commissioning agent tests the building to ensure that equipment and systems installed meet the design intent and perform as designed. Agents also observe trainings for owner's staff, often reviewing manuals and instructions to see that they gibe with sustainability goals. Finally, after completion of construction, but before the end of the warranty period, the commissioning agent retests systems and components to verify that they continue to perform as designed.

*Table 12 – Summary of Commissioning Services for Prerequisite and Credit*

| Commissioning Service | Abbreviated Commissioning (prerequisite) | Standard Commissioning (1 point) | Comprehensive Commissioning (2 points) |
|---|---|---|---|
| Design Intent Document | ✓ | ✓ | ✓ |
| Commissioning Plan | ✓ | ✓ | ✓ |
| Design Development Design Review | | | ✓ |
| Construction Documents Design Review | | ✓ | ✓ |
| Commissioning Specification Development | ✓ | ✓ | ✓ |
| Submittal Review | | | ✓ |
| Prefunctional Testing | ✓ | ✓ | ✓ |
| Functional Testing | ✓ | ✓ | ✓ |
| Commissioning Report | | ✓ | ✓ |
| Meeting Attendance | ✓ | ✓ | ✓ |
| O&M Manual Review | | ✓ | ✓ |
| Operator Training | ✓ | ✓ | ✓ |
| Systems Manual | ✓ | ✓ | ✓ |
| One-year warranty review | | ✓ | ✓ |

A comparison of various levels of commissioning required for recognition under the 2009 Collaborative for High Performance Schools Criteria rating systems for California and Texas, this table illustrates the basic and more comprehensive services available under the rubric of commissioning. *Collaborative for High Performance Schools (CHPS).*

Since commissioning entails hiring an additional consultant to the project, many owners will wonder what makes this person necessary and what part they play in sustainable renovation design. While some architects or engineers and even some contractors can accurately assess compliance with the design intent and performance of equipment, such close proximity to the building process often results in blind spots. An independent third-party agent working directly for the owner helps identify significant issues and generally leads a project to perform better than those without commissioning.

During the design phase, most projects proceed without a third-party review of the design intent.

Even constructability or quality control checks don't usually look into the basic assumptions of design or how those assumptions might affect building system performance. Energy performance, daylighting efficacy, indoor air quality, and other sustainability issues just do not exist within most quality control processes. Similarly, during construction, the volume of work and speed of communications often allow improper product substitutions to slip through, or systems startups to occur without correlation with the design intent. Finally, at the completion of construction, contractors often hand over buildings with only cursory instructions to the owner's staff, another chance for sustainable intent to be subverted by "business as usual." Be-

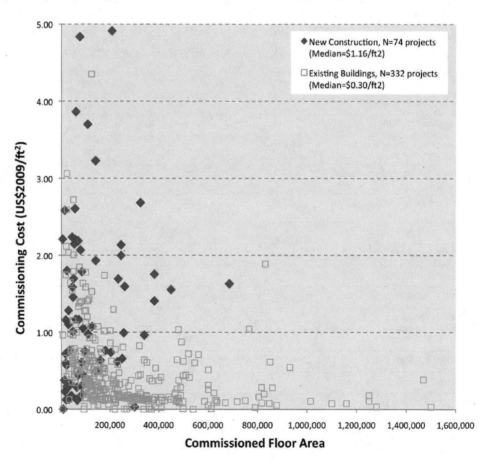

Grouped under $2/ft², with most buildings under $1/ft², commissioning costs remain a small portion of project costs while providing a great potential for benefit. *Analysis by Evan Mills, http://cx.lbl.gov.*

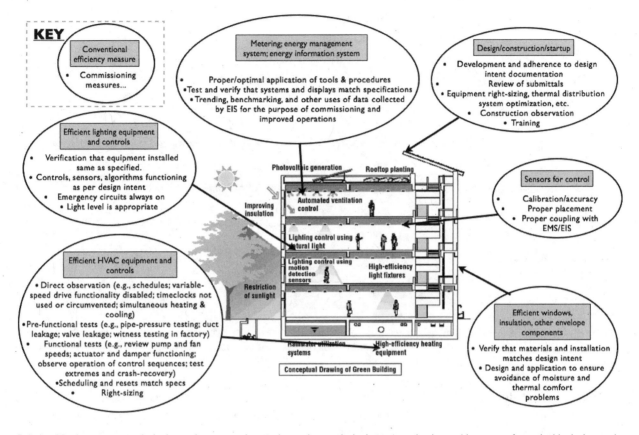

**KEY**

Conventional
efficiency measure

- Commissioning
measures...

**Efficient lighting equipment and controls**

- Verification that equipment installed same as specified.
- Controls, sensors, algorithms functioning as per design intent
- Emergency circuits always on
- Light level is appropriate

**Metering; energy management system; energy information system**

- Proper/optimal application of tools & procedures
- Test and verify that systems and displays match specifications
- Trending, benchmarking, and other uses of data collected by EIS for the purpose of commissioning and improved operations

**Design/construction/startup**

- Development and adherence to design intent documentation
- Review of submittals
- Equipment right-sizing, thermal distribution system optimization, etc.
- Construction observation
- Training

**Sensors for control**

- Calibration/accuracy
- Proper placement
- Proper coupling with EMS/EIS

**Efficient HVAC equipment and controls**

- Direct observation (e.g., schedules; variable-speed drive functionality disabled; timeclocks not used or circumvented; simultaneous heating & cooling)
- Pre-functional tests (e.g., pipe-pressure testing; duct leakage; valve leakage; witness testing in factory)
- Functional tests (e.g., review pump and fan speeds; actuator and damper functioning; observe operation of control sequences; test extremes and crash-recovery)
- Scheduling and resets match specs
- Right-sizing

**Efficient windows, insulation, other envelope components**

- Verify that materials and installation matches design intent
- Design and application to ensure avoidance of moisture and thermal comfort problems

Photovoltaic generation   Rooftop planting

Improving insulation

Automated ventilation control

Lighting control using natural light

Lighting control using motion detection sensors

High-efficiency light fixtures

Restriction of sunlight

Rainwater utilization systems   High-efficiency heating equipment

**Conceptual Drawing of Green Building**

Relationships between commissioning and energy savings: a thorough commissioning process leads to achievement of sustainable design goals through verification that systems work as intended. *Analysis by Evan Mills, http://cx.lbl.gov.*

cause of these facts, the major environmental building ratings systems all require a basic commissioning process and provide additional points for enhanced commissioning.[4]

The initial scope of commissioning will generally include review of design documents and drafting of the sustainable design intent. With more strenuous commissioning processes, the agent will re-review the design documents at a number of stages to ensure that the original design intent does not fade away due to design changes. Early in the design phase, commissioning agents help the design team set measurable sustainability goals with an eye toward energy efficiency, facilities maintenance and operation, and other sustainability characteristics. Particularly in complex projects, a consultant whose sole role prioritizes the clarification of sustainability intent should aid all team members to think more holistically, opening discussions involving the interaction of building systems. While a balkanized design intent might begin with a superinsulated energy-efficient sealed box (mechanical engineer?), sustainability discussions focused on commissioning might open up issues of daylighting and health, indoor air quality, simplified systems for easy

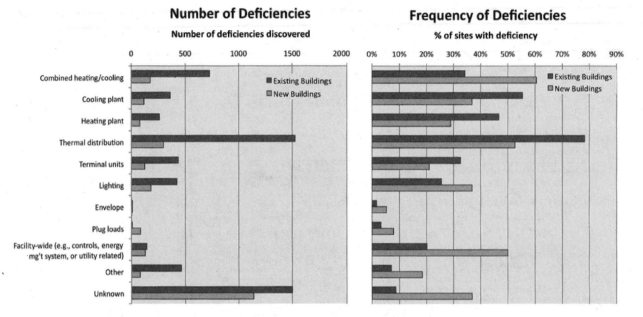

Types of problems (deficiencies) found by the commissioning process. Over half of the new buildings studied had deficiencies involving their combined heating/cooling systems, thermal distribution, or facility-wide controls. In other words, commissioning provided a process by which problems with a new building's basic function (thermal control) could be identified and remedied. *Analysis by Evan Mills, http://cx.lbl.gov.*

maintenance, and durability of systems. Ultimately, this should lead to a more balanced design approach combining available resources including natural ventilation, daylighting, durable materials, and easy-to-service systems. Commissioning states and measures the performance of integrated design.

While a commissioning plan consisting of testing, owner training, operational methods, and as-built documentation requirements develops, the agent continues to review specific aspects of the design in order to point to areas where the documents slip from the original intent. This continuing design intent check is an additional method to flag areas of disagreement or disorder for resolution. Every early chance to improve the clarity of the documents not only benefits the sustainability goals but also leads to a smoother construction process.

During construction, a commissioning agent observes installation and tests lighting and HVAC con-

trol systems to see that they work as intended. Often, the commissioning agent helps resolve disputes about how systems perform. On a recent project of ours, the commissioning agent helped the design team identify the cause of a problem in which one out of six installed HVAC package units had a computer control issue that prevented it from performing properly at morning startup, despite the subcontractor's contention that the unit had been installed properly. In fact, the units had been correctly specified and installed correctly, but because of the inherent contentiousness of a design-bid-build contract relationship, the engineer and subcontractor could only accuse each other, while the commissioning agent was able to see the issue from outside, and identify a problem that lay within the equipment. The remedy reverted to the manufacturer for resolution, based on a finding of lack of *performance* rather than an *installation* fault.

Besides the obvious benefits for better energy performance that lead from proper commissioning, CHPS identifies other benefits: [5]

- Proper and efficient equipment operation
- Better coordination between design, construction, and occupancy
- Improved indoor air quality, occupant comfort, and productivity
- Decreased potential for liability related to indoor air quality, or other HVAC problems
- Fewer occupant complaints and warranty callbacks
- Reduced operation and maintenance costs

All these benefits accrue to a project that has had careful design and carefully observed installation and startup of functional equipment. Since we know that performance of LEED-rated buildings often varies wildly from design expectations,[6] commissioning becomes an important process by which performance starts as a criterion retested numerous times throughout design and then is confirmed during the construction process.

As construction activities draw to a close, the commissioning agent is engaged in the startup of building systems. From review of pre-functional testing performed by subcontractors to the actual testing and documentation of system performance, the agent aims for the goal of smooth building operation in which the

According to an LBNL study of commissioning, the more thorough the commissioning scope, the greater the potential energy savings. *Analysis by Evan Mills, http://cx.lbl.gov.*

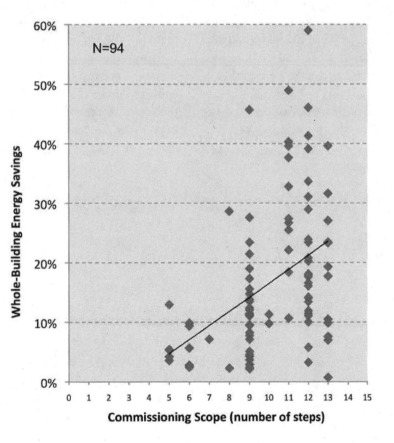

maintenance staff, building occupants, and owners understand how and why the building works the way it does and how its performance can be maintained. While it is generally the systems installers who do the training, their programs, manuals, and approaches can be overseen by the commissioning agent, bringing knowledge of the design intent to discussions of both comfort and efficiency. Without a clear picture of the sustainable operation of a building, maintenance staff sometimes reverts to past experience, potentially subverting the sustainable design intent through lack of just a few hours of effective training.

Increasingly common within the requirements of sustainability checklists, building system monitoring during the first year of use also provides invaluable information for operations and maintenance staff. Since only approximate methods can be used to simulate system operation during seasonal changes, a full year of operations provides a minimum duration needed to learn how building systems react to a wide range of conditions. Some sustainability protocols like the Living Building Challenge prioritize actual performance over design intent. While this prolongs the certifica-

tion process, actual building performance remains the sole method for verifying sustainable energy performance.

The first year of commissioning coincides with the warranty year for the construction contract. Some contracts are written to withhold a percentage of the contractor's bid until the successful completion of the first year of operation. Such a contract provision usually will be reflected in higher bids for construction projects. In the spirit of effective team creation with the contractor, scheduling and budgeting for proactive inspections and adjustments to building systems or landscape features like planting and irrigation can make the first year of building operation a continuation of the integrated project delivery rather than an occasion for argument and blame.

Grand openings of projects frequently feature thanking the lenders and investors. Without them there would be no project. But taking the occasion to thank the occupants for living through a renovation, and to celebrate the design and construction team for their hard work, is a big part of getting ready for the next sustainable renovation.

CASE STUDY

# Chicago Center for Green Technology

**Owner**   City of Chicago, Chicago Department of Environment

**Renovation Architect**   FARR Associates

**Original Building Type**   Industrial, Warehouse

**Renovation Building Type**   Office, Industrial, Assembly, Other

**Original Construction Date**   1952

**Renovation Date**   2003

**Location**   Chicago, IL

**Climate**   Humid Continental (Köppen Dfa)

**Area**   34,000 ft$^2$

**Achievement**   LEED V1.0 Platinum (38 points)

**Key Indicators**   Mixed Mode Ventilation
  Ground Source Heat Pump
  Daylighting
  Rainwater Harvesting
  Photovoltaics
  Low-Emitting Materials
  Green Roof
  Bio-Retention Field

**Energy Achievement**   40 percent less than comparable building

**Total Energy Use**   118,400 kWh/year 3.48 kWh/ ft$^2$/year   (37.46 kWh/m$^2$ year)

**Electricity After**   161,000 kWh/year   4.74 kWh/ ft$^2$/year   (51.02 kWh/m$^2$ year)

**Heating After**   33.3 kBtu/sf   10 kWh/ft$^2$/yr   (107 kWh/m$^2$ year)

**Renewables**   Photovoltaics—20 percent of electricity

On a former construction waste disposal site, the Chicago Department of Environment developed the Chicago Center for Green Technology's (CCGT), the first renovated building in the world to receive a LEED for New Construction Platinum certified rating. Housing nonprofit and for-profit environmental organizations, the building uses 40 percent less energy than comparable buildings while publicly highlighting many aspects of sustainable renovation.

Water-efficient native planting, arrayed in bioswales and a constructed wetland combine with pervious paving to slow runoff. A rainwater catchment system with 12,000-gallon cisterns provides irrigation. Heating and cooling for the building comes from a ground source heat pump system deployed under the bioswales because saturated soils have greater heat-retaining capacities. *Photography by Chris Kelly.*

A ground source heat pump system with twenty-eight 200-ft-deep wells provides heated or cooled liquid to mechanical systems. A building management system controls interior environment and shaves peak loads by dimming lights or offsetting equipment startups during high demand periods.

Abundant natural light, modulated by exterior shading and insulated, low-emissivity glazing allows reduction in electric lighting demands. High efficiency electric lighting zoned to segregate similar use areas and tied to daylight sensors and to the building management system further controls demand. An extensive photovoltaic array produces about 20 percent of the facility's electrical needs.

After abatement of abundant existing asbestos, the interior environment was further improved through the use of low–volatile organic compound (VOC) paints and adhesives. Additionally, 36 percent of building materials have recycled content. The greenhouse gas chlorofluorocarbon (CFC) is not used in any materials or building systems while hydrochlorofluorocarbons (HCFCs) are not used in any construction materials. The project helped promote the use of treated wood without the toxic arsenic-containing compounds Chromated Copper Arsenate (CCA) or Ammoniacal Copper Zinc Arsenate (ACZA). Finally, while materials were selected for their effect on indoor air quality or general environmental effect, they also were chosen to require less transportation—50 percent of materials were manufactured or assembled within 300 miles of the facility.

Photovoltaic panels provide 20 percent of building electrical use. Angled panels on the right double as sunshades, preventing hot summer sun from heating the interior while allowing low winter light to enter and warm the spaces within. Remaining roofing uses a cool roof surface to limit heat island effects. *Photography by Chris Kelly.*

## ENDNOTES

1. www.usgbc.org/ShowFile.aspx?DocumentID=1275, accessed September 7, 2010.

2. U.S. Environmental Protection Agency, www.epa.gov/lead/.

3. U.S. Environmental Protection Agency, www.epa.gov/waste/hazard/tsd/pcbs/index.htm.

4. LEED, criteria EA P1—Fundamental Building Commissioning & EA 3—Additional Commissioning; CHPS, criteria EE3.0—Fundamental Commissioning & EE3.1—Enhanced Commissioning.

5. *Best Practices Manual*, Volume V, "Commissioning," 2006 edition, Collaborative for High Performance Schools.

6. Energy Performance of LEED® for New Construction Buildings, New Buildings Institute, 2008, prepared for USGBC. This study of 552 LEED-rated buildings found that while the average energy consumption for LEED buildings met performance goals, 50 percent of buildings varied more than 25 percent from predicted values; of those, about half (25 percent of these LEED-rated buildings) performed significantly worse than designed.

# chapter 8

# HIGH PERFORMANCE RENOVATION

## TRANSFORMATION

Projections of atmospheric carbon dioxide levels lead to some very ambitious goals that must be obtained by the year 2050 to stave off the worst effects of global warming. These goals consist of rolling back our energy use to less than 80 percent of that used in 1990.

Because about 40 percent of U.S. primary energy is consumed by buildings and about half of the buildings extant today will still be in use in 2050, we propose that our efforts to sustainably renovate existing buildings be focused on holistic transformations that make our renovated buildings not just as good as new buildings, but better.

### Renovation versus Transformation

The renovations discussed throughout the rest of this book center on particular aspects of buildings, such as single components or systems that can be improved or retrofit. *Transformation* involves changing basic building systems so they leapfrog the original intent to attain more rigorous performance. Mirroring the change in expectations for building performance that occurred from the early modern period to today, we propose

that transformed buildings should look ahead thirty or even fifty years to the need for net zero or even plus-buildings—those that produce more energy than they consume. Sustainably transformed buildings will knit more closely to their bioregion, will recycle byproducts locally, and consume little if any outside energy while continuing to provide important social, cultural, and physical ties to our past and allowing us to live comfortably in the future. Thinking locally will mean understanding the whole bioregion of the town or city where we undertake projects.

As we have shown with the more modest examples throughout this book, sustainable *renovations* harness the renewable assets of their local environment. Successful *transformations* capitalize on the synergistic effects of many different systems reacting to climate and intended use. Thorough understanding of fundamental building physics and bioregional assets spur the radical transformation of an existing building, reusing the basic framework but modifying the building to respond to sun, wind, water, and air as well as to the people who will inhabit it. Sustainably transformed buildings should result in healthful and inspiring interiors, durable and protective exteriors with interconnected components that rely on the power of natural systems.

## Change of Use

Despite their fascination with novelty, Americans generally resist deeper change. In speaking about the failure of shopping malls throughout the country, Ellen Dunham-Jones and June Williamson write in *Retrofitting Suburbia*, "...*places seek to remain the same, yet by doing so they become subject to the sort of decline that can be countered only by change.*" [1] Most individuals cannot see that to resist decay communities *must* change. This necessity provides designers and community members the opportunity to retool existing buildings to enhance our future.

Evolving communities must respond to the imperatives for *sustainable* change through transforma-

tion. While some existing buildings should be torn down to reconfigure communities for a sustainable future, many buildings can fit within a sustainable framework through change of use. Driven sometimes by economic necessity, sometimes by social pressure, and occasionally by enlightened forethought, buildings undergo changes never envisioned by their orig-

▼⌄ Sited at one of the three original Levittowns, the Willingboro Library was once home to a Woolworths retail store. As part of the development of a new town center from the bones of a 1959 mall, the transformation retained the embodied energy of the building while providing a beautifully daylit library with the following metrics: Peak Electrical Demand Reduction = 57 percent, Global Warming ($CO_2$) Reduction = 44 percent, and Energy Savings = 46 percent. [2] © *Croxton Collaborative Architects. Photograph by Ruggero Vanni.*

inal builders. Whether the impetus for transforming a building comes from the need for an income stream or from development of a new, pedestrian-oriented town center, *sustainable* renovation design should hold a lead role in the vision for transformation.

When analyzing an existing building, the design team should test each feature with an eye toward the relative benefits and detriments for programmatic use, embodied energy, lifetime energy consumption, indoor environmental quality, and renewability. Features that rank high on this list, particularly those with combined prospects for programmatic change and low lifetime energy consumption, should receive high priority for retention. Those features that are not well adapted for the changed use, those that have poor en-

ergy consumption, or those that will cause problems for environmental quality, should be the first slated for demolition or removal.

Particularly in the industrialized East we have seen a number of rounds of neighborhood transformation within larger cities. Once industrial centers, these cities have undergone collapse and rejuvenation through long economic struggles that involved the wholesale repurposing of buildings. Cities like Lowell, Massachusetts, have changed from thriving centers of nineteenth-century textile industry to depressed and abandoned hulks in the mid-twentieth century to vital postindustrial regional hubs at the outset of the twenty-first century. While many of the buildings constructed during the industrial boom times were demolished during

ca 1950, 2005: Jen Library at the Savannah College of Art and Design had a previous life as a department store. Originally constructed in 1925, then renovated in the 1950s, the building was transformed into the largest art and architecture library in the country. © *The Savannah College of Art and Design, Photo by Dennis Burnet, SCAD visual media department.*

the doldrums in the 1960s and 1970s, many of the robust brick mills have been transformed from their industrial use into apartments, stores, and offices. Our task as building owners, designers, and engineers is to develop strategies that allow these buildings to take on a new life through change of use.

Reconfigured interiors provide an opportunity to improve building performance and enhance existing attributes. Fire/life safety systems often require complete overhaul because change of use usually comes with different occupancy and egress requirements. Within a changed building, mechanical and electrical systems require revision to accommodate different uses, becoming the focus for slashing energy consumption. In tandem with interior changes, added sunshades, light shelves, and new glazing transform a façade from a dumb shell to an assertive skin that regulates the effects of sunlight, moisture, and shade. Finally, elements like brick or concrete can remain as the primary cladding or, where nearing the end of their useful life, become a substrate for a new exterior insulated skin.[3]

## Additions and Deletions

When examining the suitability of a building for a new program, deficiencies are inevitably found. If they cannot be resolved within the existing building envelope, it is time to explore the possibility of an addition. Especially when presented with a featureless or mundane building, an addition can house architecturally inspiring space while providing new connections to the surroundings. An addition sometimes forms a new focus or a unique programmatic element housing a new use while reconfiguration of the rest of the existing building divorces it from its previous use.

Additions also can aid communities by infilling sites in ways that improve community configurations; providing street frontage on suburban lots, densifying neighborhoods to improve walkability, and even introducing new uses to diversify neighborhoods.[4] Especially in low-density communities dependent on the car for mobility, additions can fill the vast wastelands between widely separated buildings, complementing existing uses while allowing suburban or low-density urban areas to reach a vital level of activity that can then support such sustainable features as mass transit or district heating/cooling plants.

On the other end of the spectrum, sustainable renovations often employ a strategy of selective demolition to undo problems caused by the original building layout or to address issues of community depopulation. Shrinking cities came to the fore with the flight of East Germans after reunification. North American cities have experienced a similar, if slower decline caused by the deindustrialization in the postwar period. In places like Detroit that now feature suburban densities, strategies aim to densify existing commercial corridors and transit nodes while transitioning back to rural densities in remaining areas. This cycle back to rural uses has resulted in Detroit containing about 80 acres of agricultural land, allowing both a productive use of the abandoned land and a shortening of supply chains for food production.[6]

Another sustainable planning strategy involves the development of sustainable energy industries in small cities, capitalizing on proximity to natural resources as well as an available workforce and inexpensive land. Focusing on natural assets, depopulated areas can become regional centers for production of solar energy, wind energy, geothermal or biomass energy. Where appropriate, individual buildings can either be transformed for use in the energy sector, or deconstructed to provide area for productive land for specialized facilities.

For the City of Melbourne's (Australia) initiative to achieve carbon neutrality by 2020, researchers developed a decision chart illustrating the steps by which the city would prioritize which buildings to adapt to sustainable criteria. They noted a range of requirements for programmatic adaption of existing com-

A simple clerestory addition brings light deep into a nearly windowless dry goods store, transforming it from just a container to an enlivened space appropriate for office use.[5] © *Ted Wathen/Quadrant Studio, www. qphoto.com.*

mercial buildings. Adaptations most likely to achieve sustainable results follow these criteria:[7]

- Change of use through flexibility of the building "as found"
- Change of use through flexibility with minor adaption
- Change of use adaption/refurbishment of vacant facility
- Change of use adaption with selective demolition
- Change of use adaption with extension [addition] of the facility
- Change of use through demolition and redevelopment"

As can be seen, renovations that require selective demolition or additions are well down the list of those likely to achieve sustainability goals. So, if this holds true, demolition or addition should only be considered when other adaptations do not achieve desired programmatic results.

## Preservation of Significant Historic Characteristics

Sustainable renovations tend to focus on building technics and energy use, conserving embodied energy to some degree, but prioritizing reduction in ongoing energy use. When seeking the highest levels of energy performance, complete transformation of the building skin and internal systems is usually required. These changes come with attendant visual impacts. Historic elements of many buildings present both a challenge to technical improvements and an opportunity for preservation of cultural heritage. Older, more ornate buildings may perform more poorly than more modern, yet bland buildings, but they provide other community benefits. Their ornamentation embellishes the cityscape, while their presence can embody a community's memory, providing reminders of events past while upholding a standard of character not often found in contemporary buildings.

The relative historical merit of a building can lead to differing attitudes toward sustainable envelope improvements. Where an older, more ornate masonry building requires considerable technical challenges to be surmounted to optimize its façade; newer, less distinguished buildings lend themselves to façade optimization. *Gelfand Partners Architects.*

Cultural memory has its place in our communities, but must be balanced with other considerations. Historical merit varies widely, from issues of architectural heritage, to mainstream historical events, to exemplary evocations of vernacular history. For significant buildings, project teams should investigate a building's history to determine which features are worthy of preservation, applying standards such as the National Park Service's Secretary of the Interior's Standards for the Treatment of Historic Properties.[8] For less important buildings, the team needs to apply value judgments and consult with local preservation commissions weighing historical merit against sustainability considerations such as indoor environmental quality, energy, and water use.

As discussed previously, pre-1920 buildings tend to perform better than many newer buildings because they are more likely to have massive exterior wall systems and better-quality windows and doors with good natural light and ventilation. Often, they can be brought to a fairly high level of energy efficiency through relatively minor modifications—envelope sealing, interior insulation, weatherization, and replacement of mechanical systems. For such buildings, the important decisions will surround window replacement and interior finishes. Window replacement has a recent history of vociferous debate focusing on energy savings versus preservation and embodied energy. It appears that in most cases, weatherization of older wood windows with the addition of good quality storm windows will preserve the historic nature of the windows while only losing a few percentage points in energy efficiency.

The replacement of internal systems presents a challenge to preservation of historic interior finishes. Removal of finishes for pipes and wires often creates significant damage, so creative routing of building services is required to avoid historic areas within a building. Where finishes are sacrosanct, piping replacement can be accomplished sometimes through introduction of cured-in-place (CIP) piping rather than through removal and replacement. When new systems must be added, exposed surface piping and conduit is usually not acceptable. Introduction of decorative shielding elements can sometimes hide otherwise obtrusive modern additions.

## RETROFITTING ACTIVE ENERGY SYSTEMS

After improvements to a building's envelope, wholesale replacement of active energy systems is often the next big energy conservation goal. When combined with better insulation, improvements to daylighting, and improved solar control, lighting and heating/cooling systems can be downsized (because of smaller loads) *and* improved in efficiency. The combination of minimized sizing and efficiency gains often leads to comprehensive energy savings well over 50 percent. When a building is truly transformed, energy savings approaching 100 percent (net zero buildings) are becoming more achievable.

It must be stressed that while some systems or components can be replaced to achieve efficiencies compared to existing systems, comprehensive transformations of a building's skin combined with systems replacements achieves a significantly greater improvement. Compare the simple replacement of T-12 fluorescent lamps with more efficient T-8 lamps—achieving about 25 percent energy savings with a daylighting upgrade combined with lamp replacement achieving an 80 to 100 percent electricity savings.[9] Similarly, a 60 percent efficiency boiler can be replaced with a 90 percent efficient condensing boiler to achieve 30 percent heating efficiency gain, or, combined with envelope insulation, the boiler can be reduced in size and made more efficient, saving 80 percent.

Of course, active energy system replacement can touch on aspects of sustainability outside simple energy use. New types of systems are being developed to take advantage of regional renewable assets such as an abundance of wood fiber, or excellent solar access.[10] Optimization of active energy systems combines knowledge of systems' technical requirements along with an understanding of a particular site and its natural resources. Deep energy retrofits take advantage of synergies among passive and active energy systems, combining loads when appropriate and balancing loads across time. Responding to changing conditions within a building and harnessing local resources, complex controls predict energy transfer trends and adjust a building's systems to anticipate upcoming needs. Drawing on the resources surrounding a building, sophisticated active systems minimize the use of fossil fuels while maximizing the use of renewable resources.

## Combined Heat and Power

Combined heat and power (CHP) systems are conceptually simple but technically complex energy producers. Developed to harness waste heat from boilers or furnaces, CHP units draw heat from exhaust flues to generate steam which can then generate electricity. Conversely, some CHP systems use fuel to produce steam for electrical generation, *then* use the excess heat for domestic water or space heating or cooling. Even with today's efficient heating systems, a tremendous amount of energy still escapes through the chimney. By collecting that energy, CHP units can approach 90 percent efficiency.[11] Further, they provide an uninterruptable electrical service for much of a building's needs while reducing community pollutants by generating power without the generating and transmission losses of grid-tied electricity.[12]

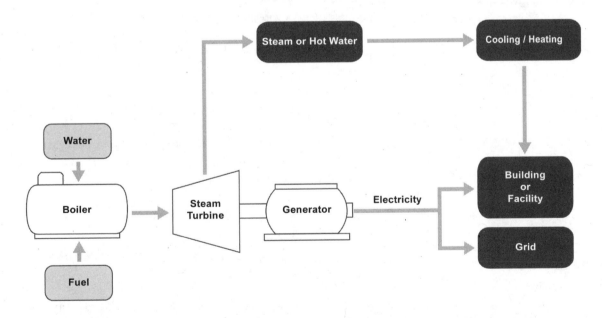

Steam boiler with steam turbine combined heat and power plant. In many regions of the country, biomass-fueled CHP systems provide the most environmentally sustainable heating and cooling option. CHP systems must be carefully coordinated with a building's other systems to provide maximum benefit. *U.S. Environmental Protection Agency.*

**HUD CHP Guide #2: Feasibility Screening for Combined Heat and Power in Multifamily Housing—Is My Building a Good Candidate for CHP?**

- Do you pay more than $0.07/ kWh on average for electricity (including generation, transmission, and distribution)?
- Are you concerned about the impact of current or future energy costs on your building?
- Is your building located in a deregulated electricity market?
- Are you concerned about power reliability? Is there a substantial financial impact to your building or residents if the power goes out for one hour? For five minutes?
- Do you have thermal loads throughout the year (including hot water, chilled water, hot air, steam, and so forth)?
- Does your building have an existing central plant?
- Do you expect to replace, upgrade, or retrofit central plant equipment within the next three to five years?

- Do you anticipate a building expansion or new construction project within the next three to five years?
- Have you already implemented energy efficiency measures and still have high energy costs?
- Are you interested in reducing your building's impact on the environment?

If you have answered "yes" to three or more of these of these questions, your facility may be a good candidate for CHP. The next step in assessing the potential of an investment in CHP is to have a Level 1 Feasibility Analysis performed to estimate the preliminary return on investment. EPA's CHP Partnership offers a comprehensive Level 1 analysis service for qualifying projects and can provide contact information to others who perform these types of analyses.

While usually pursued as part of a campus or district heating system, combined heat and power systems have become smaller in recent years, and are now applicable to individual buildings with hydronic heating and cooling systems. CHP units consist of a heat source (natural gas, biomass) that powers both a generator to produce electricity and a heat exchanger to provide useful heat.[13]

In many regions of the country, especially the Northeast and the Northwest, biomass CHP has become the system of choice. Switching from fossil fuels to a locally derived renewable fuel, biomass CHP units decrease the length of the carbon cycle from millions of years (fossil fuels) to less than 100 years (local wood pellets). Secondarily, they shorten the supply chain for

fuel from thousands of miles (petroleum) to hundreds of miles (wood heat/electricity). Lastly, by replacing municipal electrical supply, they eliminate grid distribution losses while providing more local energy production control.

Scalable from the municipal level down to an individual building, combined heat and power biomass boiler units provide a readily accessible replacement for traditional heaters and grid-tied electrical power. Within the building, a biomass CHP unit replaces a traditional water heater/boiler or furnace unit while providing a connection to the electrical supply source. Assuming that the building envelope has been transformed to reduce loads to a minimum, the biomass CHP unit would best prioritize electrical generation with "waste" heat being used to provide the minimal heat needed in the building.[14] Additionally, the federal government provides an investment tax credit for CHP projects up to fifteen megawatts.[15]

On a larger, more complex scale, biomass pyrolysis CHP operations can take advantage of even more synergies. Pyrolysis, a chemical decomposition process caused by heating organic matter in the absence of oxygen, produces two byproducts—biochar[16] and bio-oil (which can be refined to biogas[17]). Starting with agricultural waste—corn stalks, chaff, husks, leaves, stems, and the like—pyrolysis installations provide high nutrient biochar back to the farmers, increasing yields, while providing a clean fuel source. If carefully coordinated, pyrolysis captures waste heat from the pyrolysis kiln and gas-powered electricity generator to preheat dryers that start the biomass process. Gas produced by the pyrolysis kiln and the char gasifier is used to power the electricity generator. In a closed loop, the input is agricultural waste and the outputs are electricity, biogas, and heat that can all be used to serve buildings. Both the biogas and electricity can be used to either heat or cool a space. Somewhat surprisingly, the heating of agricultural waste (pyrolysis) can be used for cooling or refrigeration through the intermediary of an absorption chiller run by biogas.[18] Note that with either standard—or pyrolysis—CHP units, biomass must be restricted to woody *waste* material rather than the inappropriate use of whole, virgin trees.

## Solar Heating and Power

In order to move toward a more sustainable future, design teams need to harness the power of the sun beyond passive strategies. *Active* systems that respond to solar radiation can be used to daylight, heat, and *cool* buildings. Particular properties of existing buildings sometimes preclude these strategies, so an understanding of a building's original principles will allow designers to choose which strategy might be best suited to a building and its environment. Among the options for active solar systems are daylight tracking devices, solar fiber-optic lighting, active solar heating (hot water), and active solar cooling systems as well as the ubiquitous photovoltaic power generation.

# Biomass Liquefaction via Pyrolysis

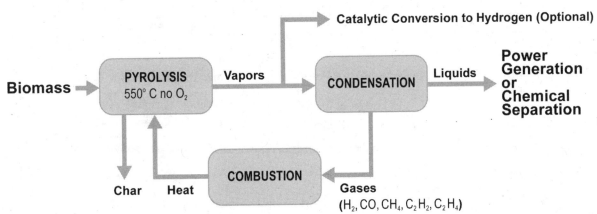

Biomass Pyrolysis: Inputs = Crop Waste, Outputs = Electricity, Heat, Biofuel. Closed-loop power generation for large installations. *U.S. Department of Energy.*

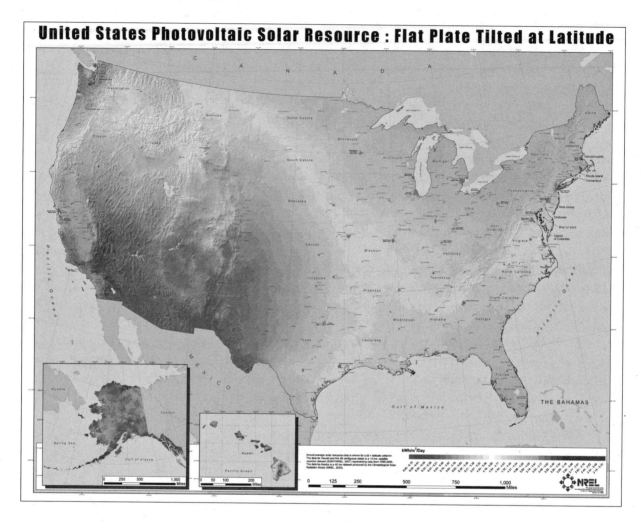

United States Photovoltaic Solar Resource : Flat Plate Tilted at Latitude

### Threshold Values Proposed to Compute the Potential for the Corresponding Solar Techniques[19]

| Solar Strategy | (Solar Irradiation during Heating Season) | |
| --- | --- | --- |
| | Threshold for Systems on Façades | Threshold for Systems on Roofs |
| Passive thermal heating | 216 kWh/m² solar irradiation during the heating season | Same as for façades |
| Photovoltaic systems | 800 kWh/m² annual solar irradiation | 1,000 kWh/m² annual solar irradiation |
| Daylighting systems | 10 klx mean daylight illuminance during office hours (8 to 18 hr) | Same as for façades |
| Solar thermal collectors | 400 kWh/m² annual solar irradiation | 600 kWh/m² annual solar irradiation |

◄Active solar energy harvesting systems rely on the availability of sunshine. Ranging from an annual average of about 4.0 kWh/m²/day (≈1,400 kWh/m²/year) in the Great Lakes and eastern part of the country to almost 7.0 kWh/m²/day (≈2,500 kWh/m²/year) in the desert Southwest, solar radiation provides ample power for many building systems. Assuming a benchmark exemplary building with only 100 kWh/m²/year load, active solar systems should be sufficient to provide net zero energy use in low-rise buildings. *U.S. Department of Energy.*

While not directly producing energy from the sun, an intriguing project from MIT in 2006 took on the challenge of retrofitting an existing 1950s curtain wall building with an active double-skin façade that incorporated a rotating anidolic reflector system to reduce power needs through daylighting.[20] The project added a second glass skin on top of the refurbished existing curtain wall. Within the gap between the skins, the designers deployed a horizontal reflector that gathered daylight from directly above the building. Relying on diffused daylight rather than on the angle of direct sunlight, this system reflects daylight deep into the interior, even on the north façade. Further, the exterior reflectors are motorized, able to respond to changing sunlight conditions.

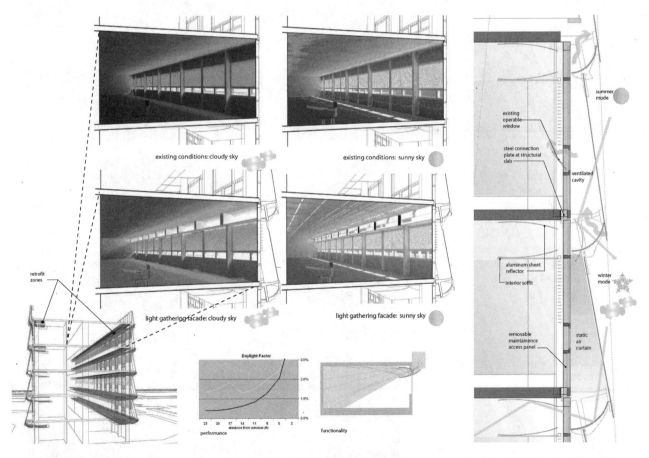

While anidolic daylighting reflectors—shaped to throw diffused daylight deep into a building—are sometimes installed in fixed position, this design project proposes to motorize them, allowing seasonal as well as daily adjustments in daylighting. Curing the ills of a typical curtain wall, the system could potentially cut lighting energy by 60 percent. *Courtesy of Edward O. Rice and Sian Kleindienst.*

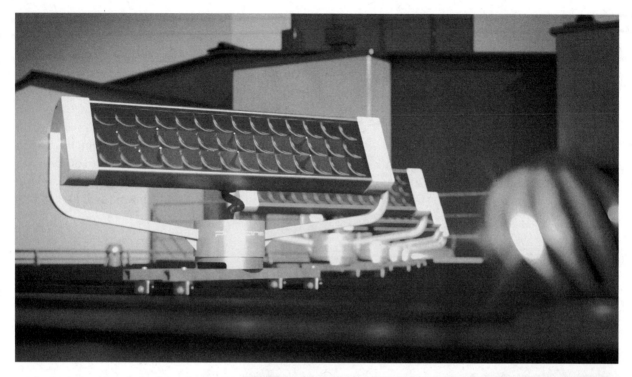

▲▶ Rooftop solar collectors channel sunlight into fiber-optic cables that snake through the building to light fixtures at interior areas. Fiber-optic daylighting is sometimes criticized for its "blue" light. Although the spectrum matches daylight, we have become accustomed to yellower interior light from incandescent lamps or even fluorescent lamps that have been tuned to more closely match incandescent. *Parans.*

Reducing lighting power requirement, heliostat daylighting employs a similar conceptual framework—the use of mirrors to reflect daylight deep into a building. However, heliostats continuously track the sun to reflect light to secondary mirrors that distribute the light within a structure. Often the daylight is terminated at reflective/refractive prisms to spread the concentrated light. Advantages of these systems are that they can provide daylight deep within buildings, but disadvantages include the required maintenance on the tracking system and the line-of-sight space needed to provide a path for the light to get from the roof to the areas being daylit.

Yet another method to transport daylight deep into a building utilizes fiber-optic cables, often called Hybrid Solar Lighting, or HSL. Usually coupled with a sun-tracking, concentrating collector on the roof, HSL systems channel daylight through fiber-optic cables to a "light fixture" that distributes the daylight within a space.

The power of the sun easily generates hot water for domestic use or hydronic heating. Low-tech flat plate collectors simply run black pipes through glazed panels, soaking up heat from sunshine. More effective *direct active* systems use controllers to regulate the time and volume of hot water, usually in conjunction with an insulated storage tank which includes a heating element to supplement solar hot water during cloudy weather or at night. *Indirect active* systems are even more efficient; they use two loops, a heating liquid (heat transfer fluid—HTF) such as glycol which is used to heat the separate reservoir of water and a second water loop from the storage reservoir to building uses. More expensive evacuated tube collectors limit heat loss when compared to flat plate collectors; however, they are not necessary in sunny climates where heating temperatures remain high. They are most effective in cloudy or cold climates where collector losses are more significant.

Solar absorption chillers provide an effective method for cooling in hot sunny climates. Using a lithium bromide mixture which boils at a very low temperature (giving up heat), a small photovoltaic panel can provide the minimal power to run the pumps and fan necessary to achieve a refrigeration cycle. Heat from solar hot water is used to re-condense the lithium bromide liquid without using a mechanical condenser (and all its energy). Solar absorption chillers run at only 10 to 20 percent of the energy required for a conventional compressor-based air-conditioner, becoming a very desirable system.[21] Additionally, this system can double as an indirect solar hot water system to provide heating hot water in the winter.

Lastly, and most commonly, photovoltaic (PV) panels provide electricity to replace grid-tied power. Often installed despite lengthy payback periods that can run to twenty to thirty years, they are a visible symbol of environmentalism. When combined with rigorous energy saving programs that eliminate wasteful building loads, PV panels can provide the last increment of renewable energy to make a building project a net zero or "plus" building. The technics of PV are well understood—orientation and solar access are most important. Panels can be either separately mounted or integrated within new building materials (building integrated photovoltaic, BIPV). More importantly, energy conversion efficiency of panels has steadily increased while cost per installed watt has steadily declined.[22] More importantly, in terms of energy expended to produce PV systems versus the amount they replace, Energy Payback Times (EPBT) run from one to three years,[23] making their overall environmental impact significantly on the plus side.

Looking toward the future, new applications may be found for solar-powered Stirling engines. While utility-scale Stirling engine installations produce electricity in a few locations, building-scale electrical gen-

The renovations at the affordable housing development Villa Nueva Apartments in San Ysidro, California, included PV arrays by Borrego Solar on 42 buildings. The 687 kW system takes advantage of roofs that slope toward the south and west, and provides 70 percent of the development's electrical needs, approximately 80,000 kWh per month.[24] *Borrego Solar Systems.*

erating units are becoming available. Often set up as combined heat and power units, Stirling engines harness heat produced by solar concentrators, producing alternating current electricity while spinning off excess heat for heat or hot water.

## Wind Power

Like solar, wind power generation provides seemingly free and endless energy. Wind power, however, comes with even more problems to overcome in developing successful applications. First and foremost, the wind does not always blow. While solar access often peaks during periods of high electrical use, wind is extremely variable and rarely aligns with needs. Therefore, wind generation should be focused on powering uses that are not time sensitive, or developed as a small component of a distributed grid-tied generation system. In a smart-grid energy scheme, wind power provides an

offset for primary fossil-fuel power generation, combining with other renewable resources like solar and tidal action to account for growing portions of our renewable power grid.

Criticism of wind power generation at the building scale has centered on discrepancies between manufacturers' claims and *in situ* performance, often attributed to turbulence caused by generators' relation to obstructions.[25] For building-integrated wind turbines this problem becomes particularly acute. Because wind turbines require fairly high cut-in (startup) wind speeds, and have mass that must be accelerated, constantly changing wind speeds caused by turbulence result in generators performing well below their rated efficiencies. Compounding turbulence losses, noise and vibrations developed by the wind generators can be translated through the building frame to elements like metal decks that amplify the sound. Isolating noise and vibrations can be especially difficult because they vary with wind speed, requiring a range of dampening elements.[26]

Overriding these concerns is the fact that wind generation is directly related to the area of wind swept out by the generator's blades. Buildings generally do not have enough available area to make building-integrated wind financially feasible. While general wind information is available (NOAA, local airport reports), individual sites must be carefully assessed for variations in wind patterns affected by local geography. Many projects install a temporary weather station to measure actual wind speeds to compare with local weather stations.

However, if turbines can be installed on appropriate sites distant from obstructions and the effects of noise, power generation can become efficient enough to warrant installation. According to the American Wind Energy Association (AWEA), the cost per kilowatt of installed grid-connected small wind energy systems ranges from about $3,000 to $6,000.[28] If these prices hold, wind power generation will remain similar in cost with photovoltaic, although rebates vary widely by region.[29] Efficiencies rise with size; power

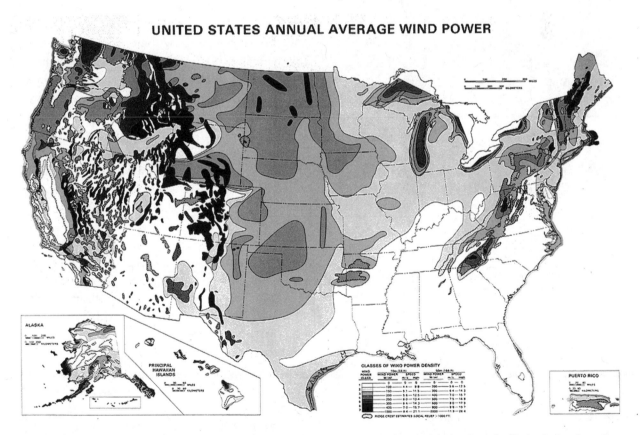

UNITED STATES ANNUAL AVERAGE WIND POWER

Average available wind varies greatly throughout the country. Local variations must also be researched to determine if a local microclimate is suitable for sustained winds. Despite common perceptions, wind generators will not work everywhere, and often encounter insurmountable obstacles in urban environments. *U.S. Department of Energy.*

These wind generators are mounted on a parking garage in a wind tunnel between two buildings. [27] This location moderates issues caused by turbulence created by the buildings, and vibration created by the turbines. While building-integrated wind generators might seem fruitful, performance often lags due to turbulent and variable winds. Larger, taller generators set away from buildings tend to perform better. *Courtesy of Windspire Energy.*

generated varies with the *cube* of wind speed, so for remote locations, bigger generators and windier sites make wind power affordable.

## Geothermal Heat Exchange

Utility-scale geothermal heating is limited primarily to the American West where geologic activity provides significant underground heat that can be tapped directly to provide heat or steam-generated power. [30] However, unless an existing project is large enough to overcome drilling expenses, direct use is less likely to be feasible than geothermal heat exchange. For individual buildings, "geothermal" energy usually refers to geothermal heat exchange (geo-exchange or ground-coupled heat pump)—the use of the nearly constant temperature of the Earth to provide a heat/cool sink that can be exchanged through a circulated liquid. Systems generally consist of a heat pump tied to a network of underground piping that allows the heat transfer liquid to either deposit heat energy in the Earth or extract it, transferring the useful energy to a building. Geothermal exchange systems work best when a building has nearly equal requirements (in terms of heat energy transfer) for both heating and cooling and deep piping installations are possible in order to reach levels of steady underground temperatures. Systems can also become effective if shallow piping runs can take advantage of seasonal fluctuations of underground temperature to overcome one-sided exchanges of heat to the Earth. [31]

While it is possible to replace the boiler and condenser of a forced air system with a geothermal heat pump, the relative value of geothermal heat exchange may be lost amid the inefficiencies of transitions from the heat transfer liquid to heated/cooled air. However, in buildings with a hydronic system, it is worth investigating whether local ground conditions allow replacement of the fossil fuel heating/cooling source with geothermal heat exchange. In many locales, especially where passive systems are not sufficient to meet the loads in an existing building, geothermal can be combined with solar hot water or PV systems to balance energy transfers. In climates with little cooling load, geothermal can

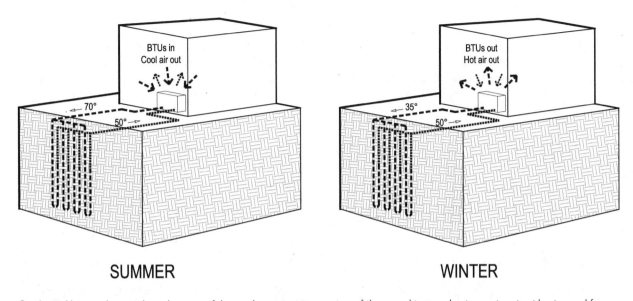

**SUMMER** **WINTER**

Geothermal heat exchange takes advantage of the nearly constant temperature of the ground to use a heat pump to extract heat or cool from the Earth to supply it to the building. Geothermal heating can be supplemented by solar hot water heating or PV to balance heat transfer and further reduce energy demand. *U.S. Department of Energy.*

be supplemented by solar hot water. Where cooling predominates, geothermal cooling can be aided by photovoltaic power.

Water bodies can also be useful heat sinks for geothermal heat pump systems, but care must be taken that the heat transfer does not change the temperature of a water body enough to affect its environmental balance. One very interesting example of using available local water resources is the Zollverein School of Management and Design in Essen Germany. Constructed in 2006, the building employs "active" insulation.[32] Rather than installing thick insulated walls, the designers take advantage of an abandoned mine that must pump water out continuously to prevent collapse. The building routes the constant-temperature water to a heat exchanger, then pumps liquid through the building walls to heat and insulate the school.

## WASTE WATER STRATEGIES

Since most existing buildings have adequate connections to municipal or project-based waste water systems, sustainability efforts are usually focused on reduction of energy use for the individual project or benefits to the overall local environment.[33] Energy reductions can be achieved through harvesting heat or usable fuel from waste water. However, looking outside the direct project benefits, waste water strategies often have an effect on communal energy use through efficiencies achieved by on-site effluent treatment, through on-site capture of the beneficial attributes of waste water, and through recharging of local aquifers or surface waters. Under the rubric of Low Impact Development (LID), stormwater management can also be used to manage and filter runoff to reduce the spread of pollutants.[34]

## Waste Water Reuse

In order to limit the environmental effects of waste water, many effluent sources can be tapped and recycled on-site. The East Bay Municipal Utility District *Watersmart Guidebook* states, "Alternative sources of water, which can be found on-site and used in these processes, may include:

- Rainwater and stormwater
- Air-conditioner condensate
- Filter and membrane reject water
- Foundation drain water
- Cooling-tower blowdown
- On-site treated grey water and wastewater

Potential uses of alternate on-site sources of water include:

- Irrigation
- Cooling-tower makeup
- Toilet and urinal flushing
- Makeup for ornamental ponds, pools, or fountains
- Swimming pools
- Laundries
- Processes
- Any other use not requiring potable water"[36]

While most "groundwater reclamation" projects are engaged at a municipal scale to replenish historic aquifers, individual projects aid these efforts by providing on-site filtration and percolation strategies where geologically appropriate. On-site biofiltration of stormwater provides benefits both in terms of groundwater recharge and in minimizing off-site treatment. Biofiltration swales can effectively transport, control, and filter stormwater, diverting it from municipal wastewater treatment systems—decreasing the pressure on existing piping systems while reducing the immense energy required to mechanically purify wastewater.[35] Further, stormwater can be detained or retained to allow recharge of local aquifers or for irrigation or other purposes.

Rainwater harvesting takes LID concepts one step further by collecting the rainwater and using it at least once before it infiltrates or leaves the site. Since rooftop drains often connect directly to sanitary systems, it may be necessary to provide a whole new drainage system to accommodate harvesting. Once collected, rainwater can be stored for nonpotable uses such as flushing toilets, irrigation, or HVAC process. Of course, because rainwater carries pollutants and particles, diversion of the first increment of each rain (first flush) and then ongoing filtration is usually required. But since each gallon saved by rainwater collection replaces imported potable water, new systems will cut off-site electrical use as well as on-site costs. In general, when a project modifies existing building services, many sources can be tapped in order to maximize water reuse (see sidebar).

## Graywater Recirculation

Graywater reuse is second only to rainwater harvesting in reduction of potable water consumption. Graywater systems typically divert drainage from all water-using fixtures except toilets (black water). Graywater often accounts for 80 percent of building waste water, so significant reductions in imported potable water can be achieved if filtered graywater can feed back into building uses such as flushing toilets, washing clothes, or machinery processes. Depending on the organic and chemical composition, graywater systems (generally high in nitrogen and organic matter) often provide subsurface drip irrigation directly, or through a storage tank. Of course, the quality of graywater directly affects the types of uses that can be undertaken. Where a building program also includes the elimination of toxic cleaning products or the use of biodegradable maintenance materials, graywater is quite appropriate for irrigation, even with minimal filtration. However, because of the possibility of pathogens, systems should avoid direct human contact with graywater.

If graywater cannot be cleaned of toxins or chemicals because of limited control over occupant activity, it can be filtered, then used for toilet flushing or, if filtered more assiduously, used for secondary washing, process loads, or irrigation.  In general, any building activities that do not require potable water can use filtered graywater.

Projects in Australia have taken a more aggressive stance toward water conservation, either employing on-site processing of black water or venturing into "sewer mining" ("water mining"), the capturing of sewage passing a site in order to reuse it after on-site purification. With the advent of small sewage processing plants (the size of a shipping container) usually using membrane filtration, project-based treatment can lead to tremendous savings in potable water use. Generally used only in arid regions with severe pressure on potable water sources, sewer mining can find applications in other regions where renewable resources can be used to power the pumps and machinery necessary.

## Reuse of Building System Water

Some innovative buildings look past graywater harvesting itself to harvesting secondary aspects of waste water, namely the heat embodied in sewage. Allied with sewer mining, waste water heat recovery systems shunt the typical waste water through a heat exchanger before it passes out of the building. Tied to the building's water heating system for either space heating or domestic hot water, the heat exchanger merely captures a product that would normally drain down the sewer.

## Living Machine Waste Water Treatment

Employed in projects that aim to reclaim waste water to reduce potable water use, or to replace traditional sewage treatment facilities, "living machine" or "eco-machine" natural waste water treatment facilities employ microbes, plants, and animals to clean waste water. Pioneered by Dr. John Todd, [37] natural waste water treatment systems typically contain a closed tank that begins anaerobic digestion by microbes, then a series of open tanks where aerobic reactions clean waste water through the actions of bacteria, zooplankton, phytoplankton, snails, and fish. Finally, water is separated from any solids in a clarifier tank, then flows through ecological fluidized beds that provide final cleaning.

Depending on climate and volume, natural waste water treatment facilities can be either inside or outside. When inside, their plant communities tend to consist of tropical plants (in northern climates where there is less sunlight available) or localized plants in more southerly areas. Typically becoming economical and energy-efficient when waste water quantities are over 100,000 gallons per day, these systems require distinct expertise when first designed, but can be managed by locally trained staff with occasional visits by experts to retune the natural systems if disrupted by unexpected inflows. When combined with local agricultural infrastructure, natural waste

An eco-machine consists of tanks containing plant and animal communities that clean waste water. Eco-machines can be indoors in greenhouses or outdoors as constructed wetlands. Ecological costs include the power needed to pump effluent into the system, routine maintenance costs, and heating costs for greenhouses in northern climates. *Gelfand Partners Architects.*

water treatment facilities can also be used for food production (mushrooms, fish, greens) by importing compost for food production and reusing waste heat from composting.

## PASSIVE HOUSE (PASSIVHAUS) DESIGN AND EXISTING BUILDINGS

Passive House ("PassivHaus" in Germany) is a set of standards for particular facets of building physics that result in an extremely energy efficient package. Developed in Europe, with the first buildings constructed in Germany around 1990, the standard primarily applies

to new houses. However, because of the readily understood standards and the superior results they engender, Passive House criteria can be applied to other building types *and* to existing buildings. The standard requires use of a superinsulated exterior that eliminates thermal bridging, an airtight envelope, and use of a heat recovery ventilation system.

With new buildings, passive solar design combined with the robust envelope can result in a building that requires almost no mechanical heating. Existing buildings without good solar orientation might not easily meet the standard. Further, some building uses require more primary energy (per square foot) than residential use. However, in general, the standard

---

### Passive House Performance Characteristics[38]

- Airtight building shell ≤ 0.6 ACH (air changes per hour) at 50 pascal pressure, measured by blower-door test.
- Annual heat requirement ≤ 15 kWh/m²/year (4.75 kBtu/ft²/year)
- Primary energy (heat, hot water, electricity) ≤ 120 kWh/m²/year (38.1 kBtu/ft²/year)

In addition, the following are recommendations, varying with climate:

- Window u-value ≤ 0.8 W/m²/K
- Ventilation system with heat recovery with ≥ 75 percent efficiency with low electric consumption at 0.45 Wh/m³
- Thermal bridge free construction ≤ 0.01 W/mK

---

provides an excellent benchmark for achievement; methods applied to Passive House designs certainly improve existing buildings of all types. It should be noted that the standard applies best to northern, temperate climates and may not adapt well to very cold climates or hot/humid climates where humidity control and cooling are paramount.[39]

Extensive insulation, envelope sealing, insulated windows, and heat recovery ventilation can be added to existing apartment buildings to meet the Passive House standard, resulting in energy savings in excess of 80 percent.[40] Some have voiced concerns about moist interior air condensing within a superinsulated wall, eventually causing structural damage. Passive House advocates note that by concentrating on insulation and especially on air barriers, the standards lead to buildings where moist interior air has no path to reach cold surfaces.[41] As noted in Chapter 4, problems with moisture inside walls tend to occur from drafts—air infiltration to a cold surface—rather than from migration of water vapor.

## Passive Solar Design

Whether designing to the Passive House standard or not, passive solar design is an essential component of high energy performance buildings. Overcoming poor solar orientation of existing buildings while taking ad-

vantage of the sun's power to heat or cool them can be a distinct challenge. When solar access is available, modifications to glazing, provision of sunshading, and even enclosure of balconies to create "winter gardens" or buffer spaces can be effective. Adding sunshading can be as important as correct glazing. Fixed sunshades come in many premanufactured configurations (see Chapter 4), while active sunshading devices are becoming more common. European companies are starting to penetrate the U.S. market, providing motorized venetian blinds and motorized awnings—systems that are relatively common in Europe.

Because of envelope thermal requirements, Passive House designs require replacement of windows in all but the mildest climates. When choosing thermal glazing, special coatings can be selected to tune the glass to the heating/cooling needs of each façade as appropriate for the climate. Generally, for passive solar heating, high solar heat gain coefficients (SHGC) and high visible light transmittance are desired in colder climates. Low SHGC with high transmittance is desirable on east or west façades where overheating is a concern or in areas with large cooling loads.

Especially in colder climates, creating glazed balconies or sunspaces facing south can provide two benefits. First, these occasionally occupied spaces buffer the main space from temperature swings. During hot

## Thermal Glazing

Passive House standards require thermal glazing. Glazing must be chosen to match the desired effect for the building location and solar orientation.

- Single glazing is about 5 to 6 W/m²K.
- Double glazing around 2 to 3 W/m²K.
- Triple glazing 0.6 to 1.0 W/m²K.

Glass with low-emissivity (low-e) coatings on the inside help prevent radiation transfer to keep occupants from feeling cold during the winter or hot during the summer. A simple test to determine where an existing low-e coating lies is to hold up a candle next to the glass—it will reveal a different color reflection at the coating.

weather, interior sunshades and operable windows will provide a shaded semi-exterior space to provide a transition from inside to outside. During cold weather, they act as solaria, heating up, often above interior needs, providing a heating source for the rest of the interior. Careful analysis must be made of the potential use, because over the years occupants begin to desire that these spaces be heated or cooled like the rest of the interior, sometimes adding energy-inefficient systems that defeat their original purpose. Therefore, new sunspaces should have a distinctly different design with "outdoor" materials to accentuate their intent as transition spaces rather than main occupancies.

Further concerns surround the tendency of passive buildings in moderate climates to overheat in hot weather, especially in renovations of buildings without solar shading. Careful attention to the interaction of glazing, insulation, and especially solar shading can overcome these concerns and should be a normal part of design of a passive solar building.[42]

## Superinsulation

The heart of Passive House criteria, superinsulation allows drastic reductions in energy use for heating and cooling. Difficulty with detailing is the greatest challenge to meeting the Passive House standard, and may prevent some projects from achieving the same

energy savings as new construction. To prevent thermal bridging, insulation should be added to the exterior of the existing walls wherever possible. In order to provide a continuous insulation barrier, eaves can be extended in order to insert insulation over the existing framing. Basements, crawlspaces, and perimeter foundations require excavation to short circuit the thermal bridge formed with the ground.

Climatic conditions must drive the details of insulation and moisture barriers to prevent buildup of water within the wall assembly. Particularly around openings, coordination of window and door location with insulation must avoid thermal bridges where cold can migrate toward the interior, providing an opportunity for midwall condensation. In hot/humid climates, careful study of dewpoints within walls and moisture management at the exterior of new insulation can drive extensive energy reductions through the power of the thermal mass to be a heat sink for interior cooling. In a renovation, the addition of insulation needs to be designed strategically so that benefits from existing thermal mass are retained and new moisture problems avoided.

In cold and moderately cold climates, large energy savings can be expected through application of exterior insulation. Where existing building energy use is dominated by heating needs, it is most affected by improvements to infiltration and insulation. If a cold climate has a significant summer cooling period or inte-

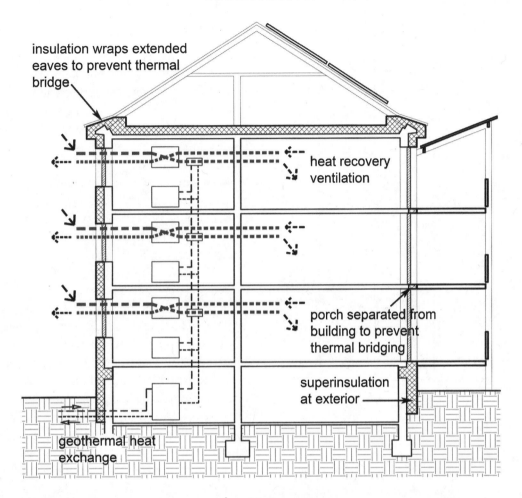

insulation wraps extended eaves to prevent thermal bridge

heat recovery ventilation

porch separated from building to prevent thermal bridging

superinsulation at exterior

geothermal heat exchange

Superinsulation and insertion of new insulated windows resulted in 94 percent reduction in energy use in an apartment renovation in Ludwigshafen, Germany. Eaves were extended to allow insulation to completely wrap the existing roof/wall intersection. Excavation at the perimeter wall allowed new insulation to extend into the ground to minimize another thermal bridge.[43] *Gelfand Partners Architects.*

rior loads dominate, exterior insulation systems could be combined with night flushing/precooling or chilled beam cooling in order to moderate diurnal temperature swings caused by occupant loads combined with high exterior temperatures.

Exterior insulation systems can be especially effective on buildings with masonry or precast concrete envelopes. While the durability of concrete and masonry exterior cladding would be lost, the benefits of thermal mass inside the insulation would greatly enhance energy savings.

Of course, some projects do not lend themselves to exterior insulation. Where unavoidable, interior insulation can be employed; however, moisture migration issues become much more complex and require special attention to detailing. Thorough analysis of moisture

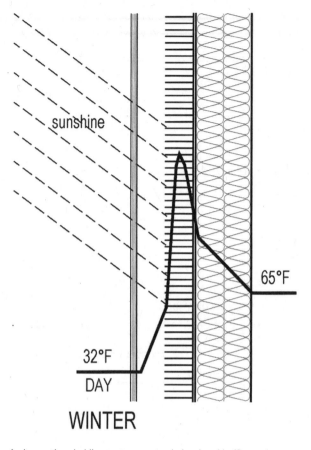

An innovative cladding system uses a dark-colored baffle sandwiched behind glass to effectively raise the temperature of the exterior of the wall to minimize thermal difference from inside to outside.[44] In winter, the sun penetrates deep into the baffles, heating the exterior surface well above the internal temperature. In summer, the higher sun angle does not penetrate as far, so the exterior temperature is not raised as much. *Gelfand Partners Architects.*

movement with particular attention to cold surfaces is vitally important, particularly since interior insulation schemes tend to leave significant thermal bridges at floor/wall intersections. Finally, as discussed in relation to windows, superinsulation schemes in warmer climates require coordination with solar shading and internal loads to prevent overheating.

## Sealing the Envelope

Sealing the envelope against air infiltration is critical to the performance of a building trying to achieve Passive House standard. Existing buildings generally experience two to seven air changes per hour through infiltration. In other words, during the heating season, leaking interior air is exchanged for exterior air so that the whole building volume must be reheated two to seven times per hour. Depending on the exterior air temperature, the building consumes tremendous amounts of energy just to heat and reheat the uncontrolled air leaking into the building. Cooling season results are similar. To prevent this uncontrolled air exchange, Passive House requires that buildings achieve 0.6 or fewer air changes per hour (ACH).

To meet this infiltration standard, edges of openings must be caulked, duct and pipe penetrations sealed, and gaskets provided at windows and doors. With these few adaptations, an existing building can expect dramatic infiltration improvements. However, there are likely to be many more openings still left in the envelope. A common scenario at this point is to run a blower door test. Generally set at a pressure of 50 Pascal, blower door tests confirm that a building has become tight enough, or provide an opportunity for deploying smoke sticks to find the locations of remaining air leaks. Marked, then filled with sealants or expanded foam, all the openings must be sealed so the building will achieve less than 0.6 ACH at 50 Pascal.

While these methods work well for buildings receiving a comprehensive insulation upgrade, two product types can simplify the insulation/infiltration procedure for buildings receiving renovations that do not remove interior finishes. If cavity walls are present, icynene or polyurethane foam—soy-based or synthetic—can be injected into wall cavities. While improving insulation, these materials also expand to fill gaps and cracks, effectively sealing the envelope. Combined with exterior insulation and a new vapor barrier, expanded foam insulation readily achieves an exterior envelope seal.

## Introducing Fresh Air—Heat and Energy Exchange

The introduction of fresh air into tight buildings is critical for both indoor air quality and human comfort. Unfortunately, the more fresh air introduced, the more energy is expended to heat or cool it to maintain comfort. Engineers have devised heat recovery ventilation systems that capture the heat or cool leaving a building and transfer it to the entering fresh air. Since tight buildings accentuate problems with interior moisture buildup, the Passive House standard and building codes require ventilation. While different jurisdictions and different occupancies will require different *levels* of ventilation, Passive House merely requires a *low-energy* ventilation system with at least 75 percent *efficiency* in terms of heat exchange.

In cold climates, active heat recovery ventilation is becoming more common, so systems are achieving much higher levels of efficiency and lower levels of energy use. Consisting of an enthalpy wheel or crossed baffles that transfer heat from outgoing exhaust air to incoming air without actually mixing the two streams, an active heat recovery system requires that intake and exhaust ducts cross at least once. In renovation projects this can be a challenge since older buildings often did not provide for room ducts at all. In mid-century and later buildings, duct routes can often be reused; however, efficiency is often lost in routing an intake location distant enough from exhaust to prevent mixing of exterior airstreams.

Warm/hot climates can use similar systems, although more care is needed to capture moisture from incoming cooled air when it condenses at the heat exchanger. Some systems employ air-to-liquid heat exchangers, essentially running a separate chiller coil (backwards) through the exhaust air to partially cool the incoming hot air. These systems are called active *energy* recovery ventilation systems and are only used in hot/humid climates.

Perhaps the most attractive option is a passive heat recovery ventilation system powered by wind and stack ventilation (see Chapter 5). Pioneered in the BedZed project near London, and best suited for cold/continental climates, a passive heat recovery system works by having exhaust and intake air pass through a high-efficiency heat exchanger just below a wind cowl that boosts airflow by harnessing the passage of wind. The cowl has a small intake nozzle with a large outflow vent that is steered downwind by a wind vane. The difference in pressure between the small intake vent and large exhaust draws air out of the building from high-level exhaust grilles while providing fresh air through low-level grilles. High-level exhaust grilles aid in ventilation through the stack effect—temperature difference between the upper and lower air within a room. Unfortunately, there is a three-story limit for effective use of passive heat recovery ventilation; otherwise the 85 percent efficient system would seem a no-brainer for most buildings in appropriate climates.

ZedFactory has also developed a passive heat recovery system for cross-ventilation; however, it is more dependent on dominant wind patterns and can be very tricky to implement because of the variations that occur around a building due to shifting winds.

## Edith Green—Wendell Wyatt Federal Office Building

**Owner**   General Services Administration (GSA)

**Renovation Architect**   SERA Architects, Cutler Anderson Associates

**Original Building Type**   Office

**Renovation Building Type**   Office

**Original Construction Date**   1974

**Renovation Date**   2013

**Location**   Portland, OR

**Climate**   Oceanic (Köppen Csb)

**Area**   526,000 ft$^2$ gross (439,000 ft$^2$ tower, 87,000 ft$^2$ parking)

**Achievement**   LEED v3 Platinum target (tracking 82 points)

**Key Indicators**   Envelope Replacement—Optimized Daylighting
   Hydronic Radiant Ceiling Heating and Cooling System
   Dedicated Outdoor Air System (DOAS)
   High Efficiency Lighting with Advanced Controls
   Plug Load Reduction
   Rainwater Catchment
   High Efficiency Plumbing Fixtures

**Energy Achievement**   60 to 65 percent less energy than comparable building

**Total Energy Use Before**   94 kBtu/ ft$^2$/yr   27.5kWh/ ft$^2$/year   (296 kWh/m$^2$ year)

**Total Energy Use After**   4.0 to 5.5mWh/year (predicted)   9.1 to 12 kWh/ ft$^2$/year

**Heating Before**   11.5 to 12.0 mBtu/year   7.85 kWh/ ft$^2$/year   (84.5 kWh/m$^2$ year)

**Heating After**   3.5 to 5.0 kBtu/year   2.84 kWh/ ft$^2$/year   (30.5 kWh/m$^2$ year)

**Water Before**   13 gallons/ft$^2$

**Water After**   5.7 gal/ft$^2$   62 percent less water than baseline

**Renewables**   287,000 kWh

**Photovoltaics**   9 percent of electricity

**Solar Thermal Collectors**   30 percent of domestic hot water

Re-skinning of the 1974 Edith Green—Wendell Wyatt federal office building achieves energy savings both directly through reduction of heat losses and infiltration and indirectly through control of heat gain and provision of daylighting to offset electrical use. *Scott Baumberger.*

Transformation of the thirty-five-year-old eighteen-story Edith Green—Wendell Wyatt federal office building illustrates how a typical office tower can benefit from modernizations involving both façade and internal systems. Tracking to reach a LEED Platinum level, the renovation upgrades the building to meet current accessibility, life safety, and seismic standards while committing to reducing ongoing ownership costs for the federal government. In developing building systems, the design team prioritized energy load reduction by improving the façade and replacing all major building systems and even specifying energy-recovery elevators.

# ENVELOPE & DAYLIGHTING

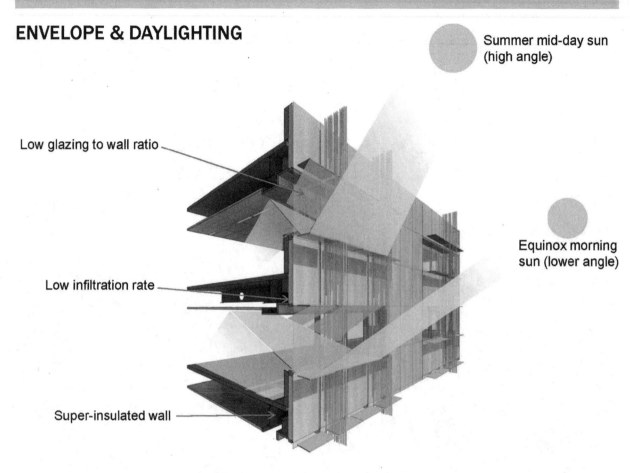

Summer mid-day sun
(high angle)

Low glazing to wall ratio

Equinox morning
sun (lower angle)

Low infiltration rate

Super-insulated wall

A new skin on the south and east walls use sophisticated sunshading to maximize daylighting while minimizing heat gain in summer. The horizontal shades act as both shading devices and light shelves, reflecting daylight into the open office floors. *Courtesy SERA Architects.*

Each façade receives a different sunshading system responding to their differing orientation. While the north façade will be skinned with insulated glazing and superinsulated wall panels, the west face will be covered with a vertical "reed" system that will block 50 percent of afternoon sun. The south and east façades include insulated glazing, superinsulated spandrel panels, and horizontal sunshade/light shelves and vertical reeds that block summer sun to minimize heat gain.

Since the building begins with large floor plates and façades are tuned to prevent solar heat gains in summer, interior cooling loads normally predominate. Lighting systems include daylight sensors and high-efficiency, optically enhanced fixtures to minimize energy use and overheating.

# SHADING STRATEGY

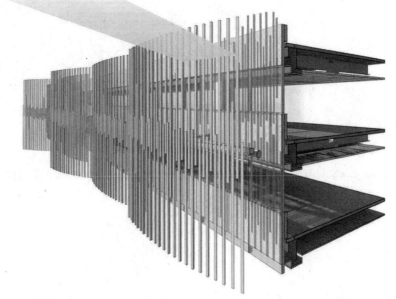

**West**
Reeds provide 50% shading

**South & East**
Combination vertical +
horizontal

**North**
No shading

The western façade receives a different re-skinning strategy. Prioritizing sunshading, aluminum "reeds" filter 50 percent of western light, minimizing heat gain from afternoon sun. Originally conceived as a vegetated screen, a careful benefits analysis revealed that inert sunshades will perform as well at blocking heat gain without the inherent risks of natural plant material. Operable sunshades were also analyzed but lower initial cost and lower maintenance cost of the fixed shading system won out in terms of lifetime costs. *Courtesy SERA Architects.*

Because of the reduction in loads, a hydronic heating and cooling system consisting of ceiling-mounted radiant panels will be used to meet interior temperature requirements. Radiant panels are supplemented by a dedicated outdoor air system providing 100 percent fresh air with heat recovery exhaust.

Solar thermal panels will provide 30 percent of domestic hot water while photovoltaic panels provide 6 percent of electricity needs. High-efficiency plumbing is supplemented by a rainwater collection system using a former gun range for storage.

# RAINWATER REUSE SYSTEM

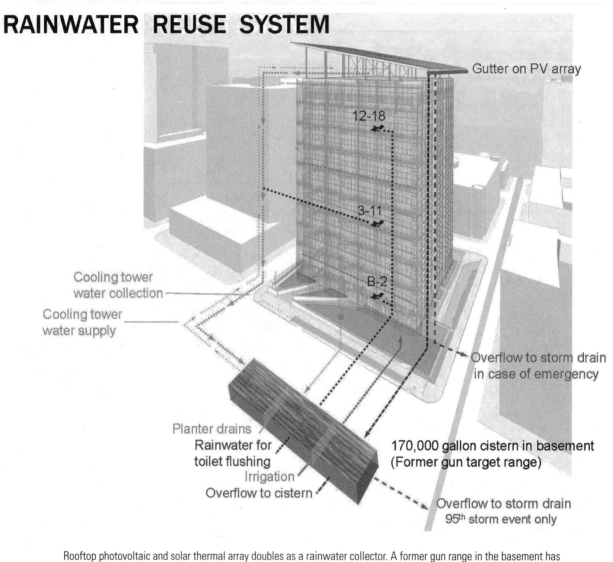

Gutter on PV array

12-18

3-11

B-2

Cooling tower water collection

Cooling tower water supply

Overflow to storm drain in case of emergency

Planter drains
Rainwater for toilet flushing
Irrigation
Overflow to cistern

170,000 gallon cistern in basement
(Former gun target range)

Overflow to storm drain
95th storm event only

Rooftop photovoltaic and solar thermal array doubles as a rainwater collector. A former gun range in the basement has been converted to a 160,000-gallon tank that will store rainwater for reuse in toilet and urinal flushing, and for irrigation. *Courtesy SERA Architects.*

CASE STUDY

# 39 Hunter Street

**Owner**  Kador Group

**Renovation Architect**  Jackson Teece Architects

**Original Building Type**  Office

**Renovation Building Type**  Office

**Original Construction Date**  1916, 1970s

**Renovation Date**  2008

**Location**  Sydney, Australia

**Climate**  Temperate  (Köppen Cfa)

**Area**  64,500 ft$^2$

**Achievement**  6 Star—Green Star Rating

**Key Indicators**  Daylighting, Atrium

    Underfloor Displacement Ventilation

    Precooling Water from Sprinkler Tank

    Peak Load Reduction—Gas Generator Coupled to Chillers

**Water Use After**  22 percent reduction (total water), 46 percent reduction (excluding cooling towers)

**Renewables**  None

A landmark in Sydney, Australia, 39 Hunter Street (formerly the Perpetual Building), originally constructed in 1916, was ripe for sustainable renovation to undo insensitive 1960s and 1970s renovations, preserve the building for future generations, and provide a model of energy efficiency. Since original light wells had been in-filled and neighboring buildings had grown up around it, daylight penetration was limited; the design team prioritized studies of daylighting, ultimately proposing development of a new atrium that allows deep penetration while highlighting preservation of significant historic material.

In order to best protect historic interior ceiling coffers and decoration, the team devised an underfloor displacement air-distribution system that minimized effect on historic fabric while providing high efficiency. Jackson Teece Architects designed a complementary "lily pad" component to provide lighting and fire protection at the crossings of ceiling

coffers while leaving the majority of the ceiling articulation exposed. For building cooling, a gas-fired generator runs one of the two chillers which cool water stored in an insulated fire sprinkler water reservoir to shave peak loads. The heating, ventilation, and air-conditioning (HVAC) system employs variable speed pumps and sophisticated controls for further energy efficiency.

Interior air quality was maximized through the specification of low-emitting materials and the minimization of the use of polyvinyl chloride (PVC). Carbon dioxide ($CO_2$) sensors are tied to the HVAC system to improve indoor air quality. Energy use is further reduced through installation of highly efficient T-5 fluorescent and light emitting diode (LED) lighting throughout. Tenant spaces are submetered to promote conservation. Finally, water is conserved through rainwater collection for toilet flushing and installation of waterless urinals and dual-flush low-flow toilets.

Presenting an historic face to the city, the interior of 39 Hunter Street contains sophisticated environmental control systems. A gas generator couples with chillers and pumps to shave peak electrical loads. A fire sprinkler water tank doubles as cold storage to further cut peak electrical demand by storing water from chillers run during the night. *Jackson Teece Architecture—Sharrin Reese.*

▲ Louvers operated by a sophisticated energy management system exhaust hot air at appropriate times, generating air circulation without any fan energy. Low-emitting paints, sealants and adhesives, and recycled carpet tiles help maintain indoor air quality. *Jackson Teece Architecture—Sharrin Reese.*

▶ Suspended acoustical ceilings from the 1960s concealed original plaster beams and decorative soffits now exposed by the renovation. Underfloor air distribution provides greater user control in open offices. Sensitive additions that complement the original decoration contain new lighting with occupancy sensors, fire protection services, and carbon dioxide sensors. *Jackson Teece Architecture—Sharrin Reese.*

Accentuating historic fabric through juxtapositions with new elements, this renovation skillfully incorporates new systems within an historic building. *Jackson Teece Architecture—Sharrin Reese.*

Reaching through eight floors, a new skylight both daylights and ventilates this historic building. *Jackson Teece Architecture— Sharrin Reese.*

# ENDNOTES

1. *Retrofitting Suburbia, Urban Design Solutions for Redesigning Suburbs*, Ellen Dunham-Jones and June Williamson, Hoboken, NJ: John Wiley & Sons, 2010.

2. Croxton Collaborative Website: www.croxtoncollaborative.com/proj_wplibrary.htm, accessed May 14, 2010.

3. *Tower Renewal Guidelines, for the Comprehensive Retrofit of Multi-Unit Residential Buildings in Cold Climates*, University of Toronto, 2009. This volume has an excellent analysis of overcladding systems on concrete residential buildings along with examples and technical details.

4. Dunham-Jones and Williamson, *ibid.*; Chapter 9 Edge City Infill: Improving Walkability and Interconnectivity.

5 (Fer) studio LLP, Louisville, Kentucky.

6. "Small, Green & Good; the Role of Neglected Cities in a Sustainable Future," Catherine Tumber, *Boston Review*, March/April 2009.

7 *Delivering Sustainability Through the Adaptive Reuse of Commercial Buildings: The Melbourne CBD Challenge*, Wilkinson, James, & Reed, PRRES, 2009.

8. Available online at the National Park Service Website: www.nps.gov/history/hps/tps/standguide/.

9. T-12 to T-8 lamp conversion calculated from www1.eere.energy.gov/femp/procurement/eep_fluortube_lamp.html, accessed August 28, 2010.

10. A useful resource is the United States Atlas of Renewable Resources produced by NREL, http://mapserve2.nrel.gov/website/Resource_Atlas/viewer.htm.

11. *Power Technologies Energy Data Book (PTEDB)*, 4th ed., NREL, 2002, www.nrel.gov/analysis/power_databook/docs/pdf/db_chapter02.pdf, accessed August 28, 2010.

12. Generation and grid transmission losses approach 68 percent, compounding the pollution produced by municipal power generation. Calculated from www.nrel.gov/analysis/power_databook/docs/excel/7_4.xls, accessed August 28, 2010.

13. U.S. EPA Combined Heat and Power Partnership, www.epa.gov/chp/.

14. For further reading, see the U.S. EPA Combined Heat & Power Partnership at: www.epa.gov/chp/basic/renewable.html.

15. www.epa.gov/chp/incentives/index.html.

16. Biochar, used by traditional Amazonian cultures to form *Terra Preta de Indio* or "Indian black earth" reintroduces carbon and other nutrients into the soil through burning of organic matter on the surface. See, www.css.cornell.edu/faculty/lehmann/research/terra%20preta/terrapretamain.html.

17. http://web.archive.org/web/20070814144750/http://www1.eere.energy.gov/biomass/pyrolysis.html .

18. Completed in 2005, the transformation of Juhnde Bioenergy Village, Juhnde, Germany, provides all electricity and heating from locally grown biofuel and waste plant material through a biogas plant with district heating network to 140 households. Updating Germany, www.bioengiedorf.de.

19. R. Compagnon, *Solar and Daylight Availability in the Urban Fabric*, University of Applied Sciences of Western Switzerland (HES-SO), Ecole d'ingénieurs et d'architectes de Fribourg, © 2004 Elsevier B.V. All rights reserved.

20. Described in: Edward Rice, "Considering Daylight in Facade Renewal: The Effect of New Measures for Daylight in the Consideration of Aging Modern-Era Facade Types," SMArchS thesis in Building Technology, Department of Architecture, MIT, June 2006, (Chapter 4.5) and in: Siân Kleindienst, "Improving Daylighting in Existing Buildings: Characterizing the Effect of Anidolic Systems," S.M. thesis in Building Technology, Department of Architecture, MIT, June 2006, (Chapter 7). Theses Advisor: Marilyne Andersen. http://dspace.mit.edu/handle/1721.1/35496 and http://daylighting.mit.edu/publications/Velux%20Poster%20Full.pdf, accessed April 15, 2010.

21. "Design and Optimization of Solar Absorption Chillers," Bergquam Energy Systems for California Energy Commission, March 2002.

22. Commercially available photovoltaic modules have energy conversion efficiencies (percentage of sunlight converted to electricity) of about 10 to 15 percent while experimental panels are reaching efficiencies of 40 percent. See http://upload.wikimedia.org/wikipedia/commons/c/c9/PVeff%28rev100414%29.png.

23. U.S. DOE, Energy Efficiency and Renewable Energy Program, Solar Energies Technologies Program: www1.eere.energy.gov/solar/pv_basics.html.

24. Courtesy Borrego Solar, www.borregosolar.com/solar-power-systems/case-studies/client-villa_nueva.php, accessed April 8, 2010.

25. *Environmental Building News*, The Folly of Building-Integrated Wind, May 1, 2009. www.buildinggreen.com/auth/article.cfm/2009/4/29/The-Folly-of-Building-Integrated-Wind/, accessed May 21, 2010.

26. *EBN, ibid.*

27. Windmills installed at Adobe Headquarters, San Jose, California.

28. AWEA Website, Small Wind, www.awea.org/smallwind/ toolbox2/factsheet_econ_of_smallwind.html, accessed May 21, 2010.

29. Database of State Incentives for Renewables and Efficiency, http://dsireusa.org/.

30. U.S. DOE Energy Efficiency and Renewable Energy Website: www1.eere.energy.gov/geothermal/geothermal_basics .html.

31. More on geothermal heat exchange, U.S. DOE Energy Efficiency and Renewable Energy Website: http://web .archive.org/web/20070625154743rn_1/www1.eere.energy .gov/geothermal/.

32. Designed by Sanaa with Nicole Berganski, project architects, and Böll & Krabel Associated Architects.

33. For more information, see U.S. EPA Guidelines for Water Reuse, Municipal Support Division Office of Wastewater Management, 2004.

34. "Bioretention Applications, Inglewood Demonstration Project, Largo, Maryland and Florida Aquarium, Tampa, Florida," Low-Impact Development Center, U.S. EPA.

35. About half of the energy cost of water is for treatment of waste water; therefore 20 to 40 Wh/gallon. Calculations based on "Energy Savings and Greenhouse Gas Reductions from the Santa Clara Valley Water District's Water Use Efficiency Programs," 2008 find that their average water use energy cost is 0.044 kWh/gallon, ≈ 40Wh/gallon. Other agencies indicate energy costs over 80 Wh/gallon, depending on size and style of municipal waste water treatment facility and water sources (well versus surface), distribution system types (gravity versus pumping).

36. EBMUD *Watersmart Guidebook*, A Water-Use Efficiency Plan Review Guide for New Businesses, East Bay Municipal Utility District, 2008.

37. See http://toddecological.com/ for further information.

38. Passive House Institute, United States, www.passivehouse.us /passiveHouse/PHIUSHome.html, accessed May 25, 2010.

39. Passive House Arrives in North America: Could It Revolutionize the Way We Build?, *Environmental Building News*, April 1, 2010, www.buildinggreen.com/auth/article. cfm/2010/3/31/Passive-House-Arrives-in-North-America -Could-It-Revolutionize-the-Way-We-Build/, accessed May 25, 2010.

40. Modernization of Old Buildings: High Energy Efficiency is Better, PassivHaus Institute, www.passivehouse.us/passive House/PHIUSHome.html, accessed May 25, 2010.

41. Modernization of Old Buildings: High Energy Efficiency is Better, Passive House Institute, U.S., www.passivehouse.us/ passiveHouse/PHIUSHome.html accessed May 25, 2010.

42. "Energy Use and Overheating Risk in Zero-Energy Renovation," Liselotte Apon, Ir. Elisa C. Boelman, Dr. Eng. MBA Christoph M. Ravesloot, Ir. Drs., Delft University of Technology, 2005.

43. Diagram after Walter Braun, www.eor.de/fileadmin/eor/ docs/aktivitaeten/2010/Energieberatertag/Vortraege/01_ Walter%20Braun_Bauen_und_Sanieren_im_21_JH.pdf, accessed February 4, 2011. Hoheloogstrasse 1 & 3 apartment building in Ludwigshafen, Germany: owned by GAG Ludwigshafen am Rhein, renovation architect Architekt Walter Braun, an 8,000-ft² multifamily building that uses 1.39 kWh/ft²/year (15.0 kWh/m²/year) in energy.

44. Diagram after: GAP-solar wall panel by Gap-solar GmbH, www.gap-solar.at/beitraege/downloads/2020_2006_ FPII%20productfolder_0502.pdf, accessed August 28, 2010.

# chapter 9

# THE FUTURE OF RENOVATION

## INTRODUCTION

Energy conservation goals must be ambitious in order to mitigate the impact of buildings on climate change, habitats, and local environments. But our solutions need to be as real as our problems. Fortunately our goal of an 80 percent improvement in building energy consumption while improving comfort, health, and productivity is realistic, and is becoming more achievable every day.

If we link the major uses of energy, the major strategies for saving energy, and the service lifecycles of building components, an environmental strategy takes shape. Even though the building stock itself turns over very slowly (in comparison to the fleet of vehicles, for example) building components such as systems, elements of the envelope, and finishes need replacement at a more rapid rate.

The building stock in the aggregate can meet the goals:

1. Low or no cost improvements to save 27 percent by 2015

2. Replacement of roofs, building equipment, and cost effective upgrades for a further 18 percent by 2025

3. Major renovations with changes in daylighting and building physics for a further 21 percent by 2040

4. Introduction of 6 quads (quadrillion Btus) of renewable generating capacity by 2040

None of the goals listed here require technology beyond what we possess right now. An ambitious renovation today could meet the 2040 performance stated here. Clearly we can hope to develop more and better materials and technology and to accomplish improvement even faster.

The improvements noted relate to the operational energy used by buildings, but that is only 80 percent of the energy consumed by buildings. Major renovations, although requiring less than new buildings, consume a large amount of energy and resources during the construction period. Attention to design for reuse, permanent flexibility, deconstruction rather than demolition, and designing partitions and equipment for redeployment are further elements of the long-term reduction of energy and resource waste by the building sector.

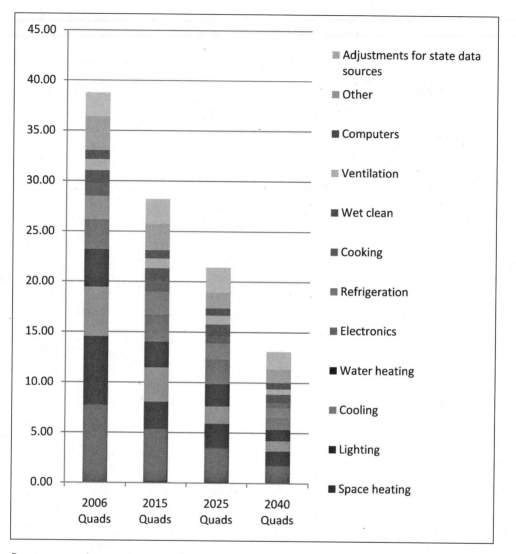

Energy conservation measures based on present day technology could save 25.68 quadrillion Btus per year, 66 percent of the operational energy used by the building sector, by 2040. *Gelfand Partners Architects.*

The sequence of improvement for any individual building varies by building type, use, and climate. Measurement and auditing of the performance of each individual building will help determine what the first step is for that particular building. But for the building stock as a whole, energy- and resource-mindful behavior, maintenance, and targeted upgrades can contribute to immediate change. There is no reason to wait and there is every reason to abandon fatalism about the scale of the improvement required.

# ENERGY CONSERVATION AND BUILDING LIFECYCLE STRATEGY

## Low and No Cost Strategies

Low- and no-cost strategies are possible to implement immediately. We are not predicting that they will be, but we are showing that it is feasible to set a near-term target such as 2015 for a 25 percent reduction in energy demand by the building sector. The combination of marketing and regulation that would be necessary to spread such an audacious goal is beyond our scope. But based on the research that has been done on energy conservation campaigns this is a possible target. It is clearly less expensive and more desirable than additional power plants.

The obvious first targets for improvements are the major energy demands of space heating, lighting, space cooling, and hot water heating. Low- and no-cost strategies such as behavior changes, lamp changes,

### 2006 U.S. Buildings Energy End-Use Splits

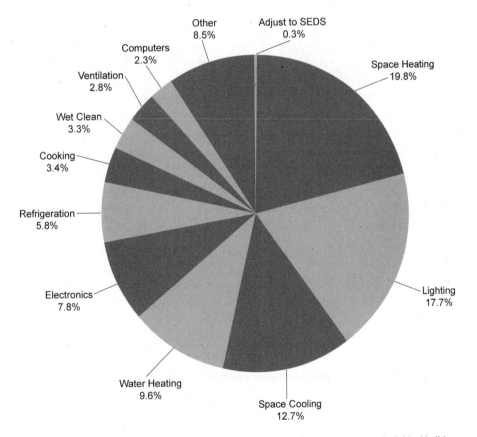

While individual buildings vary from the average energy end-use splits in this chart, each individual building will have its own highest yield uses.[1] *U.S. Department of Energy.*

**Low and No Cost Improvements**

| Energy demand | Quads | 2006 | Behavior | Quads | Retro-commissioning | Quads | Weatherizing | Quads | Upgrading equipment | Quads | 2015 Quads |
|---|---|---|---|---|---|---|---|---|---|---|---|
| Space heating | 7.68 | 19.8% | | 0.00 | 5.0% | 0.38 | 0.16 | 1.23 | 10.0% | 0.77 | 5.30 |
| Lighting | 6.86 | 17.7% | 10.00% | 0.69 | | 0.00 | | | 50.0% | 3.43 | 2.74 |
| Cooling | 4.92 | 12.7% | | 0.00 | 20.0% | 0.98 | | | 10.0% | 0.49 | 3.45 |
| Water heating | 3.72 | 9.6% | | 0.00 | 2.0% | 0.07 | | | 30.0% | 1.12 | 2.53 |
| Electronics | 3.02 | 7.8% | 10.00% | 0.30 | | 0.00 | | | | 0.00 | 2.72 |
| Refrigeration | 2.25 | 5.8% | | 0.00 | | 0.00 | | | | 0.00 | 2.25 |
| Cooking | 1.32 | 3.4% | 10.00% | 0.13 | | 0.00 | | | 10.0% | 0.13 | 1.05 |
| Wet clean | 1.28 | 3.3% | | 0.00 | | 0.00 | | | | 0.00 | 1.28 |
| Ventilation | 1.09 | 2.8% | 10.00% | 0.11 | | 0.00 | | | | 0.00 | 0.98 |
| Computers | 0.89 | 2.3% | 10.00% | 0.09 | | 0.00 | | | | 0.00 | 0.80 |
| Other | 3.30 | 8.5% | 10.00% | 0.33 | | 0.00 | | | | 0.30 | 2.67 |
| Adjustments for state data sources | 2.44 | 6.3% | | 0.00 | | 0.00 | | | | 0.00 | 2.44 |
| | 38.77 | 100.0% | | 1.65 | | 1.44 | | 1.23 | | 6.24 | 28.21 |

Targeted low and no cost upgrades could achieve a 27 percent reduction in building energy demand. *Gelfand Partners Architects.*

weatherization, and retrocommissioning have a major return in energy efficiency in these areas. Using the Kutztown and NYSERDA studies, we can target 10 percent as a goal for behavior changes such as turning off lights, fans, cooling, and electronics when not in use, and add setback thermostats, and plugstrips to turn off energy vampires.[2] Changes in cooking behavior put additional savings within reach.[3]

Retrocommissioning of heating and cooling by itself produced 20 percent efficiency improvements in rooftop units.[4] In the United States broad application of these low-investment measures could reduce building energy use by 15 percent. With water savings due to fixing leaks, both water use and the embodied energy in water could be reduced substantially, contributing another few percent to overall energy savings.

Weatherizing small buildings such as houses (over half of all buildings in the United States) yields savings of 32 percent in space heating.[5] As discussed, it is a less effective strategy in positively pressurized buildings, but will contribute substantially to the performance of the building sector as a whole.

Energy efficiency improvements for lighting are so cost effective that many owners are doing them with-

out waiting for current equipment to wear out. LED light sources need major price reductions before they dominate the market, but with the paybacks for lighting improvements today, changing to high efficiency fluorescent lighting is an interim step most building owners will want to take. Cutting lighting loads in half means cutting building electricity use overall by another 10 percent.

While appliances used to last for twenty years or more, today's appliances are more likely to last for ten. Today's refrigerators, washers, dryers, dishwashers, water heaters, stoves, and ovens, are probably going to be replaced within fifteen years. Easy improvements can come as gas appliances with pilot lights are replaced by electronic ignition and more self-cleaning ovens with their improved insulation replace existing ovens. Industry agreements without regulation would contribute to savings of .3 quadrillion Btus (quads)/year over the next thirty years even assuming no new technology.[6]

Another measure that could be adopted very early and at low cost is the introduction of cool roof coatings in cooling dominated climates. Such cool roofs (see figure in Chapter 4) could reduce cooling loads by 10 percent.[7]

# Energy and Water Savings from Standards

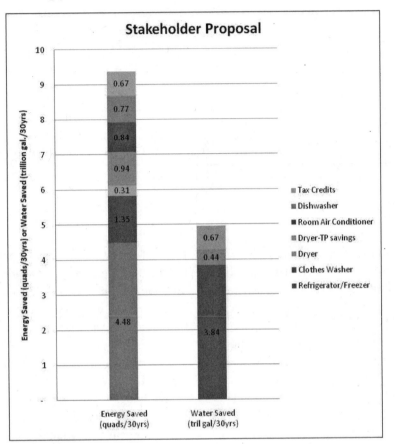

Energy and water savings from upgrading appliances will add up to substantial numbers. *Association of Home Appliance Manufacturers (AHAM).*

As noted, each building needs to be analyzed in a way that integrates its construction materials and details, occupancy, climate zone, and individual situation. But the top five low and no cost measures for the building sector as a whole are:

1. Change behavior
2. Retrocommission HVAC and water heating
3. Weatherize small buildings
4. Upgrade lighting, heating (especially controls), and appliances
5. Install cool roofs or cool roof coatings

## 2025 Improvements

Over the decades from the 1950s through the 1970s the primary heating and cooling infrastructure of buildings changed from steam and hot water heating

**2025 Improvements**

| Energy demand | Quads | 2006 | Upgrade Envelope | Quads | Upgrade equipment | Quads | Plug loads | Quads | Direct solar | Quads | 2025 Quads |
|---|---|---|---|---|---|---|---|---|---|---|---|
| Space heating | 5.30 | 7.68 | 30.00% | 1.59 | 5.0% | 0.26 | | 0.00 | | 0.00 | 3.44 |
| Lighting | 2.74 | 6.86 | | 0.00 | 10.0% | 0.27 | | 0.00 | | 0.00 | 2.47 |
| Cooling | 3.45 | 4.92 | 30.00% | 1.03 | 20.0% | 0.69 | | 0.00 | | 0.00 | 1.72 |
| Water heating | 2.53 | 3.72 | | 0.00 | 2.0% | 0.05 | | 0.00 | 10.0% | 0.25 | 2.23 |
| Electronics | 2.72 | 3.02 | | 0.00 | | 0.00 | 10.00% | 0.27 | | 0.00 | 2.45 |
| Refrigeration | 2.25 | 2.25 | | 0.00 | | 0.00 | 30.00% | 0.67 | | 0.00 | 1.57 |
| Cooking | 1.05 | 1.32 | | 0.00 | 30.0% | 0.32 | | 0.00 | | 0.00 | 0.74 |
| Wet clean | 1.28 | 1.28 | | 0.00 | | 0.00 | 10.00% | 0.13 | | 0.00 | 1.15 |
| Ventilation | 0.98 | 1.09 | 10.00% | 0.10 | | 0.00 | | 0.00 | | 0.00 | 0.88 |
| Computers | 0.80 | 0.89 | | 0.00 | | 0.00 | 10.00% | 0.08 | | 0.00 | 0.72 |
| Other | 2.67 | 3.30 | 10.00% | 0.27 | | 0.00 | | 0.00 | 30.0% | 0.80 | 1.60 |
| Adjustments for state data sources | 2.44 | 2.44 | | 0.00 | | 0.00 | | 0.00 | | 0.00 | 2.44 |
| | 28.21 | 38.77 | | 2.99 | | 1.60 | | 1.15 | | 1.05 | 21.42 |

Upgrades to building envelopes, systems, equipment, and introduction of more renewables can shave another 18 percent off building energy demand. *Gelfand Partners Architects.*

and operable windows to forced air heating and cooling. Over the next fifteen years a similar revolution in our approach to building systems can occur, substituting smart HVAC systems that work with local climates to provide building comfort with healthier air and less energy. Such system replacements should be done as current equipment wears out. Although the most substantial gains can be realized when system replacements are performed in conjunction with major overhauls of building daylighting and ventilation, such overhauls are much less common events in a building service life. However, incremental improvements in building envelopes such as insulation, weatherizing, door and window replacement, and new roofing, are almost sure to occur in this time frame.

Most of the case study examples in this book achieve improvements such as shown in the chart above. Through upgraded envelopes heating and cooling loads can be reduced. Adding insulation in easily accessed attics can be done at the same time building equipment is replaced. Restoration and improvement of operable windows can be a simple ventilation improvement in buildings of the right age. As shown in

the Empire State Building example, due to individual building circumstances, a window replacement reduced load enough that the area of space conditioned by the original equipment could be expanded. When that equipment needs replacement, a further incremental improvement will occur in building performance. It is not necessary to take all steps in all buildings in the same order.

Equipment upgrade improvements recognize the general availability of more efficient heating and cooling equipment than what will be replaced. There is a range of different efficiencies at different price points. The improvements shown are for widely available equipment, not the most cutting edge.

The further improvements in lighting recognize the kind of strategy changes in lighting that come with a more extensive renovation. In the first round of lighting upgrades, the assumptions were that lamps and ballasts were upgraded and incandescent sources replaced. To make further gains, in appropriate commercial uses, the fixtures themselves should be replaced with direct/indirect lighting and with task lighting. This kind of strategy shift allows overall light levels to be reduced as well as using the most high efficiency sources. In conjunction with such lighting changes it will frequently be necessary to replace ceiling tiles or systems. This can be done immediately but represents a larger investment. Therefore, it could be considered a second-wave strategy.

Commercial kitchens are big energy hogs. In addition to continued upgrades on the home front, it can be assumed that by 2025 commercial kitchens will also be shifting to more energy-efficient equipment and practices.

Reduction of plug loads depends upon improvement of the individual appliances, office machines, and equipment that draw power in a building. With all equipment running at current Energy Star performance or better, energy demand drops considerably. This is obviously feasible and could be brought about by either market changes or regulation in much the same way that improvements to the fleet of vehicles can. Refrigeration is a particularly large area for improvement and is highly sensitive to market changes. Although the basic refrigeration machinery and insulation are generally improved in modern refrigerators, configuration, defrosting, and icemaking are areas where more improvement is needed in order to reduce the demand by these appliances. Clearly this should be a challenge for the industry.

Although direct solar water heating has been around for a long time, it is becoming more cost effective daily. It can be shown to be cost effective in buildings right now in many climate zones. But because it is usually done in conjunction with roofing, and because it needs to overcome perception problems caused by initial systems in the 1970s, it is shown as a medium-term improvement.

Direct solar is also included in the "other" category. This is meant to recognize the increased interest by government and other institutional leaders in using solar for things like swimming pool heating, under-

pavement heating coils, larger-scale hot water heating, direct solar garbage compactors, and the like.

In a renovation that is meant to carry a building through to 2025 before further major work, depending again on the individual building, the following major improvements could be the top priorities:

1. Upgrade insulation, doors and windows, roofs, and envelope sealing

2. Upgrade building HVAC and lighting systems and strategies

3. Purchase and install Energy Saver or equivalent equipment

4. Cut energy use in major applications such as commercial kitchens and swimming pools

## 2040 Improvements

The farther that we go from the present the more speculative predictions are. However, many major renovations completed today will not be repeated at a similar scale until 2040 or after. We are designing some of the buildings of 2040 today. We have shown the European examples of renovations that have achieved 90 percent improvements in energy use. This is technically feasible in almost all buildings. From a financial point of view, it is possible to be very strategic about selection of building improvement strategy. Even when it is not feasible to make the kind of major investment represented by full envelope and system replacements, it is possible to masterplan the building improvements so that future work can be phased in with little rework.

As seen in prewar buildings, daylight and natural ventilation are effective strategies. While more efficient equipment uses less energy, using no equipment uses even less. We can learn from these buildings, restoring their strategies with modern improvements in safety and comfort, and applying their strategies to

**2040 improvements**

| Energy demand | Quads | 2006 | Major Renovation | Quads | Upgrade equipment | Quads | Plug loads | Quads | Direct solar | Quads | 2040 Quads |
|---|---|---|---|---|---|---|---|---|---|---|---|
| Space heating | 3.44 | 7.68 | 30.00% | 1.03 | 20.0% | 0.69 | | 0.00 | | 0.00 | 1.72 |
| Lighting | 2.47 | 6.86 | 30.00% | 0.74 | 10.0% | 0.25 | | 0.00 | | 0.00 | 1.48 |
| Cooling | 1.72 | 4.92 | 20.00% | 0.34 | 20.0% | 0.34 | | 0.00 | | 0.00 | 1.03 |
| Water heating | 2.23 | 3.72 | | 0.00 | 20.0% | 0.45 | | 0.00 | 30.0% | 0.67 | 1.11 |
| Electronics | 2.45 | 3.02 | 10.00% | 0.24 | | 0.00 | 40.00% | 0.98 | | 0.00 | 1.22 |
| Refrigeration | 1.57 | 2.25 | | 0.00 | | 0.00 | 40.00% | 0.63 | | 0.00 | 0.94 |
| Cooking | 0.74 | 1.32 | | 0.00 | 30.0% | 0.22 | | 0.00 | | 0.00 | 0.52 |
| Wet clean | 1.15 | 1.28 | | 0.00 | | 0.00 | 30.00% | 0.35 | | 0.00 | 0.81 |
| Ventilation | 0.88 | 1.09 | 40.00% | 0.35 | | 0.00 | | 0.00 | | 0.00 | 0.53 |
| Computers | 0.72 | 0.89 | | 0.00 | | 0.00 | 10.00% | 0.07 | | 0.00 | 0.65 |
| Other | 1.60 | 3.30 | 15.00% | 0.24 | | 0.00 | | 0.00 | | 0.00 | 1.36 |
| Adjustments for state data sources | 2.44 | 2.44 | | 0.00 | 30.0% | 0.73 | | 0.00 | | 0.00 | 1.71 |
| | 21.42 | 38.77 | | 2.96 | | 2.68 | | 2.03 | | 0.67 | 13.09 |

Major renovations make possible new envelopes, new daylighting and ventilation strategies, and new applications of direct use of renewable energy. *Gelfand Partners Architects.*

postwar buildings. Introducing atrium or courtyard daylight and ventilation into the center of existing deep buildings is clearly the kind of change that happens in conjunction with major renovation. Use of light shelves and fins on the outside of buildings also helps daylight penetrate deeper into the building, reducing the need for daytime artificial illumination. While light fixtures will almost certainly continue to improve, a further leap in performance is more likely to be achieved through reducing demand.

Passive strategies of harnessing thermal mass, effective stack and cross-ventilation, and reduction of heat gains from the sun, lights, and equipment again add significant reductions to cooling loads. Especially with cooling it is possible to reap significant rewards with geo-exchange systems and heat pumps. With heat and energy recovery ventilation it is also possible to introduce 100 percent outside air into a building while simultaneously saving energy and improving indoor air quality.

It is also safe to assume that the high performance possible in selected equipment today will be more broadly available and applicable as the years go by.

Such equipment will probably be replaced several times between now and 2040, and we assume it will become more efficient. We also suggest that major energy gains will be made as potable water use is reduced. These gains will be both local to the building and in water utility energy use.

The high-performance renovation today is as much or more a custom design as a brand new high-performance building, but the broadly applicable trends needed to produce steep declines in energy demand are:

1. Application of daylight and passive ventilation strategies
2. High-performance envelope design
3. High-performance system design
4. Energy efficient electric devices
5. Strategic application of direct use of renewable energy sources

## Building Integrated Power Generation

While it has been shown that energy conservation can reduce building energy demand to a small fraction of what it is today, further reduction or outright elimination of energy impact depends on building integrated power generation. It is not clear how the efficiency of these technologies compares between utility-scale generation and distribution and building-scale use or connection back into the power grid. With the tremendous line losses of utility-generated power, it is clear that a strong argument exists for distributed power generation. On the other hand, some of the utility-scale power-generation technologies are more efficient in themselves, and will also provide for process power and for sectors other than the building sector. It is not our goal to advocate that all buildings operate completely off the grid, although that is a possible scenario in years to come.

While 66 percent energy savings is met by the energy conservation strategies outlined above, to reach 80 or even 100 percent savings, it is necessary to generate power. The renewable technologies that are being applied today at the building level include solar energy used directly, in photovoltaic production of electricity, or in creating water or steam to turn turbines and generate electricity. Piezoelectric production of electricity is another somewhat experimental technology, while cogeneration of power and heat using biomass or other fuels is another approach. Small wind is being refined to avoid interference from the structures themselves, and to avoid transmitting vibrations and noise. Geo-exchange systems are not really power generation, but by borrowing the energy in the Earth they are another aggressive way to save generated energy. Government and utility subsidy programs are still necessary to make most of these strategies pay off financially in the near term.

While we can make the case that energy conservation in the building sector is both something we should do and something we can do, that does not mean that it is something we will do. Something of the same situation exists in renewable energy. Many promising technologies exist but few can compete without subsidy with the retail cost of power available to most users. For near-term gains, energy conservation is by far more cost effective. Though many promoters of renewable energy sources project steadily rising costs of electric power, the National Renewable Energy Laboratory (NREL) projects retail electricity prices to "stay at current historic highs through 2025."[8]

As noted, significant gains could be made on the energy conservation side by that time. But even assuming the cost of power remaining stable, NREL projects higher market penetration by renewables based on various drivers such as state renewable portfolio standards (RPS), voluntary markets, Integrated Resource Planning (IRP), and Systems Benefit Charge (SBC) subsidies.[9]

What could this mean to the achievement of the 80 percent reduction goal for the building sector? NREL looks at a theoretical maximum of 20 percent market penetration by 2020 based on the opinion in the power generation industry that integrating intermittent renewables into the grid would cause significant challenges at levels above 20 percent.[10] Note that taking buildings *off* the grid could be another approach to increasing the amount of power provided by renewables without requiring an entirely new electric power distribution infrastructure. Subtracting space heating (primarily natural gas) from total building energy use, the building sector uses about 30 quads of electrical energy, and 20 percent of that is 6 quads. If it were generated through renewables, then the non-renewable energy use of the sector drops from the total of 13 quads after energy conservation to a total of 7 quads. That is slightly beyond the 80 percent reduction we are looking for.

The point of this calculation is not prediction. It is to establish the feasibility of rolling back the human influence on climate. Applying energy conservation measures that are available today, adopting a

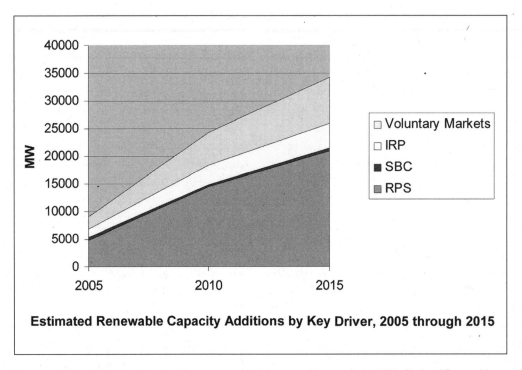

**Estimated Renewable Capacity Additions by Key Driver, 2005 through 2015**

Near-term drivers of increased renewable energy could triple renewable capacity by 2015. *National Renewable Energy Laboratory.*

schedule that is consistent with the need to replace and upgrade buildings as components age, and continuing to encourage the development of renewable energy sources, it is feasible to reduce energy use by buildings by 80 percent. As we have seen in the case studies, levels of reduction higher than 90 percent have already been achieved.

## DECONSTRUCTION

The excuse that high performance is infeasible in existing buildings is neither true nor acceptable. However, even the kinds of improvements we have described are conventional in their approach to building lifecy-

cles. We have shown many examples that demonstrate that building systems and envelopes can be improved to function much more sustainably. However, they are still being torn apart and reworked in place, inevitably producing waste.

Change is a permanent condition of human habitats. Communities grow and shrink and the activities within them shift and relocate. As the planet becomes more and more crowded, the need to maintain and restore agricultural land, to take advantage of harbors, and to protect wetlands, forests, and wilderness limits the geographies of change. People need and will continue to need to find better ways to live where they live now or within even tighter footprints.

In adapting existing buildings to their roles in a changing world, we need to assume that the world will continue changing and that the old approach of demolition and reconstruction is unlikely to remain viable. A new or renovated building built today should be planned for a future that includes more renovation. Deconstruction is the process of taking buildings apart so that their components can be reused with a minimum of processing. The first widely adopted examples of this are office landscape systems. These systems allow workstations to be reconfigured in a variety of ways as business needs change.

The first workstation systems assumed an even bright light and constant temperature over the entire office environment. That way workstations could be moved without changing other systems. As both lighting and conditioning become more specific to the workstation, its true reconfigurability diminishes.

A contemporary model calls for a lower level of ambient light over the whole space with task lighting mounted inside each workstation. The workstation also includes raceways for wire and cable. To make the workplace truly flexible, a raised floor allows both reconfigurable wiring and underfloor heating and cooling. With a

Open office systems and a grid of individually adjustable HVAC floor registers help facilitate reconfiguration of these Kansas City Power and Light workstations. © *Aaron Dougherty.*

pressurized underfloor system and a grid of salad spinner–like diffusers individual workers can adjust the conditioning of their space to their liking without the need for duct reconfiguration or complex controls.

It can be seen that in such a design it is much easier to move the office furniture around and adapt to new needs. This combination of a fixed but adaptable infrastructure and a movable kit of furnishings and equipment is permanently flexible. Taking that approach and applying it to other parts of buildings is what makes deconstruction possible. As building de-

signers work on projects for the future, such an approach would help reduce the amount of resources that needs to go into buildings on both an initial basis and in the coming years.

## CONCLUSION

No technical barrier exists to the implementation of broad energy conservation strategies in the building sector. A combination of education, regulation, and

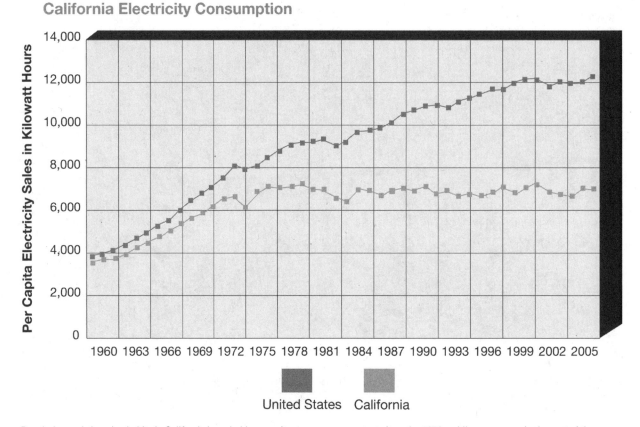

**California Electricity Consumption**

Regulation and changing habits in California have held per capita energy use constant since the 1970s while energy use in the rest of the country has increased significantly. *California Energy Commission.*

economic pressure will likely be necessary to bring about change. Where incentives, education, and regulation all combine, as in California, per capita energy use has remained level while the rest of U.S. per capita energy has climbed. With 72 percent of electricity consumed by the building sector it should be clear that the first cuts in consumption are not only possible, they have been accomplished in at least one large market. The average Californian uses only slightly more than half the electricity of the average American.

The per capita rate of energy use for Californians is slightly lower than the average rate for all developed countries.[11] It cannot be said that citizens of California, or of other developed countries, greatly sacrifice comfort or convenience. Conservation is not synonymous with sacrifice. As has been noted, discomfort is neither sustainable nor necessary.

Broadly applied, energy conservation in the building sector can make a very important contribution to the environmental health of the planet. But however broad the application must be, it will still come down to each individual building owner, manager, or user to begin work on each building. While it is not possible to say what the top five strategies are for a given existing building, it is possible to say what the first five steps might be:

1. Analyze the site constraints and opportunities of the building

2. Measure and benchmark the building performance

3. Educate maintenance staff and users on immediate changes they can make

4. Masterplan building improvements that will conserve energy and increase livability

5. Go as far as you can afford to go

CASE STUDY

# The Courtyard Portland City Center by Marriott

**Owner**  JER Portland Hotel LLC, managed by Sage Hospitality

**Renovation Architect**  SERA Architects

**Original Building Type**  Office

**Renovation Building Type**  Hotel

**Original Construction Date**  late 1970s

**Renovation Date**  2009

**Location**  Portland, OR

**Climate**  Oceanic (Köppen Csb)

**Area**  199,000 ft² (256 Guest Rooms)

**Achievement**  LEED Gold (41 points)

**Key Indicators**  Envelope Replacement

    High Efficiency Plumbing Fixtures

    High Efficiency Lighting

    Low-Emitting Materials

    Public Transportation

    Kitchen Waste Composting Program

**Energy Achievement**  28 percent less than comparable building

**Total Energy Use**  3,800,000 kWh/year  19.1 kWh/ft²/year  (205 kWh/m² year)

**Electricity Before (baseline)**  5,930,000 kWh/ year  29.8 kWh/ft²/year  (321 kWh/m² year)

**Electricity After (design)**  3,251,000 kWh/ year  16.3 kWh/ft²/year  (176 kWh/m² year)

**Heating Before (baseline)**  10,540,000 kBtu  53.0 kWh/ft²/year  (570 kWh/m²/year)

**Heating After (design)**  2,945,000 kBtu  14.8 kWh/ft²/year  (159 kWh/m²/year)

**Water Before (baseline**  2,201,197 gallons  11.06 gal/ft²

**Water After (design)**  1,713,868 gallons  8.61 gal/ft²

The Courtyard Portland City Center building by Marriott, located in Portland, Oregon, was originally constructed as an office building in the 1970s. Through a sustainable transformation, it became the first LEED Gold certified Marriott hotel, one of only nine certified hotels in the country at the time. The building employed many measures to earn this status. Prioritizing energy reduction while reconfiguring the building for hotel use, the project replaced the building skin, providing a new insulated façade with efficient windows.

▲ Rather than tearing down a vacant office building to build a new hotel, a creative design team replaced the skin and reconfigured the interior to meet the requirements of a hotel. Saving a tremendous amount of embodied energy, the new hotel's skin combines with efficient heating and cooling systems to allow the building to run at less than half the heating and one-third the cooling energy of a baseline building. *Courtesy SERA Architects.*

▶ Low-emitting materials combine with an indoor air quality management plan during construction and an outdoor air delivery monitoring system to provide a superior indoor environment without sacrificing design. *Michael Mathers.*

Inside, fluorescent lighting was installed throughout and controls improved in order to lower energy use by 28 percent compared to a standard hotel, for an annual savings of $58,000. Additionally, the hotel employs programs to reduce water usage, cutting 28 percent, equivalent to fifteen hotel swimming pools and a savings of $6,000 each year.

The materials used also emphasize sustainability, particularly the capture of the structure's embodied energy through transformation of an outdated office building to hotel use. During construction, waste was diverted from the landfill, transportation of the material was reduced by prioritization of local purchase, and use of recycled material was highlighted. Additionally, non-polyvinyl chloride (PVC) wall covering, low volatile organic compound (VOC) paints, and low urea-formaldehyde casework were installed in guestrooms to improve indoor air quality. Finally, management continues the sustainable path through use of green housekeeping materials and organic bath products. Further, the hotel encourages recycling, which they achieve through the use of uniforms made from recycled plastic bottles, food waste that is composted rather than thrown away, and placement of recycling bins in each guestroom.

A green housekeeping policy that includes use of green cleaners and organic bath products extends the attention given to sustainability during construction. Sage Hospitality continues its sustainable policy with a composting and guest recycling program. *Courtesy Sage Development.*

## CASE STUDY

# James Lick Baths

**Owner**   165 10th Street LLC, For profit

**Architect**   Gelfand Partners Architects

**Original Building Type**   Public Bath

**Renovation Building Type**   Office

**Original Construction Date**   1890

**Renovation Date**   2009

**Location**   San Francisco, CA

**Climate**   Mediterranean (Köppen Csb)

**Area**   7,400 ft$^2$

**Achievement**   LEED CI v2.0 Gold (34 points)

**Key Indicators**   Daylighting and Daylight Compensation Lighting and Controls

   Hydronic Radiant Panel Heating

   30 Percent Water Use Reduction

   Energy Star Equipment

   Building Reuse

   60 Percent Resource Reuse, Furniture and Furnishings

   20 Percent Recycled Content

   Low-Emitting Materials

**Lighting Energy Achievement**   30 percent less than comparable building (California Title-24)

**Heating and Ventilating**   15 percent less than comparable building (California Title-24)

**Total Energy Use**   245 kBtu/ft$^2$/year   71.8 kWh/ft$^2$/year   (773 kWh/m$^2$ year)

**Lighting**   0.96 watt/ft$^2$

165 10th Street is a San Francisco City Landmark. Built in 1890 by the James Lick estate as a free public bath house, it housed a men's bath, with forty bathtubs, and a women's bath with twenty tubs. Between the bathing spaces a boiler in a sunken room heated the water and a tower supported hot and cold water tanks that fed the tubs by gravity.

Gelfand Partners transformed this uninsulated light industrial space into a new office for the practice. Note the number of light fixtures replaced by the single row of high-efficiency direct/indirect lighting in the renovation. An analysis was made of on-site salvage of existing 2 × 12 framing for the new mezzanine. It proved more cost effective for offsite salvage and use of new Forest Stewardship Council (FSC) lumber in the mezzanine framing. *Gelfand Partners Architects; Mark Luthringer.*

Existing lighting fixtures were reused with new lamps, and the existing HVAC system was retrocommissioned in the south studio for a Title-24-compliant installation with no new embodied energy. *Mark Luthringer.*

After extensive damage in the 1906 earthquake and fire the building was repaired and continued as a bath until 1919. From 1919 until 1973 it was an industrial laundry, followed by a variety of offices, workshops, and stores. The two main bath spaces were divided and circulation in the building became convoluted. A wall at the base of the tower was demolished, leaving one side unsupported.

The 2009 renovation cleared the clutter of existing partitions and mezzanines. During construction openings in the brick walls appeared when sheetrock partitions were demolished. The renovation restored the original logic of the building. Boarded up ventilation louvers in the skylight curbs were reopened and a new fresh air supply introduced. Structural improvements created a new horizontal diaphragm, allowing the generous skylight openings to remain. A new concrete wall replaced the missing tower support.

Existing historic decking remains visible around the edges of new thermal and acoustic insulated panels. Wood was FSC-sourced, no added formaldehyde computer numerical control (CNC) plywood. Slots in the plywood lighten the panels sufficiently to avoid overstressing historic steel trusses while also facilitating acoustic control in the office. *Mark Luthringer.*

The improvements reinforce the basic sustainability of a daylit space that uses stack ventilation to move fresh air through the space. The new mezzanine stands apart from the adjacent wall, and new slotted FSC plywood ceiling panels float between the original roof trusses, revealing the original decking. The slotted plywood is also used in railings and wall panels throughout the space.

New lighting in the north studio space beats Title 24 by 53 percent while existing lighting on the south side remains for an average improvement of 30 percent.

In order to reduce the water consumption, on the inside, there are low-flow fixtures and high-efficiency drip irrigation for the living wall. Outside, native plants fill a new sidewalk greening planter area. Workstations were created from recycled flat panel doors, all steel was high recycled content, 74.9 percent of construction debris was diverted for salvage.

In terms of the building masterplan, next steps might include reroofing over additional rigid insulation, replacing skylight glazing with a high-performance glass, replacing existing lighting in the south studio with a daylight compensation system, and extending the radiant heating system to the south studio when the existing HVAC breaks down.

# Cox School

**Owner**   Oakland Unified School District

**Architect**   Gelfand Partners Architects

**Original Building Type**   Public School

**Renovation Building Type**   Public School

**Original Construction Date**   1958

**Renovation Date**   2008

**Location**   Oakland, CA

**Climate**   Mediterranean (Köppen Csb)

**Area**   60,000 ft²

**Achievement**   CHPS verified addition, CHPS designed modernization

**Key Indicators**   Daylighting
   New high efficiency HVAC package units

The Cox Campus in Oakland, California, houses two small schools. Built in 1958, it was planned as a neighborhood elementary school. The Oakland Unified School District has adopted CHPS (the Collaborative for High Performance Schools) standards for all new construction, and for each scope of work in a modernization. In the case of Cox, Gelfand Partners built a new CHPS-conforming addition and renovated selected systems in the existing buildings. This step-by-step approach fits into Oakland's strategy for financing the improvement of their facilities. Basic improvements are being made at all schools instead of complete renovations at only a few. However, the standards of the work that is completed meet the criteria of CHPS.

Over time, the original daylighting and heating scheme for the Cox buildings had been eliminated. Skylights were boarded up and the underfloor radiant system replaced by convectors at exterior walls. Important scopes of work were to reopen the skylights (though as vertical glazing for glare control and security), and replace the heating system. New ceilings and electric lighting were not in the budget for the renovation. However, these systems can be replaced without disrupting other work. Changes to the site also improve the play area, reduce heat island effects, and increase permeability.

The new daylighting at Cox is a critical change in the atmosphere of the school. Even without comprehensive new electric lighting, usage is reduced due to the brightness of the classrooms and school halls. When funding becomes available for the lighting replacement, more energy savings will be achieved.

Gelfand Partners replaced existing boarded-up skylights with new light monitors on the roof of this existing school. *Mark Luthringer.*

New light monitors transform existing hallways and reduce electric lighting. *Gelfand Partners Architects; Mark Luthringer.*

New light monitors also improve lighting in existing classrooms. *Mark Luthringer.*

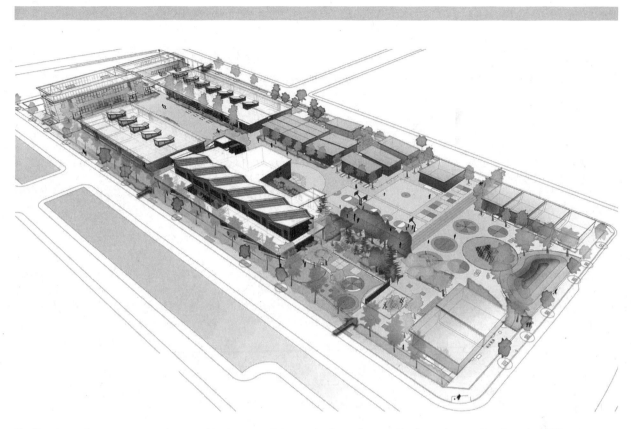

The Cox site continues to accommodate portable classrooms but new planting and permeable play surfaces and gardens give children many new ways to play and spread out over all available space. *Gelfand Partners Architects.*

## ENDNOTES

1. http://buildingsdatabook.eren.doe.gov/ChartView.aspx ?chartID=0, accessed December 17, 2010.

2. Op cit., NYSERDA.

3. www.consumerenergycenter.org/home/appliances/ranges. html, accessed December 28, 2010.

4. Op cit., Pacific Gas and Electric.

5. 2005 Metaevaluation of WAP—Past Evaluations— Weatherization and SEP Support, Oak Ridge National Laboratory, accessed December 28, 2010. http://weatheriza tion.ornl.gov/past_evaluation_2005wap.shtml

6. www.aceee.org/press/2010/08/major-home-appliance-effi ciency-gains-deliver-huge-natio, accessed December 28, 2010.

7. U.S. DOE, Cool Roof Fact Sheet.

8. National Renewable Energy Laboratory, "Energy Sector Market Analysis," www.nrel.gov/docs/fy07osti/40541.pdf, accessed February 2, 2011, p. 18.

9. Ibid., p. 25.

10. Ibid.

11. http://earthtrends.wri.org/text/energy-resources/vari able-574.html, accessed February 2, 2011.

# INDEX

**A**

additions and deletions, high performance renovation, 205–7

air conditioning. *See also* electric power; energy consumption; energy generation systems; HVAC systems
  culture, 22
  whole building design strategies, 39–40

air infiltration losses, building envelope design, 78

air leaks, facility management upgrades, 50–51

American Clean Energy and Security Act of 2009, 23

American National Standards Institute (ANSI), 142

American Society of Heating, Refrigerating, and Air-Conditioning Engineers (ASHRAE), 70–72, 110

apartment building (Linz, Austria), 105–7

appliance lifecycle, future prospects, 242

Architecture 2030 Challenge, 7, 23, 24–25

asbestos, hazardous materials abatement, construction operations, 179

ASHRAE (American Society of Heating, Refrigerating, and Air-Conditioning Engineers), 110

ASHRAE Headquarters (Atlanta, Georgia), 70–72

Athena Sustainable Materials Institute, 144, 145–46

atria, daylighting, modern buildings (late), building envelope design, 97–98

automated systems, building envelope, 11–12

**B**

BedZed project (London, England), 227

behavior change, facility management upgrades, 51–52

benchmarking. *See also* software; specific software names
  facility management upgrades, 52–55
  testing and, whole building design, 22–28

BESTEST software, building energy models, 23

Best Management Program (BMP), 119

biomass liquefaction, pyrolysis via, 211

Brundtland commission, 2

building codes
  ventilation, 36
  whole building design, 40–41

Building Design Advisor software, building energy models, 23

building energy models, whole building design, 22

Building Energy Simulation Test (BESTEST) software, 23

building envelope design, 77–108
  air infiltration losses, 78
  automated systems, 11–12
  case studies, 103–7
  daylighting, high performance renovation, case histories, 230
  functions of, 77
  insulation strategies, 78–84
    cold climate, 79–80
    continental climate, 83–84
    generally, 78–79
    hot dry climate, 83
    hot humid climate, 82
    humid middle latitude climate, 81–82
  modern buildings (late), 96–102
    daylighting, 96–98
    insulation, 99
    roofing, 101–2
    roof structure, 98–99
    window replacement, 100–101
  modern buildings (mid-century), 92–96
    curtain walls, 92–93
    insulation, 93–95
    roofing, 95–96
    window replacement, 95
  passive house design, 226–27
  pre-war buildings, 84–91
    masonry wall design, 85–86
    roofing, 89–91
    roof structure, 88–89
    thermal mass, 84–85
    window replacement, 86–88
  whole building design strategies, 38–39

Building Information Model (BIM), 31

building materials, 141–72

building materials *(cont'd)*
  environmental considerations, 141–50
    Athena Sustainable Materials Institute, 145–46
    generally, 141
    operational energy and waste, 150
    rating systems and lifecycle assessment, 142–44
    recycling, salvage, and reuse, 146–49
    resource efficiency, 149
  low-emitting materials, 151–57
  modern (late), 163–65
  modern (mid-century), 162–63
  pre-war buildings, 157–61
    plaster and partitions, 159–61
    roofing, building envelope design, 89–91
    salvage, 157–59
  whole building design strategies, 36–37
Building Owners and Managers Association (BOMA), 23
building sector
  building energy models, 23
  greenhouse gases, 4–5, 201
building systems, 109–40
  case studies, 134–39
  construction, commissioning, 193–95
  controls, 114
  functions of, 109–10
  light, 112–13
  modern buildings (late), 127–33
    daylighting, 130–32
    deep floor plates, 127–28
    electric power and controls, 133
    HVAC systems, 130, 131
    ventilation, 128–30
    water-saving strategies, 132–33
  modern buildings (mid-century), 120–27
    daylighting, 124
    electric power, 126–27
    HVAC systems, 122–24
    hydronic systems, 120–21
    ventilation, 122
    water-saving strategies, 124–26
  pre-war buildings, 114–20
    daylighting, 118
    electric power, 120
    steam and hydronic systems, 115–17
    ventilation and fire safety, 117
    water-saving strategies, 118–20
  service lives of, 8

  thermal comfort, 110–11
  water use, 112
  whole building design strategies, 39–40
building system water, high performance renovation, 221. *See also* water use

**C**
California Sustainable Building Task Force, 12–13
Canadian Waste Water Association (CWWA), 118
carpet, low-emitting materials, 155
Carpet and Rug Institute (CRI), 141
change of use, transformation, high performance renovation, 202–5
Chicago Center for Green Technology (Chicago, Illinois), 197–99
climate. *See also* specific climates
  building envelope, whole building design strategies, 38–39
  insulation strategies, building envelope design, 79–84
  materials, whole building design, 36–37
  passive house design, 223–24, 227
  thermal mass, 84–85
  whole building design, 19–22
climate change. *See* global warming
codes
  ventilation, 36
  whole building design, 40–41
cold climate
  insulation strategies, building envelope design, 79–80
  pre-war buildings, 84
Collaborative for High Performance Schools (CHPS), 26, 141, 175–76, 195
color rendering index (CRI), 113
combined heat and power (CHP) systems, energy systems retrofitting, 209–11
comfort, renovation benefits, 10–12
Commercial Buildings Energy Consumption Survey (CBECS) Database, 23
commissioning, construction operations, 191–96
concrete, low-emitting materials, 152
condensation
  building envelope, whole building design strategies, 39
  curtain walls, modern buildings (mid-century), 92–93
construction. *See* new construction
construction operations, 173–200
  commissioning, 191–96
  debris removal, 185–86
  demolition and investigations, 176–77

demolition documents, site discussions versus, 177–78
hazardous materials abatement, 178–85
    abatement process, 182–85
    asbestos, 179
    lead, 179–80
    polychlorinated biphenyls (PCBs), 180–82
occupied projects, 186–91
    elevators, 189–91
    notification, 189
    phasing, 187–89
    relocation, 186–87
    separation and noise, 189
sustainability, 173–74
team assembly, 174–76
continental climate, insulation strategies, 83–84
controls, building systems, 114
correlated color temperature (CCT), 113
costs
    facility management, 9–10
    green buildings, 12–13
Courtyard Portland City Center Marriott Hotel (Portland, Oregon), 252–54
Cox School (Oakland, California), 259–63
Cradle to Cradle (C2C) approach, 37, 142
crawlspaces, insulation, 93–95
culture
    high performance renovation, 207–8
    whole building design, 19–22
curtain walls, 92–93

**D**

daylighting
    advantages of, 10
    benchmarking, 27–28
    high performance renovation, case histories, 230
    modern buildings (late)
        building envelope design, 96–98
        building systems, 130–32
    modern buildings (mid-century), building systems, 124
    pre-war buildings, building systems, 118
    solar heat and power, energy systems retrofitting, 213–16
    whole building design strategies, 32–34
daylight savings time, 51
debris removal, construction operations, 185–86
deconstruction process, future prospects, 248–50
deep floor plates, modern buildings (late), building systems, 127–28

deletions, transformation, high performance renovation, 205–7
demolition, construction operations, 176–77
demolition documents, site discussions versus, construction operations, 177–78
design problem, whole-building design concept, 17–19
developing nations, global warming, 14–15
disassembly, modern buildings (mid-century), building materials, 162–63
disposal reduction, late modern buildings, 164–65
DOE-2 software, building energy models, 23
Dunham-Jones, Ellen, 202

**E**

earthquake, materials, whole building design, 36
ecomachine waste water management, 221–22
Edith Green--Wendell Wyatt Federal Office Building (Portland, Oregon), 228–32
electric power. *See also* air conditioning; energy consumption; energy generation systems; HVAC systems; lighting systems
    modern buildings (late), building systems, 133
    modern buildings (mid-century), building systems, 126–27
    pre-war buildings, building systems, 120
elevators, occupied projects, construction operations, 189–91
Empire State Building (New York, New York), 86–87
encapsulation, hazardous abatement process, 182–85
energy consumption. *See also* air conditioning; energy generation systems; HVAC systems
    building envelope, whole building design strategies, 38–39
    building sector, 4–5, 201
    facility management upgrades
        behavioral change, 49–52
        benchmarking, 52–55
    future prospects, goal-setting, 239–40
    green buildings, 13
    statistics on, 250
    submetering (electricity), 51
energy generation systems, 208–19
    combined heat and power (CHP) systems, 209–11
    future prospects, 246–48
    generally, 208–9
    geothermal heat exchange, 218–19
    solar heating and power, 211–16
    wind power, 216–18
EnergyPlus software, building energy models, 22, 23
Energy-10 software, building energy models, 23

Energy Star, 23, 59–60
envelope. *See* building envelope design
environmental considerations (materials), 141–50
    Athena Sustainable Materials Institute, 145–46
    generally, 141
    operational energy and waste, 150
    recycling, salvage, and reuse, 146–49
    resource efficiency, 149
Environmental Protection Agency (EPA), 54, 59, 64, 65, 143
existing buildings, 6–10
    future prospects, goal-setting, 239–40
    renovation versus replacement, 8–9
    sustainability, 6–8

**F**
facility management, 49–76
    behavior change, 51–52
    benchmarking, 52–55
    case studies, 70–75
    existing building renovation, 9–10
    green perspective on, 49–51
    HVAC systems, 60–61
    LEED-EBOM, 62–69
        generally, 62–63
        indoor air quality, 63–65
        integration of program, 65–69
        regional issues, 65
    lighting systems, 56–59
    plug loads, 59–60
    retrocommissioning, 55–56
    water use, 62
Federal Energy Management Program, 119
fiber-optic lighting systems, solar heat and power, 213–15
finance
    existing building renovation, 7–8
    facility management, 9–10
    green buildings, 12–13
fire safety, pre-war buildings, building systems, 117
flooring, low-emitting materials, 155–56
Forest Stewardship Council (FSC), 142
Franklin, Benjamin, 51
future prospects, 239–63
    case studies, 252–63
    deconstruction process, 248–50
    goal-setting, 239–40
    lifecycle strategy, 241–48
        energy generation, 246–48

        2025 improvements, 243–45
        2040 improvements, 245–46
        low and no cost, 241–43

**G**
Gardsten Apartments (Sweden), 42–44
geothermal heat exchange, energy systems retrofitting, 218–19
glaciers, retreat of, 1–2, 14
glazing. *See also* insulation
    modern buildings (late), building envelope design, 100–101
    passive house design, 223–24
    sun-shading strategies, 88
global warming
    evidence of, 1–2
    response to, 14–15
graywater, waste water management, 220–21. *See also* water
    use
green buildings
    comfort, 12
    economics of, 12–13
    facility management upgrades, 49–51
GREENGUARD Environmental Institute (GEI), 142
greenhouse gases
    building sector, 4–5, 201
    global warming, 2–3, 14
green roofs. *See also* roof structure
    future prospects, 242–43
    modern buildings (late), building envelope design, 101–2
    pre-war buildings, building envelope design, 89–91
grout, masonry wall design, building envelope design, 85–86
gypsum wallboard, recycling, 165

**H**
hazardous materials abatement
    construction operations, 178–85
        asbestos, 179
        lead, 179–80
        polychlorinated biphenyls (PCBs), 180–82
    late modern buildings, 163–64
    process of, construction operations, 182–85
    summary chart, 181
HCFCs, insulation strategies, building envelope design, 81
health, renovation benefits, 10–12
heating. *See* electric power; energy consumption; energy generation; HVAC systems
heliostat daylighting, solar heat and power, energy systems retrofitting, 215

HEPA (high efficiency particulate air) filters, 155
Herman Miller, 10
Herman Miller Building (Zeeland, Michigan), 73–75
Heschong-Mahone study, 10
high efficiency particulate air (HEPA) filters, 155
high performance renovation, 201–38
    case histories, 228–36
    energy systems retrofitting, 208–19
        combined heat and power (CHP) systems, 209–11
        generally, 208–9
        geothermal heat exchange, 218–19
        solar heating and power, 211–16
        wind power, 216–18
    passive house design, 222–27
        generally, 222–23
        sealing the envelope, 226–27
        solar power, 223–24
        superinsulation, 224–26
    transformation, 201–8
        additions and deletions, 205–7
        change of use, 202–5
        historic
            characteristics, 207–8
            renovation compared, 201
    waste water, 219–22
Hines (real estate developer), 13
historic characteristics, transformation, 207–8
Home on the Range (Billings, Montana), 103–4
hot dry climate
    insulation strategies, building envelope design, 83
    pre-war buildings, 85
hot humid climate
    insulation strategies, building envelope design, 82
    pre-war buildings, 85
humid middle latitude climate, insulation strategies, building
    envelope design, 81–82
hurricanes, global warming, 14
HVAC systems. *See also* air conditioning; electric power;
    energy consumption; energy generation systems; ven-
    tilation
    construction, commissioning, 194–95
    daylighting, pre-war buildings, building systems, 118
    design problem, 17
    facility management upgrades, 50, 51, 60–61
    future prospects, 242, 243–44
    modern buildings (late), 127, 130, 131
    modern buildings (mid-century), building systems, 122–24

    pre-war buildings, building materials, 161
    retrocommissioning, facility management upgrades, 55–56
    thermal comfort, 110–11
    whole building design strategies, 35–36, 39–40
hydronic systems
    modern buildings (mid-century), building systems, 120–21
    pre-war buildings, building systems, 115–17

**I**
ice caps, melting of, 1–2
indoor air quality
    health, 10
    ventilation, passive house design, 227
    volatile organic compounds (VOCs), 151–52
industrialization, global warming, 14–15
insulation. *See also* glazing
    building envelope design, 78–84
        cold climate, 79–80
        continental climate, 83–84
        generally, 78–79
        hot dry climate, 83
        hot humid climate, 82
        humid middle latitude climate, 81–82
    modern buildings (late), building envelope design, 99
    modern buildings (mid-century), building envelope design,
        93–95
    pre-war buildings, 84–91
    superinsulation, passive house design, high performance
        renovation, 224–26
    types of, summary chart, 82
Intergovernmental Panel on Climate Change (IPCC), 14
international perspective, global warming, 14–15
investigations, construction operations, 176–77
irrigation
    modern buildings (mid-century), building systems,
        125–26
    waste water management, high performance renovation,
        220

**J**
James Lick Baths (San Francisco, California), 255–58

**K**
Kansas City Power & Light Headquarters (Kansas City,
    Missouri), 137–39
Kats, Greg, 12–13
Koeppen Climate Classification system, 19, 20

**L**

landscaping, irrigation, modern buildings (mid-century), building systems, 125–26
late modern buildings. *See* modern buildings (late)
Lawrence Berkeley National Laboratory, 10
lead, hazardous materials abatement, construction operations, 179–80
Leadership in Energy and Environmental Design (LEED). *See* LEED (Leadership in Energy and Environmental Design)
Le Corbusier, 92
LED systems
    building systems, 112–13
    facility management upgrades, 58–59
LEED (Leadership in Energy and Environmental Design). *See also* United States Green Building Council (USGBC)
    commissioning, 195–96
    construction operations, 175–76
    facility management upgrades, 62–69
        generally, 62–63
        indoor air quality, 63–65
        integration of program, 65–69
        regional issues, 65
    USGBC, 50–51, 54, 143
Legionnaire's Disease, 63
lifecycle considerations
    environmental assessment
        Athena Sustainable Materials Institute, 145–46
        building materials, 142–44
    future prospects, 241–48
        2025 improvements, 243–45
        2040 improvements, 245–46
        integrated power generation, 246–48
        low and no cost, 241–43
lighting systems. *See also* electric power
    building systems, 112–13
    construction, commissioning, 194
    facility management upgrades, 56–59
    future prospects, 242
    solar heat and power, energy systems retrofitting, 214–15
    whole building design strategies, 39–40
living machine waste water management, 221–22
Los Altos School District, 26
low cost strategies, lifecycle strategy, future prospects, 241–43
low-emitting materials, building materials, 151–57
Low Impact Development (LID), 219, 220
Loyola Elementary School (Los Altos, California), 29–31

**M**

maintenance
    operational energy, 150
    replacement versus, building materials, 147
Marlton Manor (San Francisco, California), 32, 34
masonry, salvage, pre-war buildings, building materials, 157–59
masonry wall design, pre-war buildings, building envelope design, 85–86
materials. *See* building materials
Mazria, Edward, 23
McDonough and Braungart, 37
Mediterranean climate, pre-war buildings, 84–85
MERV (Minimum Efficiency Reporting Value), 123
metals, low-emitting materials, 152–53
mid-century buildings. *See* modern buildings (mid-century)
Minimum Efficiency Reporting Value (MERV), 123
modern buildings (late)
    building envelope design, 96–102
        daylighting, 96–98
        insulation, 99
        roofing, 101–2
        roof structure, 98–99
        window replacement, 100–101
    building materials, 163–65
    building systems, 127–33
        daylighting, 130–32
        deep floor plates, 127–28
        electric power and controls, 133
        HVAC systems, 130, 131
        ventilation, 128–30
        water-saving strategies, 132–33
modern buildings (mid-century)
    building envelope design, 92–96
        curtain walls, 92–93
        insulation, 93–95
        roofing, 95–96
        window replacement, 95
    building materials, 162–63
    building systems, 120–27
        daylighting, 124
        electric power, 126–27
        HVAC systems, 122–24
        hydronic systems, 120–21
        ventilation, 122
        water-saving strategies, 124–26
moisture, building envelope, 39
mold, carpet, 155

**N**

natural materials, low-emitting materials, 152

Neimeyer, Oscar, 92

new construction, existing building renovation contrasted, 7–9

no cost strategies, lifecycle strategy, future prospects, 241–43

noise, occupied projects, construction operations, 189

Normand Maurice Building (Montreal, Canada), 134–36

notification, occupied projects, construction operations, 189

**O**

occupancy rates, green buildings, 13

occupied projects (construction operations), 186–91

    elevators, 189–91

    notification, 189

    phasing, 187–89

    relocation, 186–87

    separation and noise, 189

oceans, global warming, 14

Omicron Office (Vancouver, Canada), 166–68

operational energy, environmental considerations, building
    materials, 150

Operations Report Card (ORC), 26–27

**P**

partition systems, pre-war buildings, 159–61

passive house design, 222–27

    generally, 222–23

    sealing the envelope, 226–27

    solar power, 223–24

    superinsulation, 224–26

perimeter slabs, insulation, mid-century modern buildings,
    93–95

phasing, occupied projects, construction operations, 187–89

photovoltaic power, energy systems retrofitting, 211–16

Pilkey, Orrin, 14

plaster, pre-war buildings, 159–61

plastic sheeting, occupied projects, 189

plug loads, facility management upgrades, 59–60

plumbing fixtures

    modern buildings (mid-century), 124–25

    pre-war buildings, 119

pollution

    control of, 4

    indoor air quality, 10

polychlorinated biphenyls (PCBs), 180–82

pre-war buildings

    building envelope design, 84–91

    masonry wall design, 85–86

    roofing, 89–91

    roof structure, 88–89

    thermal mass, 84–85

    window replacement, 86–88

    building materials, 157–61

        plaster and partitions, 159–61

        salvage, 157–59

    building systems, 114–20

        daylighting, 118

        electric power, 120

        steam and hydronic systems, 115–17

        ventilation and fire safety, 117

        water-saving strategies, 118–20

productivity. *See* worker productivity

pyrolysis, biomass liquefaction via, 211

**R**

rainwater. *See also* water use

    high performance renovation, case histories, 232

    waste water management, high performance renovation,
        219–22

rating systems, environmental considerations, building mate-
    rials, 142–44

recycling

    building materials, 146–49

    late modern buildings, 164–65

regional issues, LEED-EBOM, 65

relocation, occupied projects, construction operations,
    186–87

renovation

    benefits of, 10–15

    existing buildings, 6–10

rents, green buildings, 13

replacement, maintenance versus, building materials, 147

resilient floors, low-emitting materials, 155–56

resource efficiency, environmental considerations, building
    materials, 149

retrocommissioning, facility management upgrades, 55–56

reuse

    building materials, 146–49

    late modern buildings, 164–65

roofing

    modern buildings (late), building envelope design, 101–2

    modern buildings (mid-century), building envelope design,
        95–96

    pre-war buildings, building envelope design, 89–91

roof structure. *See also* green roofs
    modern buildings (late), building envelope design, 98–99
    pre-war buildings, building envelope design, 88–89
Russell, Bertrand, 17

**S**
salvage
    building materials, 146–49
    pre-war buildings, building materials, 157–59
science, global warming, 1–3
Scientific Certification Systems (SCS), 142
sea level change, global warming, 14
separation, occupied projects, construction operations, 189
sick building syndrome, 10, 163
site discussions, demolition documents versus, construction
    operations, 177–78
snow melt, global warming, 14
SoFlo Office Studios (San Antonio, Texas), 169–71
software. *See also* benchmarking; specific software names
    benchmarking databases, 22–28
    building energy models, 22
    Building Information Model (BIM), 31
    facility management upgrade benchmarking, 52–55
solar heat and power
    energy systems retrofitting, high performance renovation,
        211–16
    passive house design, 222–24
    roofing, pre-war buildings, building envelope design, 89–91
    thermal mass, 84–85
SPARK software, building energy models, 23
steam systems, pre-war buildings, building systems, 115–17
stone, low-emitting materials, 152
student performance, daylighting, 10
submetering (electricity), 51
suburban development, 29
sun-shading strategies
    daylighting, modern buildings (late), 97–98
    glazing, 88
    high performance renovation, 230
    passive house design, solar power, 223–24
superinsulation, passive house design, 224–26
sustainability
    benefits of, 10–15
    construction operations, 173–74
    defined, 1–3
    existing buildings, 6–10
    materials, 36–37
    urgency of, 4–5

**T**
Taut, Bruno, 77
team assembly, construction operations, 174–76
testing. *See also* software; specific software names
    facility management upgrades, 52–55
    whole building design, 22–28
thermal comfort, building systems, 110–11
thermal glazing, passive house design, 223–24. *See also*
    glazing
thermal mass
    climate zones, 84–85
    wall construction, 79
thermostats, mid-century modern buildings, 126–27
39 Hunter Street (Sydney, Australia), 233–36
Thurber, James, 49
Todd, John, 221
transformation (high performance renovation), 201–8
    additions and deletions, 205–7
    change of use, 202–5
    historic characteristics, 207–8
    renovation compared, 201
Trees Atlanta Kendela Center (Atlanta, Georgia), 45–47

**U**
United Nations, Brundtland commission, 2
United States Environmental Protection Agency (EPA), 54, 59,
    64, 65, 143
United States Green Building Council (USGBC), 50–51, 142,
    143

**V**
ventilation. *See also* HVAC systems
    modern buildings (late), building systems, 128–30
    modern buildings (mid-century), building systems, 122
    passive house design, 227
    pre-war buildings, building systems, 117
    whole building design strategies, 35–36, 39–40
vinyl flooring, low-emitting materials, 155–56
volatile organic compounds (VOCs), 151–52

**W**
wall finishes, low-emitting materials, 156–57
waste
    debris removal, construction operations, 185–86
    materials sustainability, 36–37
waste reduction, late modern buildings, 164–65
waste water, high performance renovation, 219–22. *See also*
    water use

Water Efficiency Best Management Program (BMP), 119
waterproofing, masonry wall design, 85–86. *See also* building envelope design
water use
    building systems, 112, 221
    conservation strategies
        modern buildings (late), building systems, 132–33
        modern buildings (mid-century), building systems, 124–26
        pre-war buildings, building systems, 118–20
    facility management upgrades, 49–50, 62
    high performance renovation, case histories, 232
    waste water, high performance renovation, 219–22
water vapor, building envelope, whole building design strategies, 39
whole building design, 17–48
    benchmarking, 22–28
    building codes, 40–41
    building energy models, 22
    case studies, 42–47
    climate and culture, 19–22
    concept of, 17–19

strategies, 29–40
    building envelope, 38–39
    building systems, 39–40
    daylighting, 32–34
    Loyola Elementary School example, 29–31
    materials, 36–37
    ventilation, 35–36
Williamson, June, 202
window replacement
    modern buildings (late), 100–101
    modern buildings (mid-century), 95
    pre-war buildings, 86–88
wind power, energy systems retrofitting, 216–18
wind scoops, ventilation, 36
wood, low-emitting materials, 153–54
worker productivity, daylighting, 10

**Y**
Young, Rob, 14

**Z**
ZedFactory project (London, England), 227

**WILEY BOOKS ON**
## Sustainable Design

JOHN WILEY & SONS, INC. provides must-have content and services to architecture, design and construction customers worldwide. Wiley offers books, online products and services for professionals and students. We are proud to offer design professionals one of the largest collections of books on sustainable and green design. For other Wiley books on sustainable design, visit www.wiley.com/go/sustainabledesign

## ♻ ENVIRONMENTAL BENEFITS STATEMENT

This book is printed with soy-based inks on presses with VOC levels that are lower than the standard for the printing industry. The paper, Rolland Enviro 100, is manufactured by Cascades Fine Papers Group and is made from 100 percent post-consumer, de-inked fiber, without chlorine. According to the manufacturer, the use of every ton of Rolland Enviro100 Book paper, switched from virgin paper, helps the environment in the following ways:

| Mature trees | Waterborne waste not created | Water flow saved | Atmospheric emissions eliminated | Soiled Wastes reduced | Natural gas saved by using biogas |
|---|---|---|---|---|---|
| 17 | 6.9 lbs. | 10,196 gals. | 2,098 lbs. | 1,081 lbs. | 2,478 cubic feet |